Continued on back

FURTHER EXPLORATIONS
IN PERSONALITY

FURTHER EXPLORATIONS IN PERSONALITY

Edited by

A. I. RABIN
JOEL ARONOFF
ANDREW M. BARCLAY
ROBERT A. ZUCKER
Michigan State University

A WILEY-INTERSCIENCE PUBLICATION

JOHN WILEY & SONS, New York · Chichester · Brisbane · Toronto

Library of Congress Cataloging in Publication Data:

Main entry under title:

Further explorations in personality.

  (Wiley series on personality processes)
  "A Wiley-Interscience publication."
  Includes indexes.
  1. Personality. I. Rabin, Albert I.
BF698.F85   155.2   80-19407
ISBN 0-471-07721-6

Printed in United States of America

10 9 8 7 6 5 4 3 2 1

This book celebrates the work of
Henry A. Murray
and commemorates the 40th anniversary
of the publication of his seminal
EXPLORATIONS IN PERSONALITY

Contributors

JACK BLOCK, Professor
Department of Psychology
University of California, Berkeley

NORMAN S. ENDLER, Professor and Chairman
Department of Psychology
York University

NORMAN GARMEZY, Professor
Department of Psychology
University of Minnesota

DANIEL J. LEVINSON, Professor of Psychology
Department of Psychiatry
Yale University

DAVID C. MCCLELLAND, Professor
Department of Psychology and Social Relations
Harvard University

LOIS BARCLAY MURPHY, Research Consultant
Children's Hospital
Washington, D.C.

ROBERT W. WHITE, Professor of Psychology (Emeritus)
Harvard University

Series Preface

This series of books is addressed to behavioral scientists interested in the nature of human personality. Its scope should prove pertinent to personality theorists and researchers as well as to clinicians concerned with applying an understanding of personality processes to the amelioration of emotional difficulties in living. To this end, the series provides a scholarly integration of theoretical formulations, empirical data, and practical recommendations.

Six major aspects of studying and learning about human personality can be designated: personality theory, personality structure and dynamics, personality development, personality assessment, personality change, and personality adjustment. In exploring these aspects of personality, the books in the series discuss a number of distinct but related subject areas: the nature and implications of various theories of personality; personality characteristics that account for consistencies and variations in human behavior; the emergence of personality processes in children and adolescents; the use of interviewing and testing procedures to evaluate individual differences in personality; efforts to modify personality styles through psychotherapy, counseling, behavior therapy, and other methods of influence; and patterns of abnormal personality functioning that impair individual competence.

IRVING B. WEINER

University of Denver
Denver, Colorado

Preface

An event of major significance in the history of psychology took place in 1938. It was the publication of the seminal *Explorations in Personality* by Henry A. Murray and a group of collaborators. The book before you—*Further Explorations in Personality*—is the result of an intellectual feast that took place on the fortieth anniversary of that historical event, on the campus of Michigan State University. For this occasion we invited seven leading contributors to the field of personality and asked them to reflect and report on the current state of the field and to trace present developments to the antecedents published forty years earlier. We were fortunate to meet with the enthusiastic response of the contributors who saw the value in taking stock while maintaining the historical perspective.

The first part was designed to serve as a bridge between the past and the present, between the *Explorations* of 1938 and the current volume. This task was superbly accomplished by Robert White, a member of Murray's original group of collaborators, who presents the historical context with style and grace.

The remainder of the book follows the tripartite division in the program of the conference that took place in East Lansing. The second part of the volume is concerned with "continuities and discontinuities" of personality. Two papers, by Jack Block and Daniel Levinson, deal with very recent research in this area. The third part, "Experimental Studies of the Person and the Situation," consists of the papers by Norman Endler and David McClelland. The fourth and last part of the book is about "coping and its failures," which is covered by Lois Murphy and Norman Garmezy.

Serious students of personality will readily note that some of the most crucial issues in the field are addressed in these papers. We believe that their stimulating and scholarly nature will serve readers by aiding them to join us in the "further explorations" that is an ongoing process. It is anticipated that this will be the first in a series of volumes to report the biennial proceedings of Michigan State University's series of the Murray Lectures in Personality.

A. I. Rabin
Joel Aronoff
Andrew M. Barclay
Robert A. Zucker

East Lansing, Michigan
August 1980

Acknowledgments

The editors wish to acknowledge the indispensable assistance of Marc Van Wormer in organizing and running the conference. Enthusiastic support for the enterprise came from Dr. C. L. Winder, Provost of Michigan State University, Dr. Gwen Andrew, Dean of the College of Social Science, and Dr. John Wakeley, Chairman of the Department of Psychology. The additional support of Dean Keith Goldhammer (Education), Chairman Norbert Enzer (Psychiatry) and Director Fred Cox (Social Work) is hereby acknowledged. Dr. Gaston E. Blom not only chaired one of the sessions, but also helped in the editing. Kenny Bertram and Zoli Zlotogoski also assisted the conference committee and the editors in numerous ways. We are grateful to all of them for they made possible the conference and the volume upon which it is based.

With the exception of the first named editor, whose ideas and perseverance sparked the development of the conference and this volume, the listing of editors was decided alphabetically.

A.I.R.
J.A.
A.M.B.
R.A.Z.

Contents

PART FOUR.   COPING AND ITS FAILURES

FURTHER EXPLORATIONS
IN PERSONALITY

PART ONE

Historical Perspective

The paper by Robert White, which constitutes the first section of the book, is a very appropriate introduction to what is to follow. As a member of the original group of collaborators who, under the leadership of Henry Murray, produced the seminal *Explorations in Personality,* White is in the best position to provide the historical context and perspective of the work as well as the guidelines of transition to the present *Further Explorations in Personality.* He recreates for the reader the atmosphere of excitement and creativity which pervaded the pioneering work at the Harvard Psychological Clinic under Murray's leadership.

White guides us systematically, chapter by chapter, through the complex and voluminous *Explorations.* Beginning with a brief description of the organismic and dynamic conceptions of personality and the underlying propositions of these conceptions, he continues with a more detailed elucidation of the nature of the numerous variables that issue from this theoretical framework. This is followed by a review of the original methodology, which consisted of numerous measures, in combination with interview data and personal documents, designed to arrive at a profound and complex assessment of individuals. The introduction of the "diagnostic council" as an innovative approach to the study of persons and the sensitivity to the relation and interaction between researcher and subject were further extensions of the investigative process. The overall concern with the subjects' imaginative processes in developing the various research methods was particularly salient. In general, White gives us a glimpse into the inner workings and the struggles that characterized the creation of *Explorations.*

Although attention was called, forty years ago, to the study of personality as dynamic and proactive, dealing with whole persons, along the temporal dimension, much of the work in the field since then is characterized by White as "studying personality without looking at it." He bemoans the fact that so much work is devoted to single variables or

1

correlations among pairs of variables, without attending to the richness and complexity of human functioning. The production of much equivocal and trivial research is a direct consequence of the social conditions that demand fast results and prompt publication. He makes a plea for the study of personality the "long way," with numerous interrelated variables and over time. It is hoped that this admonition will serve as an antidote to the study of personality without looking at it and will inspire respect for the study of personality as a "large" enterprise.

CHAPTER 1

Exploring Personality the Long Way: The Study of Lives

Robert W. White

In one of the world's greatest plays, Hamlet tries to deflate Polonius by giving him a version of the Rorschach Test. The record reads as follows.

HAMLET.   Do you see yonder cloud that's almost in shape of a camel?
POLONIUS.   By the mass, and 'tis like a camel indeed.
HAMLET.   Methinks it is like a weasel.
POLONIUS.   It is backed like a weasel.
HAMLET.   Or like a whale?
POLONIUS.   Very like a whale.

Forty years ago, when *Explorations in Personality* came over the horizon, psychologists took another version of the Rorschach Test. Some observers thought that as a report of scientific work the book was as awkward and unpredictable as a camel. Others, noticing a tendency to burrow into unconscious motivation, considered that it was backed like a weasel. But only those can be credited with superior form perception who saw that it was very like a whale.

It was indeed a whale of a book. It contained more words than *Moby Dick*. Like Melville's novel, the story of a whaling voyage that was also a voyage through the deeps of allegory, *Explorations* was a book about research which also unfolded a profoundly important conception of personality. This conception was organismic when the rest of psychology was atomistic. It included a sophisticated view of human motivation when others were stuck with drives and instincts. It required wholistic and imaginative methods of assessment when others were adding up scores on paper-and-pencil tests. And it led to the construction of a far-reaching ego psychology at a time when psychoanalysts had barely begun to think about ego psychology.

3

EXPLORATIONS IN PERSONALITY: THE BACKGROUND

Whence came such a striking advance? The title page of *Explorations* bore a long list of authors, as if to acknowledge every member of the ship's crew down to the cabin boy, but the rest of us knew that only the first-named author, called by some of us in those days "The Skipper," could have imagined and created such a book. Considered as a psychologist of personality, Henry Murray's background was decidedly unorthodox. In the first place, he was aware early of a "bent of empathy and curiosity toward all profound experiences of individual men and women." Such a bent would never have drawn a student to the brass instrument psychology of Murray's undergraduate days. In fact, it led him to choose history as his field of concentration and medicine as his subsequent career. After medical school he spent two years in the practice of surgery, followed by five of research in physiological chemistry. As a physician interested in research he developed a deep respect for painstaking diagnosis by multiple methods, for detailed and systematic case histories, and for the careful delineation and classification of the processes under study. His studies in embryology especially brought home to him not only the organismic way of thinking but also the spontaneity and creativity that lie at the very basis of life.

Murray's career was not, however, destined to go straight forward in biochemical research. He continued to be fascinated by "the dispositions and thoughts (rather than the bodies) of human beings," an interest that drew him to study depth psychologists such as Herman Melville, Sigmund Freud, and Carl Jung. He recognized Freud's monumental contributions and incorporated several of the most important ones in his own work. But he was also much impressed by Jung, with whom for a while he worked, whose writings he characterized as "a hive of great suggestiveness," and whose emphasis on fantasy influenced the like emphasis in *Explorations*. Murray was clearly moving into personality, but by routes which almost any psychologist of the 1920s would view as dangerously unorthodox.

It is remarkable that this maverick was ever allowed to become a member of the Harvard faculty. In fact he owed his entrance to another maverick, Morton Prince, who in his late years hit upon the idea of starting a clinic where undergraduates might be taught abnormal psychology with the aid of clinical demonstrations. Prince had become well-known for his work on hysteria, multiple personality, and unconscious mental processes (Prince, 1905, 1921); his patients were unusually suitable for dramatic clinical teaching. The proposed innovation was viewed with dismay by the Psychology Department. Probably it would never have come into existence had not Prince almost forced it on the university by providing an endowment. From the start it was separately housed at a safe distance from the Yard, a sensible arrangement inasmuch as Prince and the psychologists were unlikely to stay long on speaking terms. Prince selected Harry Murray to be his assistant, and when Prince died three years later Murray found himself in charge of the Harvard Psychological Clinic.

It is interesting to draw a comparison between what might have been expected to happen and what actually did happen during the ensuing nine years. At the outset, research was in progress that lay fairly close to Prince's interest in hysteria, hypnotism, and the unconscious. It could be expected that the tradition would continue, very likely expand to related topics, and lead to a series of papers and dissertations that might eventually begin to mollify the experimental psychologists. The Harvard Psychological Clinic would become known for its contributions in a specialized area and, if it heeded the ideals of its parent discipline, for the technical soundness of its research. But this was not what happened. I was present as a graduate student during the year before and the year after Prince's death, then absent for the next three years in a teaching position. When I returned, it was to a wholly different world. Everyone was talking about needs, variables, and a mysterious process called thematic apperception. Strange people were wandering in and out, neither staff, patients, nor students, but simply personalities undergoing study. The ship had radically changed its course.

When I recovered from my initial confusion I learned that certain important decisions had been made during the time I was away. First, because it was hard to interpret the results of an experiment when one knew nothing else about the subjects, the scheme had been adopted that all experimenters should use the same pool of subjects. Each worker could thus see his or her own findings in the light of what the others had discovered. Second, the interpretations could be further enriched if one knew still more about the subjects, so it was decided to study them as individuals by means of interviews and tests. The third decision was the big one. If a lot of different workers were going to use each other's findings, there had to be a common language, a common scheme of variables, adequate to account for what was significant in personality. To accomplish such a purpose it was necessary to decide what really was significant, then work out a taxonomy to bring observation under orderly control.

In hindsight it is easy to see what it was in Murray that fell into this new shape. There was the research physician's respect for detailed histories, multiple assessment, and careful description of variables.

There was the curiosity, inspired alike by Prince, Freud, and Jung, about the realms of unconscious motivation and fantasy. There were the influences of history, literature, and the arts. There was Murray's own special fascination by the profound experiences in people's lives. But it was the necessity to arrive at systematic description that gave these diverse interests their new creative shape: the vision that the time had come when it might be possible to develop a full-length, full-depth, dynamic, scientific account of human personality. A comprehensive system was the ultimate goal, and it was time to start putting up the scaffolding.

Not everyone who was around at that time got swept up in Murray's vision. Behaviorism was still sufficiently new to be preached with fervor by those whose chief article of faith was scientific purity. Fred Skinner and I entered graduate school the same year, but Skinner, who also had his visions, had already been converted by reading Pavlov, and almost anything Murray said was simply pretext for an argument. Freud's theories, academically suspect, had a few hardy advocates, but seemed altogether too schematic to support a descriptive study of personality as a whole. McDougall's still influential ideas about instinct and social behavior commanded some respect, including that of Morton Prince, but likewise failed to provide the requisite taxonomy (McDougall, 1908). Only Gordon Allport's scholarly and humane treatise, which came out a year before *Explorations,* seemed to recognize the complexity of its subject, but did not propose any large design for learning more about it (Allport, 1937). In this atmosphere I and several others can be described as entranced by Murray's program, which did propose a large design and recognized the full range of human experience as we all knew it: failures and frustrations, but also achievements and victories; fears and fixations, but also feelings openly expressed; impulsiveness and play, but also organization and work; present concerns, but also plans and hopes and creative fantasies. It was a tall order for science, but anything less now seemed like nibbling around the edges of personality.

GENERAL CONCEPTS

The fundamental ideas behind this enterprise were set forth in a chapter entitled "Proposals for a Theory of Personality." This chapter gave evidence of the senior author's determination to leave no stone unturned: following an initial statement that there would not be space for a thorough presentation, the chapter ran to 106 pages. There were twenty-five primary propositions, eight arguments for using the idea of unconscious processes, twenty-three reasons for preferring the concept of need to that of observable action. If this strikes us today as something of a snow job, we must recall the huge weight of academic inertia and scientific resistance that in those days opposed any move toward a dynamic psychology. At a time when the study of personality was almost invariably cross-sectional, derived from batteries of tests, it was necessary to insist upon the time dimension and the ever-changing character of an organismic system. At a time when behavior was being classified by actones—externally observable actions—it was important to insist upon its dynamic, striving character, its movement toward certain end-states. At a time when unconscious mental processes were generally dismissed as ridiculous, it was relevant to bring up all possible evidence for their reality. Considering the work it had to do, the second chapter of *Explorations* may not have been unnecessarily long. Heavy machinery was needed to clear the way for the new venture.

The most basic conviction set forth in this chapter was the organismic one that living beings must be studied as living wholes. Personality is a dynamic process, a constantly changing configuration of thoughts, feelings, and actions. Because of this, it must be studied over periods of time, in recognition of which Murray often referred to his intentions as the study of lives. In addition to his organismic convictions, Murray was hospitable to field theory, at that time being brought to the attention of psychologists by Kurt Lewin (1935). Thoughts, feelings, and actions most often take place in a social environment and have to be understood as interactions with others. This conviction came to have even greater importance to Murray in his later work, when he studied two-person interactions and formulated them as single systems with equal attention to both participants. Finally, with personality thus seen as something happening rather than something fixed, concepts had to be introduced that implied movement and striving. A dynamic conception of personality meant a conception of needs, and the taxonomy required to make consistent observations was chiefly, though not entirely, a taxonomy of needs.

THE VARIABLES OF PERSONALITY

The third chapter of *Explorations* was a systematic exposition of these variables. This chapter was shorter, running to only an even 100 pages. But there can be little cavil about length when one considers the nature of the task and the scrupulous care and imagination with which it was accomplished. So thorough was the description that two or three pages of small type were required for each need. Listed first would be the different desires that expressed the need and the effects it tended to produce. Then would come the associated feelings and emotions, the trait-names and attitudes commonly used to describe the need, the press most likely to activate it, and the actions, often in great detail, by which it might be recognized. In keeping with the organismic point of view, there would then be listed the most common fusions of this need with others, the needs most likely to join with it in a subsidiary relation, and the needs to which it might itself be subsidiary. Common conflicts came next, such as need for Autonomy with need for Affiliation, followed by an enumeration of social and institutional forms through which the need might be expressed, for instance the need for Deference in organized religion and in hierarchical business and political systems. Then followed the appropriate statements in a questionnaire which had been devised as a quick if not very accurate means of measuring strength of needs: for need for Achievement, for example, "I work like a slave at everything I undertake until I am satisfied with the result"—an item, we can imagine, that sprang straight from the senior author's heart as he struggled with this huge taxonomy. Finally came a list of sentiments expressive of the need, the two following being representative of need for Affiliation: "A man's wealth is measured by his friendships," and "Wherever you go plant companionship as thick as trees."

The taxonomy included twenty needs that had been used in the actual studies, with seven more that were beginning to seem necessary for completeness. There were also eight latent needs which were considered to be repressed versions of certain of the manifest needs; for instance, repressed need for Dominance, taking perhaps the form of omnipotent dreams and fantasies. Freud's concepts of Ego Ideal, Narcissism, and Superego were included, and then there was a list of general traits or attributes like Conjunctivity-Disjunctivity and Impulsion-Deliberation. The list of variables had grown from one which was originally much shorter. The making of finer discriminations was an inevitable consequence of using the scheme in rating actual subjects. I recall the excitement of the day when Superego was divided into two variables. Subjects who betrayed anxiety and guilt over things they had done seemed to qualify for high ratings on Superego. But what about subjects who never felt guilty because they always behaved as the superego required and seemed perfectly content to do so? In such people Superego looked even stronger, yet it seemed absurd to give the guilty ones merely a middle rating. The problem was solved by fission, yielding two variables: Superego Conflict and Superego Integration, the latter signifying that superego and ego were allied in guiding behavior along acceptable lines. Another valuable discrimination occurred with respect to the commonly used variable of submission, which Murray divided into need for Deference, a willing, admiring submission, and need for Abasement, a forced, unwilling submission. In like fashion, extraversion-introversion came apart under the test of diagnostic use, yielding a variable called Exocathection-Endocathection and another called Intraception-Extraception.

I have often gone back to this chapter on the variables of personality, and it still seems to me, as it did forty years ago, an astounding intellectual feat. How could anyone think of all those instances and examples, make all those beautiful discriminations, exhibit such a prodigious familiarity with the ins and outs and roundabouts of human behavior? To have cast all this in systematic form, and to have tested the scheme by use with fifty subjects, brought the psychology of personality at one stride to an entirely new level of effectiveness and promise. It may be that the need concept is not the final resting place of personological theory and that the enduring trait variables will assume a different form as knowledge advances. Indeed one would expect that this scheme, like any set of scientific variables, would evolve in the course of time and use. But the important thing, the revolutionary thing, in 1938 was that this carefully wrought, encompassing scheme existed at all. A magnificent vista was opened for future research on personality.

Probably most of us, dazzled by Murray's taxonomy, imagined that the variables would be promptly and widely adopted by other workers. But what we heard from others was at first a series of complaints. How could you use such a large number of variables, how could you even remember them? Some workers, whose memory span was apparently limited to three items, continued to see in personality only an ego, an id, and a superego. Others accepted what had been done but turned it all into a questionnaire for quick results. We came to realize that growing up with a scheme, living through each of its proliferations, was very different from being confronted by the whole thing in its completed form. Time was required for the third chapter to infiltrate the thinking of students of personality. But a good deal of it is now part of their working vocabulary, and whole books have been written about single needs.

METHODS OF STUDY: THE LONG WAY

Securing the information about a person that was implied by Murray's concepts and variables was bound to be a large enterprise. The chapter on procedures made no claim to brevity: it ran to 206 pages. But this time the senior author can be absolved from possible charges of long-windedness. In this chapter the collaborators came into their own, each being allowed to write up the experiment or test on which he or she had worked. The plan allowed for the inclusion of all experiments in progress. Among these were tests of sensorimotor learning, abilities, level of aspiration, hypnotic susceptibility, emotional conditioning, the violation of prohibitions, and a good many more. The subjects' life histories to date were investigated by a written autobiography and by interviews on childhood, family relations, sexual development, and present dilemmas. Thus described, the procedures contain nothing especially surprising, but three features were decidedly unusual. The first was the inclusion of a large number of tests of imagination. The second was the use of a diagnostic council to bring multiple judgments to bear on the assessments. Finally, unusual care was taken to understand each subject's relation to the individual experimenters and to the study as a whole.

The outstanding item in the tests of imagination was, of course, the Thematic Apperception Test (TAT). Many psychologists today remember *Explorations* chiefly as the launching platform for that test. The method had just been invented by Morgan and Murray (1935); Murray has always acknowledged the central contributions made by his highly creative long-time collaborator, Christiana Morgan. In *Explorations* this test was joined by a whole series of procedures concerning imaginal productivity, including an original ink blot test, a test on the production of similes, a completion of the plot of Hawthorne's story, *The Minister's Black Veil,* a musical reveries test, and a dramatic productions test conducted by Erik Erikson during his two-year visit to the Clinic on his way to his own remarkable career. Never before, it can be surmised, had such a concerted attempt been made to stimulate a subject's imagination and thus to creep up on the possible shape of his or her latent needs and unconscious fantasies. In later years psychologists complained that the Thematic Apperception Test was ill suited to clinical diagnosis, especially with laconic patients, but with a gifted college population it proved to have impressive power. I shall have to confess that once in a while I had misgivings about our interpretative ventures. After spending many days on the material provided by a certain subject, and working out an interpretation which, if not quite up to Jung's standards, compared fairly well with Freud, I happened to meet the subject ambling along the sidewalk, a relaxed, cheerful late adolescent who looked as if he didn't have a care either in the world or in the unconscious. As we exchanged greetings I thought to myself, "Am I making all this up?" But I hope you will allow that perhaps I wasn't making it all up, that it was at least an earnest attempt to account for the evidence contained in the diverse imaginative productions.

The use of a diagnostic council was no novelty to a veteran of medical staff conferences. It had not, however, been offered before in the study of personality, presumably because the information collected was so sparse and superficial as hardly to deserve a conference. But with mountains of data, and with variables that did not show themselves in just one way, it would have been perilous indeed not to rely on multiple judgments. The diagnostic council of *Explorations* consisted of seven people whose duty it was to become familiar with all the material on each subject. A taxing aspect of this duty was the rating of each subject on a six-point scale on each of the variables. This was done in conference with the goal of reaching consensus on each rating. You can easily imagine that these conferences were not brief, that argument and the calling up of evidence could develop a good deal of heat, and that the ultimate consensus might be surrounded by a halo of frayed tempers. Interpretations, conclusions, the development of the total picture, went through the same strenuous mill, and the life history that emerged as the final product was thus protected from the risk of purely personal bias by resting on a foundation of collective judgment.

It was a planned feature of the research that each subject should be exposed to a lot of different people. The interviewers and the testers included older men and women and younger men and women extending down to the subject's own age. There was plenty of individuality among those who had gathered to work at the Clinic; the subjects encountered great variety of personality and style. How they responded to their different interogators seemed an important part of their own individuality. With an older woman some of the young men maintained an air of businesslike competence; others seized this opportunity to pour out their woes. It was interesting to see which person a subject would pick for a relation of special confidence and to speculate on the reasons for this choice. Much is lost in personality research if those who meet the subjects think of themselves neutrally as experimenters and fail to see the meeting as a significant personal interaction.

Because the study of personality owes so much to clinical investigation, it would have been easy for most of us to act like clinicians, overlooking the important difference between a patient and a subject. It is an unusual situation to study the lives of paid subjects without undertaking to help them. The clinician, who offers the boon of health, is expected to look for symptoms, defenses, and self-deceptions; for the sake of recovery the patient can endure being seen in an unfavorable light. But if we are simply studying personality we cannot be so presumptuous. We have to take people as they really are, as wholes, and we have to listen appreciatively while they tell us what they think they are. Being paid, the subjects in *Explorations* had a modest economic motive, but in the few cases where this was the limit of their interest they provided only a minimum of information. We learned that we could not study personality successfully unless we could induce the subjects to blossom in our presence. They did not do this if they thought we were looking for faults. They blossomed when they found that we appreciated their strong points, laughed at their sallies, sympathized with their setbacks, showed an interest in their TAT narrations, remembered the details of what they told, and generally accepted their pictures of themselves. And we really had to be capable of this appreciation. Even if we thought there might be more underneath, we had to be able to accept self-pictures and respect the subjects for what they had thus far made of their lives. Sometimes that was quite a lot.

The information derived from these intensive studies of individuality took a number of forms. There were scores on standard tests and quantitative as well as descriptive results from the several experiments. There were ratings on a six-point scale for all the variables used in the studies. The last twenty-eight of the fifty subjects, all college men, were used for various rank-order correlations, especially with the experimental results, though so small a group was obviously not ideal for this treatment. On each subject the whole material was formulated into a life history. The original intent was to include several life histories, and seven were fully prepared for publication. Each one, however, seemed to require the 100 or more pages characteristic of the chapters in *Explorations,* and we were forced to yield to the publisher's protests by including only one life history. Murray envisioned a time when scientific psychology would be able to write abstract biographies, expressed in a generalized notation derived from a common conceptual scheme. Such biographies would be the scientific contribution to understanding personality, in contrast to, though much indebted to, the literary contribution. This goal was clearly far in the future. The case history included in *Explorations* was more literary than abstract. Yet the conceptual scheme and the variables of personality ran through it in a way that provided a foretaste of what might ultimately be possible.

Although the methods used in *Explorations* have sometimes been described as clinical, and the whole enterprise as bringing clinical insights and wisdom to bear on personality, Murray's vision was actually much broader. Ego psychology, even in Freud's schematic version, comprises what is normal, realistic, and constructive in personality; it is the ego that takes over when psychoanalysis has liquidated the neurotic inhibitions. *Explorations* contained a sophisticated ego psychology, taking account of proactions, constructive growth, plans, the organization of behavior to achieve distant goals. At the beginning of an historical period when, as it turned out, clinical psychology suddenly became a large and significant profession, this emphasis was tremendously important. It provided a means of counterbalancing the clinician's habit of looking for symptoms and neglecting the signs of strength and competence. I remember how hard it was to keep clinical students, when studying a relatively normal person, from pouncing on possible symptoms and in their minds turning a merely awkward sophomore into an acute patient in need of instant treatment. The force of the clinical habit of mind is illustrated in the following incident. An instructor not long ago was using my book, *Lives in Progress* (White, 1975), with a graduate class, encouraging free discussion of the cases described. After one of these sessions a middle-aged woman came forward and said that she was the Joyce Kingsley whose case they had been discussing. In consternation, the instructor thought, "She thinks she's in the book, she must be paranoid! How do I handle this?" Fortunately he stayed his clinical judgment long enough to discover that he was indeed talking to Joyce Kingsley, who after bringing up her children had gone back to school, and who now wanted to write her term paper on her relation with her mother, which as a consequence of the class discussion she had come to see more clearly. No paranoia here; rather, an impressive example of ego strength.

If time and its own strengths have conferred on *Explorations in Personality* a certain august quality, the circumstances of its origin were anything but august. By no means did it issue from ivy-clad Harvard temples of learning. The Harvard Psychological Clinic occupied a yellow frame building, formerly a dwelling house, described by Murray as belonging to the Rutherford B. Hayes period of American architecture. The otherwise plain entrance was momentarily beautified in the spring by a vine of purple wisteria, which led one worker to say, "Wisteria outside, hysteria inside." Inside, to be sure, the style and decoration were considerably less simple, evoking comments that ranged from comfortable and interesting to eccentric. The people who worked at the Clinic were indeed a motley crew. Besides the senior professor, then only an assistant professor, and the inevitable graduate students, motley enough in themselves, there was a male Freudian analyst and a female Jungian analyst with their respective patients, there were a sociologist and two anthropologists, and there were representatives of literature, craftsmanship, and other interests unusual on a scientific team. There was a series of cats who received names such as "Need," "Press," and "Thema." There was a dog who politely slept in the Jungian analyst's office during therapy and enabled patients to reach their own emotional problems more quickly by first projecting them on the dog. In this informal atmosphere there was a lot of talk, a lot of excitement, a lot of argument. There was much failure of minds to meet, often happily followed by learning to meet, not always in agreement but at least in understanding. Most important, no doubt, was the sense of being launched on a large and significant mission, the development at last of a real way, even though an exceedingly long way, to understand personality.

How did it happen that such an unusual group of people came together in the first place and stayed together long enough to see the completion of *Explorations?* This happy result is not explained by support from the university, which was small. It is not explained by a foundation grant or by the circumstance of the separate building, though these were both helpful. I hesitate to introduce a variable which the author of *Explorations* did not include in his original conceptualization of personality, but the Harvard Psychological Clinic cannot be understood without it. This variable is *charisma,* and I shall describe it by quoting from the dedication of *The Study of Lives: Essays on Personality in Honor of Henry A. Murray,* presented to him on his seventieth birthday (White, 1963). We said there that we would "always remember with excitement and gratitude our sojourn in the high invigorating climate created by his infectious zest, wide-ranging awareness, bountiful powers of creation, and staunch fidelity to the increase of human understanding." Perhaps some day we shall understand charisma and learn the conditions under which it is most likely to flourish. In the 1930s we certainly did not understand it, but I should like to claim credit for those who were at the Clinic during those years that at least we knew it when we saw it.

MURRAY'S METHODS AND THE SOCIOLOGY OF RESEARCH

I shall presently mention the far-reaching influence of *Explorations in Personality* during the forty years since its publication. But first, with this description of methods fresh in mind, I want to reflect on the incongruous difference between the scene I have described at the Harvard Psychological Clinic and the atmosphere that typically prevails in university graduate schools, where a great deal of current research on personality is done. For the truth is that the influence of *Explorations* has not been as great as it should have been if psychologists had truly absorbed what was written there. Right now, there are hundreds of research projects, supposedly about personality, which show no trace of organismic thinking, of field theory, or of awareness of complexity. Worse still, they show no evidence that the investigators are really curious about people and have looked at personality as it shows itself in friends, in oneself, and in everyday life. The basic format is to give two tests and examine their correlation. Of course there are many elaborations upon this design, introducing experimental situations, different treatments, and highly sophisticated statistical procedures. But none of these entail any real personal contact with the subjects or any attempt to think of them as more than momentarily living people. For some time I have described this type of research as *studying personality without looking at it.* Psychologists who are satisfied to work this way have either not read *Explorations* or have pushed it aside into some category which they do not feel obliged to take seriously.

Studying personality without looking at it goes energetically forward even when its results are equivocal or clearly trivial. Every so often the literature on some topic is reviewed and given such a bad evaluation that you would think the whole thing would come to a stop. Paul Mussen has recently done this for the development of prosocial behavior in children (Mussen, 1977). There has been plenty of research, but most of it looks to Mussen like "wasted effort" spent on "trivial issues." The attempt to isolate factors, the use of artificial laboratory situations, and the underlying cause-effect model of explanation, appear badly misplaced in the study of behavior acknowledged to be "complex, intricate, multiply determined, and influenced by interacting factors." "To answer socially relevant questions," Mussen continues, "requires the study of real children making real responses in the real world;" it calls for "observations of naturally occurring social behavior" and "in-depth study of its correlates."

The heavily researched topic of birth order provides a second example of studying personality without looking at it. There are literally hundreds of papers attempting to establish correlations between birth position and this or that test or contrived situation. In a review of this ample literature Schooler (1972) characterized virtually the whole enterprise as having "essentially negative results" and concluded that when full allowance is made for factors such as number, age, sex, and spacing, "the apparently simple independent variable of birth order becomes immensely complex." Breland (1977) puts his finger on another source of complexity when he comments that "research to date has ignored much of the social process that occurs in the family environment," a statement that reinforces the conclusion of a review by Adams (1972) that what is now needed is longitudinal research with "whole families."

Criticisms of this sort express the same humanistic wisdom that is found in *Explorations in Personality*. Why, then, does this have to be rediscovered topic by topic, after decades of trivial research? Why does an investigator not foresee, before plunging into a narrowly conceived project, that the results cannot be of any real significance? The answer lies, I believe, in the social conditions that surround research when it is done in university graduate departments.

By social conditions I mean in this connection the particular circumstances under which investigators of personality do their work. A large part of this research is currently done by graduate students who are candidates for degrees. Another large part is carried out by young college and university teachers trying to make a name for themselves in a now fiercely competitive profession. The graduate student cannot afford to linger over the degree and thus remain unqualified for scarce jobs if they appear. The assistant professor must have an eye for quick publication in order to be in line for scarce appointments or promotions. To say this is not to blame these workers; their careers are at stake. But it is important to be aware of how their self-interest affects their choices of research problems.

Common to both groups is the heavy pressure of time. In making a choice, preference has to be given to problems that can be completed soon. This rules out longitudinal research by definition. It tends to rule out problems for which it is necessary to know a lot about the people serving as subjects; the study of individuals and families, if properly done, is necessarily time-consuming. These considerations of time put a premium on the use of personality tests and of contrived laboratory situations, both of which make it possible to learn a little about people quickly. Especially with tests it is possible to gather a large sample, and the computer stands ready to assist with extended manipulations of the data.

The researcher's situation, furthermore, is not conducive to cooperative enterprises. Besides taking more time, group research makes it harder to claim the desired individual credit—whether the graduate student has proved worthy of the degree or the young teacher worthy of promotion. And even at the level of tenured appointments, where such considerations are supposedly transcended, the system does not work to bring together a group of like-minded people intent upon a common enterprise. In view of their teaching responsibilities, university departments properly aim for diversity. If an appointment is made in personality, surely the next one must be in physiological psychology. The largest working group that is likely to form consists of one professor and a handful of graduate students, and the latter, at least, are in a hurry.

The conclusion follows that a university graduate department tends to provide an environment largely unsuitable for the proper kind of research on personality. It favors the small, the constricted, the technical, the unimaginative sort of research that neither requires knowledge derived from looking at personality, nor adds to that knowledge. Those who have stuck to the idea of really exploring personality have generally found it necessary to make special arrangements such as separate research units or institutes, associated perhaps with universities but not wholly dependent on them for staff and funds. Thus the earliest large offspring of *Explorations* were the studies reported by Murray and the OSS Assessment Staff in *Assessment of Men* (1948), a government-financed project for selecting candidates for intelligence assignments; the Institute for Personality Assessment and Research at Berkeley, directed by Donald MacKinnon and financed partly by contract work; and the studies of Vassar students directed by Nevitt Sanford, which were a project of the Mellon Foundation. From *Explorations* we learned, and should always remember, that the study of personality must be a large enterprise approached with freedom and largeness of mind.

ENDURING INFLUENCE

In spite of the frequently unfavorable conditions for research of this kind, *Explorations in Personality* has indeed had a wide and lasting influence. To summarize this influence would obviously be a prodigious task, and I shall confine myself to the merest hints. As a first hint, take the names of some of the co-authors on the title page forty years ago and recall what they have done: Donald MacKinnon, Nevitt Sanford, Jerome Frank, Saul Rosenzweig, Walter Langer. Then add more names from among those who worked at the Clinic in later years: Robert Holt, Sheldon Korchin, Gardner Lindzey, Fred Wyatt, Thelma Alper, Bert Kaplan, Morris Stein, Anthony Davids, Charles McArthur, Doris Gilbert, Margaret Riggs, Stanley King, Douglas Heath, and many others. It detracts not at all from the constructive originality of these people's mature work to recall that they were nurtured at the Harvard Psychological Clinic. An influence of *Explorations* can certainly be claimed on the thinking of those who, like Erikson, came with sophisticated ideas and went on in directions that were decidedly their own: Eugenia Hanfmann, Jerome Bruner, Brewster Smith, Silvan Tomkins, Daniel Levinson, and Edwin Shneidman. And I expect that there are still others, like Elliot Jacques, John Money, and Daniel Horn, who became well-known in very different fields, who owe a little something to their sojourns in Cambridge. There is also David McClelland who, although he came late to Harvard, was the earliest to see the possibilities of using thematic apperceptions to measure systematically the strength of needs. Finally, it would hardly be fair to omit the name of Harry Murray from a list of those who were influenced by *Explorations in Personality* and who continued to carry its vision forward during the ensuing forty years.

The influence of *Explorations* has always been on the side of complexity. Against all the influences that make for oversimplification, this book asserts and repeatedly demonstrates that personality is a complex organization and cannot be properly studied by simple short-cuts. It agrees with H. L. Mencken's tart statement: "For every complex problem there is an easy answer, and it is wrong." Complexity is, of course, inherent in organismic thinking and in the idea of constant interaction and exchange with the environment. *Explorations* stands as an enduring caution against cutting too quickly one's moorings in naturalistic description in order to secure some quick result. It enjoins looking at personality, looking carefully and long, before presuming to have arrived at fresh knowledge. It teaches us to be serious about taking people as wholes, as they are and as they think they are. Another of its messages is the dynamic one: people have needs, they are engaged in strivings, they are trying to produce end-states and reach goals. Furthermore, *Explorations* speaks for the importance of development over time: personality is not a fixed thing but a configuration undergoing perpetual change. Lastly, this seminal book was a powerful argument for proaction, as contrasted with reaction. Its vision of human nature included the planning, organizing, building, imagining, dreaming, creating activity without which we cannot understand either individuals or the civilization they have constructed. These were the directions of its influence.

In the end, however, we cannot suppose ourselves able to set bounds on this influence. A book is a teacher. Many books are indeed the written forms of what has been previously taught through speech. *Explorations* has been for forty years an important teacher of all those who sought to understand personality. As Henry Adams wrote: "A teacher affects eternity. He can never tell where his influence stops." We can never tell where the influence of *Explorations* is going to stop. We can be sure only that it has not stopped yet.

REFERENCES

Adams, B. N. Birth order: a critical review. *Sociometry*, 1972, **35**, 411–439.

Allport, G. W. *Personality: a Psychological Interpretation.* New York: Holt, 1937.

Breland, H. M. Family configuration and intellectual development. *Journal of Individual Psychology,* 1977, **33**, 86–96.

Lewin, K. *A dynamic Theory of Personality.* New York: McGraw-Hill, 1935.

McDougall, W. *An Introduction to Social Psychology.* Boston: J. W. Luce, 1908.

Morgan, C. D., and H. A. Murray. A method for investigating fantasies. *Archives of Neurology and Psychiatry,* 1935, **34**, 289–306.

Murray, H. A. *Explorations in Personality.* New York: Oxford University Press, 1938.

Murray, H. A. with staff, *Assessment of Men,* New York: Rinehart & Co. 1948.

Mussen, P. Choices, regrets, and lousy models. *A.P.A. Division on Developmental Psychology Newsletter,* December 1977, 9–15.

Prince, M. *The Dissociation of a Personality.* New York: Longmans, Green, 1905.

Prince, M. *The Unconscious: the Fundamentals of Human Personality, Normal and Abnormal.* New York: Macmillan, 1921.

Schooler, C. Birth order effects: Not here, not now! *Psychological Bulletin,* 1972, 78, 161–72.

White, R. W. (Ed.) *The Study of Lives: Essays on Personality in Honor of Henry A. Murray.* New York: Atherton Press, 1963.

White, R. W. *Lives in Progress: a Study of the Natural Growth of Personality,* 3rd ed. New York: Holt, Rinehart and Winston, 1975.

PART TWO

Continuities and Discontinuities in Normal Personality Over Time

While the debate in the social sciences over its proper topics, terminology and scope underlines the absence of a great order-giving figure, there are still major nodes of work that indicate a recurring question—or part of reality—that continues to demand attention. Certain papers are written time after time and, although new definitions are offered, others continue to rewrite the same paper. Behind the definitions of personality stands a simple observation: an individual's life often seems to have a common theme. Phenomenologically at least, there seems to be continuity in the subjective and objective events of a person's life. Our personality theories are attempts to meet this sense that something is organizing this continuity. The two chapters in this section, in very different ways, tackle the twin elements of this observation. Block's chapter deals with the empirical side of the question: is there, in fact, continuity in people's concerns over significant periods of a person's life? Levinson's chapter asks what kind of ideas, what sort of construct system, will be the most helpful in comprehending the agent of this continuity?

There are two important contributions that Block's paper makes to this discussion. First, in answer to those, such as Mischel (1968), who question the size of correlations between measurements of a personality variable over time, and thus question the utility of a construct such as personality, Block provides a set of empirical results of quite a substantial magnitude. In this chapter, Block reports the results of a major longitudinal study examining the stability of personality characteristics over significant periods of time. In his book, *Lives through Time,* Block (1971) presented a large set of findings that dealt with the continuity of personality from adolescence to the mid-thirties. These data constitute one of the major resources available for examining the question of stability of personality and provide a massive data base to support the observation that for many people important continuities run throughout much of their lifetimes. In this chapter, Block presents the results of the latest assessment of these people, now in their early to late forties. Thus, there is an impressive amount of data available covering thirty to thirty-five years of these people's lives. As Block indicates, methods and theories change over time, and specific questions that are urgent now were not prepared for when the study was begun in 1929 and 1932. However, given a set of limitations that Block specifies, he again is able to present impressive evidence that characteristics of people noted in their early years are still present when the sample reaches the years of full adult maturity. The data are clear and provide us with compelling evidence on the stability of personality and encouragement to institute even more ambitious longitudinal projects for the future.

The second contribution of the chapter lies in key aspects of the method that was used. Perhaps because of the range of types of data that were collected on this sample of people, a technique had to be developed that could incorporate an inundating range of interview, test, rating, and anecdotal information. Thus, to reach summarizing judgments, Block used a Q-sort procedure of personality ratings, made by multiple judges examining a wide range of information on a particular subject. This expanded base for determining personality characteristics fits very well with the position taken recently by Epstein (1979), who argued that it is not a meaningful test of the power of personality variables to expect them to predict the highly specific behavior measured in most experiments. Epstein argued that it is the nature of personality to control general classes of responses over a wide range of possible behaviors rather than permit the prediction of a single event. Epstein shows, in a fairly limited context, that when judgments are pooled across a range of comparable behaviors the power to predict these judgments from a personality variable is *very* high. In Block's study, rather than simply examine if the score on a single test (such as a dominance scale) predicted future scores on that test, he required that judgments be based on a wide range of comparable behaviors, as Epstein suggests. It is very likely that the impressive level of Block's results are the result of the type of information upon which the Q-sort was performed rather than being due to the specific merits of the Q-sort as a specific evaluation procedure.

* * *

Block's data lead to an empirically based typology which is organized by observable clusters of attributes. Levinson, on the other hand, contributes to the examination of consistency of personality by addressing the ways in which we might most productively think about the human life course. Levinson argues that before we examine the levels of correlations we must first ask what sort of variables we should be correlating. The most important questions that guide his thinking in this chapter are how to determine the unit through which life is lived and the necessary sequential order of life's concerns. In his book, *Seasons of a Man's Life* (1978), and in this chapter, Levinson identifies biography as the proper study of psychosocial development.

In its usual reading we think of biography as the account of the events in a person's life. Similarly, when we envisage these events in more theoretical forms, we think of the psychological structures and their inter-relationships that constitute the elements of our theories of personality. Because of our usual directions of thinking, Levinson's term "biography" announced in the title to his chapter "Explorations in Biography" may lead us away from the radically new construct that he has suggested as the basic element in conceptualizing personality.

Because Levinson writes so easily, in order to become most clear about his intentions it is important to underline the connection that Levinson makes with Murray's major book. In sorting out the elements needed to explain personality, Murray outlined two separate classes of variables which he felt were needed to explain personality: need and press. A construct such as need is very congenial to our present way of thinking. Whatever our theoretical persuasion, we think of "forces" (motives, drives, instincts, etc.) in the person as the basic elements that energize and control behavior. Press is a bit more remote to psychologists, which probably explains why some find it so easy to conceive of variables in the situation determining the individual's behavior. Murray phrased his conceptual analysis of the human life pretty much in terms of interaction of these discrete classes of events. However, Levinson's goal is different; he is both more ambitious and more integrative in attempting to develop a single construct that will include the two.

Thus, as Levinson stresses, his goal is to find some construct that allows him to incorporate his knowledge of personality and of society, without reducing one to the other. The central new idea he introduces is that of the life structure. Levinson begins by noting his initial theoretical need: "I sought to develop a sociopsychological perspective on the life course, a perspective that gives equal weight to the personality, the sociocultural world, and the relationship of person and world." This is a goal that has been sought by many throughout this century. As the specialty areas in social sciences developed, a small element in each has always argued that essential aspects of the phenomena in which that discipline was interested were being lost, and so these small elements have always called for interdisciplinary perspective. The result of this trend is a group of social scientists in each specialty area "aware" of the work of the others. Thus we have had psychoanalytically minded anthropologists, sociologists who spoke familiarly of the Self, and psychologists who knew that if they included social class as an independent variable in their research they would be able to report a significant difference. The outcome of this interdisciplinary awareness resulted in books, courses, and fields notable for the conjunction "and," as in "Culture *and* Personality." What has been missing is an interdisciplinary concept. It is this concept that Levinson tries to provide with his idea of the life structure.

The biography that Levinson provides, first of Murray's course of development, and then his own, makes two different types of contributions to us. His account of how the elements of an interdisciplinary program were developed through the radical idea of a Department of Social Relations at Harvard outlines the history of the most important organizational effort to close in on a multifaceted approach to the life course. But more important, this brief history provides a marvellous illustration and case study of the new idea that he wishes to introduce. While it is interesting to read these accounts as a personal tale of academic struggle and success, their more important value is as a demonstration of the social and personal elements that enter into one person's life structure. Just as McClelland's description, in a later chapter, of Richard Alpert's incarnation as Ram Dass provides a key illustration of McClelland's major theoretical point, so, too, should Levinson's extended biographical summary be read as an attempt to provide the reader with the materials that will make concrete the definition of the life structure that he provides later in the chapter.

The key definition is given on p. 69 where the life structure is defined

as the *person's relationships with various aspects of the external world.*
This apparently simple phrase bears much reflection. As Levinson
emphasizes, it is "the relationship itself, rather than the person or the
external world" that is the unit. The innovation is that the definition
moves away from our usual modes of thinking which see the processes
of one field subsumed under the processes of the other (i.e., the self seen
as the introjection of social norms or the group as the resultant of the
behavior of its members). Although, obviously, stimulated by ideas such
as Murray's, this focus on the relationship is a radical departure from the
more discrete concepts of need and press. A person's biography, then, is
the life structure built up as sets of relationships between the person and
past, present, and future others, organized around central themes that
provide the direction for selecting and modifying experience. The extended biography that Levinson provides is most helpful in understanding such a long unit of analysis. While he does not provide information
on his pre-university years, and so we do not know why the interdisciplinary road was chosen, his account of his personal biography is that of
a life structure that begins with a hoped-for interdisciplinary project,
"The Authoritarian Personality," and ends with its realization in "Seasons of a Man's Life." This account is rich in indicating how his social
world is selected by his early sets of relationships and provides major
sources of augmentation of these relationships as his life progresses.

Methodologically, Levinson's present work can be, and has been,
criticized for falling short of the usual procedures on which scientific
evidence is based. However, it is premature to raise these concerns for
Levinson is providing a description and model of the initial stages of the
research process that is usually missing from our books on research
method. Levinson, drawing from Murray's experience, argues that when
beginning an exploration all possible sources of investigation should be
used. Thus, he cites the model of Murray as a hybrid clinician-humanist-
scientist, willing to utilize all modalities to outline the coordinates of a
new terrain which might later be subjected to a more rigorous examination. The value of Murray's exploration is proven by the fact that it has
guided much of the scientific work in personality for the last forty years.
Levinson's work, especially his scheme of sequential life stages, is
equally clear in providing a set of bearings for examining the adult life
span. This descriptive scheme now permits a consideration of the
methods most appropriate for its examination and stimulates a broad
front of research projects. Its value, as happened for Murray's scheme,
will be judged later by the research that it will have evoked.

REFERENCES

Block, J. *Lives through Time*. Berkeley, CA: Bancroft, 1971.

Epstein, S. Explorations in personality today and tomorrow: a tribute to Henry A. Murray. *American Psychologist,* 1979, **34,** 649–653.

Levinson, D. *Seasons of a Man's Life,* 1978.

Mischel, W. *Personality Assessment.* New York: Wiley, 1968.

CHAPTER 2

Some Enduring and Consequential Structures of Personality

Jack Block

Thirty years ago I was a graduate student at Stanford University, and Henry Murray—three thousand miles away—was one of my teachers. *Explorations in Personality* (Murray, 1938) was then ten years old but, because of the war, its perspectives, its conceptual and empirical accomplishments, and its generative possibilities were only beginning to register on psychology.

It was a heady time; the study of personality in ways that were scientifically honorable and yet sufficiently *psychological* had been shown by Murray and his unusual set of co-workers both to be feasible and to be exciting. The conditions of being human, the concerns of being human, the characteristics of being human have all been matters of preoccupation over the ages for the philosophers. The revolutionary clinician, Freud, had moved these issues appreciably toward a theoretical integration. And now Murray and his colleagues were showing the way to a scientific study of human beings that was rich enough to do justice to the complexities of the motivational and behavioral phenomena involved.

In the intervening years it seems fair to say that we have fallen away from the high and simple optimism of those times. The reasons for this are many, complexly intertwined, and perhaps should have been anticipated as psychology has gone its expansive and scattered way. Personology (as Murray would call the study of personality) was never promised to be a rose garden. When shallow gardeners, eager for quick and easy harvest, encountered more thorns than flowers for their efforts, many turned away from the field and toward the cultivation of easier territories. Then too, psychology is subject to recurrent, essentially ideological cycles of emphasis, reflecting different views of how one should attempt to understand humankind. We have recently been going through a phase when the very observational basis of personology has been seriously argued as no more than a projective attribution by personologists, having little or no relation to the people being studied. And it must be acknowledged that personologists, even committed ones, have sometimes been forgetful of, or have found it difficult to construct or to find the necessary conditions for fair study of adaptive, value-optimizing psychological systems. Which is what, formally speaking, people are.

In this time when personality psychologists are milling around, fending off their critics and yet dissatisfied with the state of their field, it is instructive (and I must say, embarrassing,) to read again *Explorations in Personality.* The English philosopher, Alfred North Whitehead, once said: "Everything important has been said before by someone who did not discover it." The American psychologist, Jack Block, has remarked: "Everything important has been said before by someone who *did* discover it." And the world-weary French novelist, Andre Gide, has sighed: "It has all been said before, but you must say it again, since nobody listens." Listen again to the Henry Murray of forty years ago and judge his pertinence for today.

(I quote Murray almost verbatim, changing or adding words only to gain grammatical flow. The ideas are his and almost all the words, to be found in the first chapter of *Explorations*) Said Murray:

The life history of a single [person is the] unit with which the discipline [of psychology] has to deal . . . The psychologist will never fully understand an episode [of behavior] if it is abstracted from . . . the developmental history of the individual . . . (Although) the prevailing custom in psychology is to study one function or one aspect of [behavior] at a time—and this is as it must be [because of the need for detailed information] . . . the psychologist who does this should recognize that he is observing merely a part of an operating totality, and that this totality in turn, is but a small temporal segment of a personality . . . A specific situation serves to isolate, or dissect, a specific part of personality. This part can be rarely understood by itself but it can be studied as a clue to the general structure of the personality . . . Psychology must construct a scheme of concepts for portraying the entire course of individual development, and thus provide a framework into which any single episode—natural or experimental—may be fitted. (Murray, 1938, pp. 3–4)

Characterizing the then current state of personology, Murray noted that

There is no agreement as to what traits or variables are significant . . . There are few generally valued tests, no traits that are always measured, no common guiding concepts. . . . The literature is full of accurate observations of particular events, statistical compilations, and brilliant flashes of intuition. But taken as a whole, personology is a patchwork quilt of incompatible designs. In this domain men speak with voices of authority saying different things in different tongues, and the expectant student is left to wonder whether one or none are in the right. (Murray, 1938, p. 6.)

Murray warned of the difficulties confronting the investigator of personality: "There are limitations of time, of the variety of conditions and of the number of experimenters, of the necessity of observing a subject many times if one is to know that subject well." He noted "the peculiar effect of the laboratory situation," the presence of experimenter effects and the difficulty of estimating them. He resignedly accepted the attention by psychologists to only a small fraction of what is going on in behavior and anticipated the fruitlessness of focusing on tiny behavioral actions, however "objective," that are divorced from context, arguing instead for the necessity, despite all attendant complications and dangers, of *interpreting* behavior. He proposed procedures for rising above the idiosyncratic perceptions and understandings of psychologists so that the needed interpretation by psychologists of an individual's behavior could achieve an independent and valid status. He was sensitive to the variability of behavior of individuals and sought the factors within a person or context that would make seemingly "inconsistent" behaviors coherent. He was aware of the need to study intensively many and diverse individuals if one is to discover the variety of adaptive modes and relationships of which people are capable. He offered one of the very first psychological conceptualizations of the environmental contexts in which individuals must function, with his concept of "press." He was the progenitor of both enduring principles and enduring techniques for what came to be called personality assessment, with its many fruitful applications. And, he offered a theoretical scaffold for a field trying to rise toward both science and meaning. All of this is quite a lot, and nothing on this galloping list will seem outmoded to close observers of the field.

But enough of these tributes to Murray, his thinking, his work, and his values. In science, a more significant homage is the influence a man's work has on the subsequent shape of the field. I wish to talk now of some of my own research squarely in the Murray tradition, the study of *Lives through Time*, (Block, 1971).

There are many useful and intriguing ways to be a psychologist. Good fortune and choice have immersed me in longitudinal inquiries. As Murray so firmly understood, psychological knowledge must be imbedded in a developmental (i.e., temporal) framework. And if we are to address developmental questions in ways that permit inferentially clean or compelling answers, it is clear that longitudinal studies are required. The findings from correlational analyses, cross-sectional or cohort comparisons, or experimental studies can be of great importance but, for many issues, these approaches do not offer results that can logically substitute for the implications to be drawn from prolonged, systematic study of the same individuals over time. *Post hoc* clinical reconstructions or armchair ratiocinations regarding life development may contain much truth and wisdom but also, they may not. Such efforts are only mental exercises whose incremental truth value is undecidable unless tested by an appropriate empiricism, which must be longitudinal.

The questions to which longitudinal study seeks to respond are many: Is the set of character fixed early or late or never? Is the parenting a child receives influential in shaping how, as an adult, life is lived? Can especially fortunate or tragic or otherwise interesting life outcomes be anticipated early on? What are the conditions and consequences of personality change? Do we all proceed through the life course in more or less the same way or are alternative, psychologically tenable routes taken; and, if so, why? What are the pushes and pulls, the surges and the abatements characterizing the inexorably encountered stages of a human life? What are the adaptive functions, common and different, by which individuals respond to and upon their changing world and changing self-recognitions? In short, and simply put: Why do people turn out the way they do?

Questions such as these lie behind the wide and demanding lay interest in psychology. They are, ultimately, fair questions, even if sometimes naively put, and they deserve far more serious scientific attention than yet has been granted them.

The particular focus of the present paper is on the question of the "continuity" or "discontinuity" (or both) of normal personality. Over time and over context, can the various and diverse behaviors of an individual be recognized as importantly influenced by enduring aspects of character? The issue is a centrally important one and, in its current manifestation, can be traced back to the consistency-inconsistency issue as posed by Mischel (1968) more than ten years ago. Mischel's primary emphasis was on the consistency or inconsistency of behaviors, from situation to situation. By introducing the dimension of time, the question of consistency-inconsistency converts into the question of continuity-discontinuity.

There are many facets to this issue, many ways to engage it. Here I shall restrict myself simply to bringing to bear some findings issuing from the longitudinal archives of the Institute of Human Development at Berkeley.

In order to have perspective on the relationships I shall be reporting, it is necessary to understand something about the longitudinal studies from which they derive. In 1929, Jean Macfarlane started a study, which became longitudinal, of a random sample of babies born in Berkeley. The sample was intensively studied through high school, and richly detailed information exists in the files for each of the subjects. A full description of the Macfarlane study and its sampling and data collection procedures, is contained in the monograph by Macfarlane (1938).

In 1932, Harold E. Jones and his colleagues initiated their own study, of fifth-grade children attending elementary schools adjacent to Berkeley. These children, born in the early 1920s, were intensively studied through high school and, again, much information is in the files for each subject. A description of the design and orientation of the Jones study, as initially conceived, is presented by Jones (1938, 1939a, 1939b).

In the late 1950s, the subjects from the two separate studies were again evaluated at the Institute of Human Development (IHD), under support from the Ford Foundation. The subjects then were, in the one sample, about 31 years old and, in the other sample, about 38 years of age, a total of 171 individuals, 84 men and 87 women.

I came on the IHD scene in 1960, my interest in longitudinal studies kindled by Harold and Mary Jones. To integrate the long-collected but still little used information, it was necessary to impose a research design and invoke a method to make scientifically usable data from the extensive longitudinal archival material. This was not an easy task; protracted, tedious, obsessive labors by many psychologists were required before reliable and independent data characterizing the subjects at different times became available and could be used in a variety of ways to examine a host of longitudinal questions. Some years ago, in a book called *Lives through Time* (Block, 1971), I reported on this effort and, among other things, on some findings regarding the continuity and discontinuity of personality from adolescence to the mid-thirties. I shall be drawing on some of these earlier reported results in this chapter.

It seems to be a characteristic of longitudinal studies that they go on. In the late 1960s, the Institute gathered new information and evaluations on the subjects who were then, in the Macfarlane sample, about 42 years old and, in the Jones sample, about 49 years of age, a total of 146 individuals, 70 men and 76 women. The research design and the method employed successfully for *Lives through Time* were reapplied so as to achieve comparability of the data in this last assessment with data from the earlier assessments. I am grateful to have been permitted by the Institute to have access to these most recent data, costly in many ways and contributed by so many. I shall be reporting, for the first time here, some linkages of this assessment of the subjects when well into their forties with earlier assessments of the subjects going back as far as thirty or thirty-five years, to early adolescence.

The research approach employed necessarily was conditioned by the nature and limitations of the already secured information stored away in the Institute archives. Over the years, an impressively large quantity of diverse information had been accumulated for each subject. The files bulk large and are filled with folder after folder of material: interest and attitude check lists, anthropometric measurements, X-rays, intelligence test records, teachers' ratings, Rorschach responses, tracings of psychophysiological reactions, ratings of the home and mother, silhouettes of body builds, sociometric records, photographs, muscular coordination indices, interview protocols from subjects, parents, teachers and spouses, news clippings involving the subjects, free play observations, and more, much more. The sheer volume and breadth of the archival material gathered during the course of these two longitudinal studies is inundating.

Yet, for many purposes, the information collected during the longitudinal studies and deposited in the archives was insufficient or otherwise inadequate. Given a focal concern with personality and its development, much of what was filed could confidently be ignored as irrelevant. The archival material remaining while still widely ranging, was usually not in the form of data, that is, quantified or otherwise comparable and contextualized information permitting analysis and evaluation. The task of regularizing and transforming the IHD archival material into usable data was a formidable one, onerous sometimes beyond a simple or polite description.

There were several problems: For every subject, there are at least some missing procedures or there is missing information, generally for extenuating reasons, but creating large difficulties when analyses are necessary. There were procedural changes over the years, often for the better, but such changes prevented direct comparability of behaviors or performance over the years. Then too, the conceptual language and the professional concerns when the longitudinal studies were started are quite different from the conceptual language and foci of contemporary personologists; the resulting problem was to let information collected in another time, for another purpose, speak to the conceptual questions of today. Yet another problem was, if only it could be managed, a fundamental resource and strength, namely, the abundant naturalistic data available for each subject. For each of the longitudinal subjects, over the many years of the study, there had developed a file and record of anecdotes about his or her behavior in school, or social settings, of news clippings about the subject's various doings, of remarks made that an observing psychologist had thought it relevant to jot down, of the subject's private aspirations and fears as conveyed during interviews or the many informal encounters with staff members, and so on. This kind of information, although haphazard and not strictly comparable from subject to subject, was most abundant and alive. In a fundamental way, the richness of these longitudinal studies lies in the close observation and recording of subject behaviors in their natural world rather than merely in the tests and situations to which the subject samples had been exposed. The dossiers on the subjects, each containing a wealth of information uniquely pertinent to a particular life, were vivid and compelling. But how could these motley archival records, different for each subject, be employed so that comparative analyses became feasible?

The response to these several problems involved the use of personality ratings, contributed by multiple judges, via the Q-sort procedure, for each of three, and now four, entirely separate and therefore independent assessment periods. There are several features to this response, all of which require at least brief comment.

The enterprise of psychology is not yet ready to escape its reliance upon considered opinion as a basic kind of datum about people. Observations and impressions of an individual as coded in the form of a rating by a personality assessor are simple to use, applicable in diverse and experimentally untrammelled circumstances, can be derived from various, not strictly comparable kinds of information, so long as information is sufficient, and can be directed toward the indexing of unusual and most complex psychological dimensions. And finally, when well done, personality ratings are impressively valid with regard to criteria or concepts presently not measurable by alternate means within psychology.

A deficiency of personality ratings as they often have been employed is that they have been predicated on the impressions or formulations of a single observer whose judgmental idiosyncrasies were unknown. (Murray was well aware of this general problem, and in *Explorations in Personality* sought a solution through what he called a diagnostic council, a group of psychologists meeting together to form a consensus judgement about an individual who was well-known to all of them.) Data derived from solitary psychologists may not be reproducible and hence not fall within the scientific domain. But judgments derived independently from each of several raters rise above this limitation because their arithmetic consensus has the reproducibility required, without losing the important individual perception of the contributing observers (Block, 1961; 1978, Chapter 2).

The Q-sort procedure (Block, 1961; 1978) is simply a set of mildly technical rules for the scaling, by a judge, of a group of personality-descriptive variables (called Q-items) in relation to a particular individual. The ultimate ordering of the Q-items expresses the judge's formulation of the personality of the individual being evaluated. The method prevents the intrusion of extraneous and obfuscating categorizing or response biases of the judges. If a carefully evolved set of Q-items is employed, the method permits the comprehensive description, in contemporary psychodynamic terms, of an individual's personality in a form suitable for quantitative comparison and analysis.

The research analyses initially were constrained to the information available for three, and now four, cleanly partitioned time periods: early adolescence (i.e., the junior high school period, ages 13 and 14), middle adolescence (i.e., the senior high school period, ages 15 through 17), the period when the subjects were in their thirties, and now, in addition, the period when the subjects were in their forties. Strict partitioning of the archival material available for a subject means that assessments of a subject's personality during each of the time intervals are strictly independent and one therefore can have faith in the relationships subsequently found between time periods. Long-term Institute personnel who knew the subjects over many years, however deep their knowledge of them, could not for this very reason offer evaluations of the subjects at a particular time that were uninfluenced by their judgements of what the subjects once were like or turned out to be. To achieve relationships across time that could not be said to be "contaminated" by prior or subsequent knowledge, it was necessary to bring in 36 experienced psychologists having no prior acquaintance with the longitudinally studied subjects and to restrict the informational base on which they predicated their personality assessments.

Specifically, from all the information available for each subject, there were assembled four dossiers, one for each of the designated time periods. The dossiers were strictly independent and nonoverlapping; no information in one dossier was carried over into another. The material for a particular subject at a particular age was evaluated by (usually) three clinical psychologists, each functioning independently. No psychologist evaluated a subject at more than one age and, moreover, the combinations of psychologists judging each particular age were permutated extensively, using the large pool of psychologist-judges available, to prevent the possible introduction of systematic judge effects. Psychologists expressed their descriptions or formulations of each subject using the California Q-set. Interjudge agreement was generally acceptable, stereotype effects were negligible, and consequently, for each subject at each time period, the several Q-formulations were arithmetically averaged. Thus, a consensually based and reproducible composite personality description was available for each subject, at each of four time periods. Further extensive information regarding the research design, the procedures employed, and the quality controls applied as the data were developed is available in *Lives through Time* (Block, 1971).

Given the care and logic underlying the generation of these personality assessments, it would appear difficult to explain away substantial relationships empirically found to exist between time periods. Such relationships cannot be attributed to the effects of common data, common Q-sorters, or the subtle influences of stereotypes. Rather, such relationships, if obtained, can most readily be understood in terms of enduring qualities within the subjects studied, qualities that were behaviorally manifest in diverse ways, but were recognizable in their implications by experienced clinical psychologists.

And just what are the findings? They are many, surprising, and implicative; more than can be reported here alone. I have chosen in this presentation to highlight only a few features of the relationships that have emerged, emphasizing the connections between personality in early adolescence and personality in the mid-forties.

Let us first consider simply the correlations over time of the orderings of the subjects with respect to the personality variables on which they were assessed. For conceptual purposes, these correlations are in many ways unsatisfactory: they fail to allow for unreliability of measurement which attenuates relationships; they fail to allow for lawful developmental changes and transformations; and, as overall summarizing indices of relationships, they are easily misled. Nevertheless, these simple correlations over time, if recognized as minimal statements about the enduringness of personality qualities, are of interest.

For the male sample, from the junior high school period to the mid-forties, an interval of thirty to thirty-five years, 54% (49/90) of the personality variables are correlated beyond the .05 level of significance (one-tailed); 31% (28/90) are significantly correlated beyond the .01 level; and 13% (12/90) are significant beyond the .001 level. For the female sample, the corresponding figures are 62% (56/90) reaching the .05 level; 32% (29/90) significant beyond the .01 level; and 12% (11/90) beyond the .001 level of significance.

To provide some quick, sketchy sense of the psychological content of the significant relationships, for the male sample, the variable "is self-defeating" correlates .46 from Junior High School to the mid-forties; the variable "has a high aspiration level" correlates .45; the variable "genuinely values intellectual and cognitive matters" correlates .58; the variable "has fluctuating moods" correlates .40; For the female sample the variable "esthetically reactive" correlates .41 from junior high school to the mid-forties; the variable "is cheerful" correlates .36; the variable "pushes and tries to stretch limits to see what she can get away with" correlates .43; the variable "is an interesting, arresting person" correlates .44. All of these correlations are lowered or attenuated by the inevitable presence of unreliability of measurement. Reasonable allowance or correction for this attenuation indicates these correlation values would move up appreciably as the quality of measurement is improved.

The preceding analyses evaluate the consistency of the ordering of individuals over time with respect to each of a number of personality variables. A perhaps better, more holistic, and more psychological way to evaluate characterological congruence over the years is to study the ordering or salience of personality variables within an individual at different times. With the present data, this approach requires simply correlating the Q-composite formulation, consisting of 90 variables, of a subject for the junior high school period with the comparable Q-composite formulation of that individual when in the mid-forties.

For the seventy male subjects, the character congruences as expressed via correlations range from −.51 to .73, with a mean of .30. For the seventy-six female subjects, the across-time correlations of their character formulations range from −.42 to .76, with a mean of .31. Again these values are lowered by the presence of unreliability. With better specification at each time of the personalities of the subjects, the across-time correlations would rise appreciably.

Nevertheless, the figures are useful. They indicate *great* variation from person to person, some individuals being impressively predictable thirty to thirty-five years later from their character structures in early adolescence while other individuals are unrecognizable in later years from their junior high school descriptions. This very great range in intra-individual consistency over time makes foolish the computation of an "average" consistency or continuity; an average is useful only if the scores on which it is based have a small range. We should not be asking the question: Are people consistent over time? Some are and some are not. We should be asking instead such questions as: What kinds of people are consistent and what kinds are not? Is consistency a sign of positive change or a sign of failure to grow? Is inconsistency an indicator of positive change or of negative change or is it simply a sign of transformation? Can we identify the conditions and circumstances related to various kinds of personality change and personality continuity?

I have made some efforts with these data to study such deeper and more differentiated questions. I do not consider my analyses to be entirely satisfactory, in part for methodological reasons and in part because the data base simply is not comprehensive or sensitive enough to be able to respond to all the psychological issues involved. Nevertheless, by employing a relatively unused approach, some relationships are uncovered that are of appreciable interest.

The approach I have employed is a typological one. However, the concern has not been to establish types of personality but rather to study types of personality *development*. Personality types change and evolve in lawful ways over time. We are interested in tracking the developmental trends manifested by these various modes of personality organization and the alternate life paths taken. A personality type early is a personality type later, although perhaps a different one. We need to be able to plot the various separate trend-lines of our personality types, attending both to the cross-sectional comparisons available at each slice of time and to the directions and the significance of the changes observed over the years.

Skipping a lot of methodological and statistical detail that can, however, be found in Chapter 7 of *Lives through Time*, let me hasten on by saying types of personality development were identified by applying inverse factor analysis to the junior high school and mid-thirties Q-sort data considered conjointly. *Lives through Time* (Chapters 8 and 9) reports in detail the nature of the various types discerned, the developmental progressions they manifest, their familial origins, their life concomitants with respect to marriage, work, sickness, and the like, and other independent psychological data.

I cannot present here all the developmental types found and all the data that surround the types, testifying to the incisiveness of this particular way of cleaving nature. What I shall do for three of the male types and for three of the female types is to describe them as they were evaluated in early adolescence and as they are evaluated by entirely new data in their mid-forties, ten years older than they were when reported on in my earlier account in *Lives through Time*.

One male type I earlier called *ego resilients,* individuals who had manifested a long-standing characterological integrity and resourcefulness. In junior high school, these boys had been evaluated as having the following statistically distinguishing qualities when compared with the remaining boys: they were dependable, productive, ambitious, bright, valued intellectual matters, were likable, had wide interests, were poised, straightforward, sympathetic, introspective and philosophically-concerned, warm, socially perceptive, and reasonably satisfied with self.

In their mid-forties, as studied anew, these boys as men are statistically distinguished by the following qualities, when compared to the remaining men in the sample: they are productive, ambitious, bright, value intellectual matters, are likable, have wide interests, are introspective and philosophically-concerned, concerned, socially perceptive, turned to for advice, and reasonably satisfied with self. They appear to have lost some of their earlier differentiating warmth and sympathy (but are by no means deficient in these qualities—they tend to become emotional while watching an empathy-inducing film); they value their independence and their objectivity; they evaluate situations in motivational terms. Surely there is great personality congruence for these individuals over the years. Moreover, on the California Psychological Inventory (CPI), taken when the subjects were in their mid-forties, the early-defined ego resilients score significantly higher on the scales measuring dominance, self-acceptance, sense of well-being, intellectual efficiency, and psychological mindedness, among others. The CPI is a well-established and impressively validated instrument. These CPI differences provide separate and further support for an enduring and consequential structure of personality, observed from early adolescence.

Another male type I have called *unsettled under-controllers,* to indicate the pervasive impulsivity and changeableness within these individuals. In junior high school, these boys were significantly more rebellious, talkative, hostile, they had unconventional thought processes, they tested the limits of the situations in which they found themselves, they were verbally fluent, extrapunitive, irritable, self-dramatizing, negativistic, and generally undercontrolled.

In their mid-forties, these subjects as men, when compared to the remaining men in the sample, are again significantly distinguished as under-controlled, rebellious, testing of limits, hostile, self-dramatizing, expressive, deceitful, and unpredictable. On the CPI, they score significantly higher on scales measuring dominance, social presence and self-acceptance and significantly lower on socialization, self-control, achievement via conformance, and femininity. Over the last ten years, they have had more changes of jobs than the other men. Again we have powerful evidence for an enduring and consequential structure of personality, observed from early adolescence.

A third male type I labeled *vulnerable over-controllers* to indicate the excessive constriction and little margin characterizing these individuals. In junior high school, these boys were significantly more over-controlled, aloof, thin-skinned, ruminative, uncomfortable with uncertainly, distrustful, unvarying of their roles, submissive, defeatist, and introspective.

In their mid-forties, these subjects, when compared to the remaining men in the sample were significantly more withdrawing when frustrated, they were self-defeating, unvarying of their roles, self-pitying, fearful, constricted, bothered by demands, despondent, and projective. On the CPI, they scored significantly higher on over-control and good impression and significantly lower on scales measuring social presence, self-acceptance, and sense of well-being. This group tended to contain the bachelors of the sample, to a significant degree. More evidence, I suggest, for an enduring and consequential structure of personality, observed from early adolescence.

A first female type I have designated as *female prototypes,* a term intended to convey the exemplary way in which these individuals have manifested the qualities our culture at the time prescribed as appropriate for females. During junior high school, these girls had been evaluated as significantly more likable, poised, gregarious, cheerful, dependable, warm, productive, giving, sympathetic, fastidious, attractive, socially perceptive, reassuring, protective, and aware of their social stimulus value.

In their mid-forties, these women, significantly more than the other women in the sample, are evaluated as poised, cheerful, feminine, charming, socially perceptive, aware of their social stimulus value, giving, likable, warm, attractive, interested in the opposite sex, with wide interests and a good sense of humor. On the CPI, they score significantly higher on scales measuring dominance, sociability, social presence, self-acceptance, responsibility, tolerance, and achievement via conformance; lower on scales implying neurotic tendencies. They have had more children than their sample peers. Overall, these results testify again to an enduring and consequential structure of personality, observed from early adolescence.

A second female type I have called *vulnerable under-controllers,* to describe a group of individuals homogeneous in their unmodulated impulsivity of action and reaction coupled with a plaintive submissiveness that leaves them open to exploitation by others. In junior high school, these girls were significantly more under-controlled, self-indulgent, changeable, talkative, self-dramatizing, limit-testing, irritable, rebellious, brittle, self-pitying, affected, and hostile.

In their mid-forties, these subjects as women, when compared to the other women in the sample, are significantly more under-controlled, unpredictable, self-defeating, rebellious, self-indulgent, self-dramatizing, extrapunitive, socially obtuse, unconventional, and lacking in fastidiousness. On the CPI, they score significantly lower on responsibility, socialization, femininity, and ego-control. They married earlier, more often and less satisfactorily, smoke a great deal, and weigh a bit too much. Another set of results indicative of an enduring and consequential structure of personality, observed from early adolescence.

A third female type I have referred to as *hyperfeminine repressives,* because the essence of this kind of personality is a repressive but unarticulated character structure, fitful emotionality alternating with emotional blandness, and sexuality that is both unwitting and deliberate.

During junior high school, these girls were significantly distinguishable as feminine, repressive, dependable, uncomfortable with uncertainty, comparing of self to others, submissive, withdrawing, emotionally bland, dependent, fearful, and concerned with their physical appearance.

In their mid-forties, these women, when compared to the other women in the sample, were significantly more fastidious, somatizing and concerned with their body, thin-skinned, withdrawing, fearful, brittle, distrustful, self-defeating, bothered by demands, self-pitying, moralistic, negativistic, over-controlled, and they feel victimized. On the CPI, they score higher on psychoneurosis and neurotic over-control and lower on dominance, social presence, self-acceptance, tolerance, flexibility, achievement via independence, and intellectual efficiency. They have had significantly more menopausal surgery. A final set of findings evidencing an enduring and consequential structure of personality, observed from early adolescence.

In this rapid accounting of a half-dozen empirically discerned types of personality development, I have chosen to emphasize those where adult character structure is strongly foreshadowed by adolescent character structure. This is not always so, of course; some of the types I am not reporting upon (e.g., the *cognitive copers,* a female type; the *belated adjusters,* a male type) display fundamental characterological transformations over the years and in ways that can be related to a stage conceptualization of personality development such as that of Jane Loevinger (1976). My reason for stressing "continuity" here is by way of compensating for what I believe to be an exaggeration in recent discussion of the evidence and reasons for personality "discontinuity."

I happen to think that the recently created polarity between continuity and discontinuity is an unfortunate one. The terms require close definition and consistent utilization if discussion is to be fruitful; too often to date, neither condition has characterized debate.

The idea of continuity in personality development, as I believe the term to be generally understood by personologists, means that early character structure has lawful implications, not necessarily direct or obvious, for later character structure. No personality psychologist contends that later experiences, later environmental contexts, and everyone's inevitable passage through the sequence of biologically and societally imposed stages of life do not have important influence on behavior and even on personality organization and reorganization. What is contended is that how experience registers, how environments are selected or modified, and how the stages of life are negotiated depends, importantly and coherently, on what the individual brings to these new encounters—the resources, the premises, the intentions, the awarenesses, the fears and the hopes, the forethoughts and the after-thoughts that are subsumed by what we call personality.

The idea of discontinuity in personality development, as I understand the term to be used by protagonists of this view, asserts there is a lack of implication of early development for later development: early character structure tells us little or nothing about later character structure and later behavior or capacities. One line of explanation offered for behavioral discontinuity conjectures that new orientations, new dispositions, new capacities "emerge" from unique processes. Another line of explanation for discontinuity suggests that changes in the environmental surround or life context elicit and direct behavioral changes over time. Both of these projected explanations are, in principle, unexceptionable but both re-quire serious conceptual formulation followed by relevant empiricism. At this time in the apparently intensifying discussion of continuity and discontinuity, it really must be said that there is no positive, explicit, predicted evidence that a particular set of earlier events or conditions or qualities will not influence later behavior or attitudes on the world.

Instead, discontinuity advocates attempt to advance their position by citing (sometimes seemingly selectively) instances of apparent failure of the continuity position. The argument appears to be that, if the con-tinuity position has failed, the discontinuity position is strengthened. We should all have learned the fallacy of this kind of reasoning in our first statistics class; one cannot use a failure to find a relationship (of continuity, for example) as strong proof for the null hypothesis (of discontinuity). There are many reasons why relationships fail to be found, thus showing a failure of "continuity" or "consistency." Perhaps the easiest way is simply to do inadequate research: by using unreliable or invalid measures, small or irrelevant samples of subjects and of situations, and insensitive or inappropriate techniques of analysis, one can readily generate meaningless "evidence" for behavioral discon-tinuity and inconsistency. I have written on this problem elsewhere (Block, 1977).

It is time now to move beyond the "either-or" arguments that have characterized the continuity-discontinuity debate, with their repetitive demonstrations in support of one side or another. We should move on to more and closer study of lives as they are shaped and forged and led, to identify the factors within and beyond the individual that influence the evolving and mutating life. Toward that psychological end, the past ways of psychology as a science will have to change.

The institutional arrangements and larger social setting for psychologi-cal investigation have been more than slightly discouraging of intensive and sustained personality research. Then, too, the academic reward structure has seemed to encourage research that is quick and easy and dramaturgic. The serious scientific study of lives cannot proceed this way. Another essay and another time is required to consider the many facets of this problem and what should or can be done to develop the possibilities of a genuine personology.

In the meanwhile, it is good to remember that the returns from personality research will depend on what is invested in personality research. Those returns could, I anticipate, well justify the investment many psychologists have been reluctant to make. Murray well understood the problems and the pleasures of personology in his observation: "One must know a lot to comprehend a little."

ACKNOWLEDGMENT

Preparation of this paper was supported by National Institute of Mental Health Research Grant MH 16080 and by a James McKeen Cattell Fellowship. Raymond Launier and Alice Brilmayer provided inestimable help, under great temporal pressure, in analyzing the data newly reported here. I am grateful to Paul Mussen and Dorothy Eichorn for graciously permitting me access to these data, from the most recent assessment of the subjects being studied at the Institute of Human Development.

REFERENCES

Block, J. *Lives through Time.* Berkeley, CA: Bancroft, 1971.

Block, J. Advancing the psychology of personality: Paradigmatic shift or improving the quality of research? In D. Magnusson and N. S. Endler (Eds.), *Personality at the Crossroads: Current Issues in Interactional Psychology.* Hillsdale, NJ: Lawrence Erlbaum Associates, 1977.

Block, J. *The Q-Sort Method in Personality Assessment and Psychiatric Research.* Springfield, IL: C.C. Thomas, 1961; Palo Alto: Consulting Psychologists Press, 1978.

Jones, H. E. The California adolescent growth Study. *Journal of Education Research,* 1938, **31,** 561–567.

Jones, H. E. The adolescent growth study. I. Principles and methods. *Journal of Consulting Psychology,* 1939(a), **3,** 157–159.

Jones, H. E. The adolescent growth study. II. Procedures. *Journal of Consulting Psychology,* 1939(b), **3,** 177–180.

Loevinger, J. *Ego Development: Conceptions and Theories.* San Francisco: Jossey-Bass, 1976.

Macfarlane, J. W. Studies in child guidance. I. Methodology of data collection and organization. *Monographs of the Society for Research in Child Development,* 1938, **3,** (6, Whole No. 19).

Mischel, W. *Personality Assessment.* New York: Wiley, 1968.

Murray, H. A. *Explorations in Personality.* New York: Oxford University Press, 1938.

CHAPTER 3

Explorations in Biography: Evolution of the Individual Life Structure in Adulthood

Daniel J. Levinson

Our purpose is to celebrate one of the masterworks of American psychology and to apprehend its continuing importance for our own and others' labors. Its chief author and architect, Henry A. Murray, gave it the felicitous title, *Explorations in Personality*. Although personality is indeed the primary focus of this grand inquiry, its scope is much broader. As I shall indicate shortly, Murray came to see it also as a study of biography. Since 1966, my colleagues and I have been studying the lives of men (and, more recently, women). The major aim of this research is to form a theory of individual psychosocial development in adulthood. The initial results have been reported in *The Seasons of a Man's Life* (Levinson, 1978). The subtitle might well have been, "explorations in biography."

I would like to show the connection between Murray's *Explorations* and my *Seasons*, and to identify biography as a crucial common theme. I'll begin with Murray's work of the 1930s, briefly describing its historical-intellectual context and its relevance for psychology and social science. Then I'll give a brief account of my own biography, from graduate school in the early 1940s, when I was first introduced to Murray's explorations, until the mid-1960s, when I was ready to start my own. Finally, I will review the theory, methods, and findings yielded by my biographical inquiry into the adult life course. It will be evident that Murray and his creative collaborators have had an enormous influence on my personal-professional development as well as my work.

Robert White, in his introductory paper, has given a rich, personal account of Murray's enterprise from the perspective of a younger collaborator (who later succeeded Murray as Director of the Harvard Psychological Clinic). Another evocative, insightful account by a member of the original staff group has been given by Nevitt Sanford

(1980). I offer the perspective of another generation, the one that followed White's. The perspective of each generation reveals part of the truth, while reflecting its particular place in a historical process. In the belief that generations are important in collective life, as in individual biography, I want to make explicit the way they are operating here. Henry Murray was born in 1893, and turned 85 in the year of this conference. Most of his collaborators in that pioneer work were some ten to fifteen years younger and are now about 70 to 75 years old. The next generation, of which most of the contributors to this volume are a part, is now about 55 to 60 years old. We look to the succeeding generation, now around 40 years old, and the one emerging at around 30, to take up, modify further, and hand on the legacy we have received from Murray and his predecessors such as Freud (born 1856) and Jung (born 1875).

HENRY MURRAY AND HIS EXPLORATIONS

Explorations in Personality was published in 1938, after four years of collaborative research and writing. Its research leader, primary author and guiding genius was Henry Murray, at the time of publication a 45-year-old assistant professor at Harvard and head of its Psychological Clinic. His numerous colleagues were for the most part young psychologists in their late twenties and early thirties, just the right age to become deeply if ambivalently attached to a brilliant, charismatic, caring mentor. In these days when mentoring and intellectual fellowship are so scarce, those early years of the Harvard Psychological Clinic have a rich "Garden of Eden" flavor.

Murray devoted much of his early adulthood to becoming a physician and physiological researcher. In his late thirties, he finally recognized his true calling and moved into psychology. His major aims were to bring depth psychology into academic, "scientific" psychology, and to form links between the clinic and the laboratory. Murray described his intellectual origins and aims with characteristic modesty, irony and chutzpah:

> In short, then, we might say that our work is the natural child of the deep, significant, metaphorical, provocative and questionable speculations of psychoanalysis and the precise, systematic, statistical, trivial and artificial methods of academic psychology. Our hope is that we have inherited more of the virtues than the vices of our parents (Murray, 1938, pp. 33–34).

Murray's pluralistic style is reflected also in his dedication of the book to Morton Prince, Sigmund Freud, Lawrence J. Henderson, Alfred N.

Whitehead, and Carl G. Jung. A remarkable imagination, indeed, to be animated by this motley crew! And, what is even more remarkable, their diverse qualities are truly reflected in the book. It contains the vision that led Morton Prince, a psychiatrist, to found a psychological clinic devoted primarily to research. There is Henderson's dedication to a scientific outlook centered in biology but encompassing psychology and social science as well. We find the philosophical breadth of Whitehead, who sought to place the scientific enterprise within a larger intellectual-humanistic framework. Finally, the book exhibits the psychological profundity of Freud and Jung; they were split apart by almost everyone else, yet amicably joined in Murray's mediating mind. Murray admired Freud's efforts to be rational about the irrational, to develop a systematic, empirically grounded theory of the unconscious. He was attracted as strongly (though perhaps more illicitly) to Jung's fertile imagination, less controlled than Freud's but more wide-ranging, more mystical and open to outrageous ideas, and more questioning of nineteenth century rationalism. (It took me another thirty years to discover Murray's wisdom in joining them, and many others are at last beginning to see the same light.)

Taken together, these qualities suggest the kind of person that Murray actually is: a hybrid clinician-humanist-scientist, seeking to build a rigorous science of personology yet keenly aware of the mysteries of the human psyche that elude the scientist's measurements. His energies went predominantly to the quest for scientific, universally valid theory and knowledge, but perhaps his greatest love was for the unique biography of Herman Melville—a project which forms a continuing thread in his life work.

It is important to place *Explorations* in social and historical context. During the 1930s American psychology was vitally affected by the international politico-economic situation. The importing of ideas from Europe had been going on for many years, but was now intensified by the immigration of many Europeans in psychology and related disciplines. One major intellectual current was logical positivism, a philosophy of science that academic psychology found congenial and useful in furthering its claim to scientific legitimacy. A second major current was psychoanalysis. G. Stanley Hall invited Freud to lecture at Clark University in 1908, and over the next twenty-five years a small but growing number of Americans went to Europe for psychoanalytic treatment and study. It was only in the 1930s, however, with the large-scale immigration of psychoanalysts and analytically oriented psychologists, that American psychology began to regard the human personality as a fit subject for study.

Between 1935 and 1939, four exciting new books served to define and legitimize personality as a significant field in American psychology. The first, published in 1935, was Kurt Lewin's *Dynamic Theory of Personality,* a collection of papers originally written in German. Lewin sought to integrate Gestalt cognitive psychology with psychoanalysis, using an experimental rather than clinical method. Although the subsequent work of Lewin and his followers was more in social psychology than personality, his "field theoretical" approach had great influence and was assimilated into other viewpoints.

In 1937, Gordon Allport's *Personality* became the first definitive textbook for this infant field. His scholarly approach gave balanced, critical consideration to many theories and research methods. Through his judicious leadership, he played a singular role in bringing the field of personality from the edges into the mainstream of academic psychology.

Barely a year later, in 1938, Murray followed Allport to provide Harvard's other contribution. I shall return to this in a moment. First, let me note the fourth book: *Frustration and Aggression,* by Dollard, Doob, Miller, Mowrer, and Sears, published in 1939. This was, I believe, Yale's first major contribution to personality theory. A special significance of this work is that it came from a bastion of American behaviorism, led by Clark Hull, and was written by some of his most brilliant students. They attempted here to assimilate psychoanalysis into Hull's brand of stimulus-response learning theory.

These four books, then, broke the ground for the study of personality in academic psychology. A common theme was the attempt to connect psychoanalysis with other theories and methods indigenous to academic psychology. Lewin assimilated certain psychoanalytic ideas into Gestalt psychology and general cognitive theory, while using naturalistic experimental methods. The Yale group tried to join psychoanalysis with behavoristic learning theory. Allport, the omnivorous scholar, tried to create a new theoretical edifice with building blocks from many theories. He gave impetus to the use of paper-and-pencil tests, personal documents and other nonexperimental techniques for personality study.

While affirming the immense importance of all these works, I would say that *Explorations* was the most original, profound and far-reaching of the four. Though grandiose in some respects, it had a grandeur, a breadth and nobility of vision that has not been matched since in American psychology. We must go back to William James for a conception of comparable richness and scope.

Murray and his collaborators placed their stamp on the study of personality for the next twenty or thirty years. Their influence was extended during the 1940s by World War II and its aftermath, when clinical psychology was established as a new field of psychology and a new profession. Projective tests became a major element in the technology of clinical research and practice. Murray contributed the Thematic Apperception Test (TAT) and other devices, as well as a theoretical rationale for their use. The subtitle of *Explorations* is relevant here: "A clinical and experimental study of 50 men of college age." This was the most massive effort yet undertaken to develop a clinical approach in personality research, and to link it with a more traditional experimental approach.

Clinical psychology is now a powerful field within our discipline, though still rather deviant from the norms of our academic culture. The quality of deviance is not surprising when we realize that clinical psychology got beyond its infancy only in the 1940s, and that it had an alien quality from the start, representing as it did a psychodynamic, nonbehaviorist orientation and an interest in the real world more than the laboratory. The early investigators of personality, Murray in particular, created an intellectual-ethical outlook that permitted the assimilation of personality psychology and clinical work into the "scientific" academic world. It took Harvard some ten years after the publication of *Explorations* to offer Murray a full professorship; in the culture of academic psychology he represented with singular force the mythic powers of the unconscious. It took even longer for his ideas to gain legitimacy in psychology at large. The tensions are still with us.

One of Murray's special contributions was to place the study of personality on the boundary between the experimental laboratory, the psychometric laboratory, and the clinical office. This boundary was for him the most exciting domain for theory and research. He facilitated work on the boundary by creating an appropriate culture and social structure—a team of multiple investigators, representing multiple viewpoints, utilizing multiple techniques in the intensive, collaborative study of a relatively small sample of subjects. In his experimental methods he produced lifelike situations of personal significance for the participant. In his clinical research methods he sought to evoke fantasy material from the depths of the personality, and his research staff learned the art of disciplined freedom in the imaginative interpretation of personality. With regard to theory, he tried to develop a conceptual framework in which a limited number of concepts would be systematically used in the scientific analysis of individual lives. There was a creative quality in each facet of his approach. The great creativity, however, was in the effort to integrate them, to combine all this diversity within a single, comprehensive design. No initial effort of this kind could be entirely successful, but these explorations gave a noble model that deserved emulation and further development.

Over the years, Murray's example has often been admired but rarely followed. Few have been able to work on the boundary he defined or to generate the intellectual-social structures required for this work. Personality research has been fragmented into experimental, psychometric and clinical factions. The scientific ethos in academic psychology has continued to emphasize the precise measurement of a few variables within a tightly controlled research design, and to limit the exercise of imagination, the disciplined use of interpretive skill, and the search for new modes of conceptualization. What we need most, now as then, are his vitality, his breadth of vision, his intellectual daring and courage.

FROM "EXPLORATIONS IN PERSONALITY" TO "EXPLORATIONS IN BIOGRAPHY"

To build a bridge between Murray's explorations of personality in the late 1930s and my explorations of biography over the last ten or fifteen years, I must briefly recount some of my own biography. When *Explorations* appeared, I was an 18-year-old student at U.C.L.A., just discovering that psychology was a domain of science and not solely an aspect of literature. In that excellent Psychology Department I got involved in social psychology and in the Olympian struggles between Tolman and Hull regarding the nature of learning in rats and men. Over the course of an undergraduate major and a year's graduate work, however, I was not taught that personality is a significant element of psychology. This was probably the experience of students in the great majority of psychology departments at that time, and especially the "best" departments.

In 1941, I went to Berkeley and entered a new world. Edward Tolman, Egon Brunswik, Robert Tryon, and other great teachers introduced me to fantastic ideas and broadened my horizons. My remarkable new discovery, however, was the human personality. Nevitt Sanford and Else Frenkel-Brunswik were the mentors who led me to the inner world of the psyche and gave their blessing to my hopes of becoming a "personality psychologist." Both of them, in their early thirties, were apperceived as persons of unlimited wisdom and maturity by the 21-year-old novice who stood hesitantly (if also brashly) on the threshold of their intellectual mansion. Sanford had been at Berkeley for a year, fresh from graduate school and postdoctoral research at Harvard, where he had worked with Murray on *Explorations*. Frenkel-Brunswik, too, was a recent arrival. At the University of Vienna she had worked with Charlotte Buhler on the human life course, and had been involved in psychoanalytic and logical positivist circles. In graduate school I also met Erik Erikson, a young psychoanalyst and recent collaborator of

Murray's. His psychosocial view of personality and the life cycle was a seed that has been increasingly fertile in my work over the years.

During my second year at Berkeley (1942–1943), Sanford and I began a small study of anti-Semitism, financed by a munificent grant of $500 from an anonymous donor. Frenkel-Brunswik had a fellowship the same year, which she spent chiefly at Harvard with Murray, Allport, Kluckhohn and others. On her return in 1943, filled with the intellectual excitement of her travels, she joined forces with Sanford and me on the anti-Semitism research. Murray had a symbolic yet powerful presence in our small group. His multimethod approach, and many of his concepts, were brought to bear in our work on this study. We developed scales and other questionnaire techniques to measure known variables. Intensive interviewing and projective techniques enabled us to identify new variables, to generate new hypotheses and to measure the more subtle, often unconscious aspects of personality. (For a summary of our early work on this project, see Frenkel-Brunswik and Sanford, 1946.)

In 1944, as I recall, the project expanded once more. We had been approached by Max Horkheimer, head of the Frankfurt Institute for Social Research (in exile) and Scientific Director of the American Jewish Committee. He invited us to expand our investigation with funds from the American Jewish Committee, on condition that we accept as a collaborator his younger colleague, Theodor W. Adorno, then a relatively unknown philosopher-sociologist. At that point our theoretical approach and research methods were well defined, and our initial findings provided empirical grounding for a larger study. Adorno, though not well versed in our methods, contributed a sociological perspective and a wide-ranging, fertile imagination. Personally, this was an important step in the effort to join psychology and sociology.

The main product of that enterprise was *The Authoritarian Personality,* published in 1950 (Adorno et al., 1950). The decade of the 1940s had been a time of tremendous vitality and innovation in personality-social psychology, and likewise of tremendous change and liberalization on the international scene during and after World War II. Our book appeared as this era was ending and a new one beginning. The new era was characterized by pedestrian conformity and a decline of imagination in politics, art, and science. Personality-social psychology, reflecting the societal change, retreated from the exciting vistas that had emerged in the 1940s and became increasingly preoccupied with method and the measurement of narrowly defined variables. Psychology moved out of society and back into the laboratory. This is an old theme in psychology, as in other sciences. The efforts to achieve scientific legitimacy, and to work within a prevailing ideology of science, are in continuing conflict with the desire to study significant new problems that lie beyond the scope of currently conventional theories and methods.

A new chapter was starting in my life as well. In 1950 I became a faculty member in the Department of Social Relations at Harvard. This department, formed only a few years earlier, was devoted to the integration of sociology, cultural anthropology, and social and clinical psychology. The main creators and carriers of its vision were the psychologists Harry Murray, Robert White, and Gordon Allport, the sociologist Talcott Parsons, and the anthropologist Clyde Kluckhohn. My central interest was in personality, but I wanted to situate the person in a social context. In the research on authoritarianism I had begun to conceive of ideology as a reflection both of personality and of external shaping forces. I had also been engrossed in the work on culture and personality by anthropologists such as Mead, Kluckhohn, and Linton, and by unorthodox psychoanalysts such as Kardiner, Erikson, Reich, and Fromm. My own vision was expanding, but I did not yet know how difficult the road would be and how far it would lead.

Murray, too, had been trying to forge conceptual links between person and society. This was, indeed, the mandate and mythos of the Social Relations Department. There were many collaborative seminars and research projects, the collaboration usually occurring across disciplinary lines rather than within a single discipline.

My appointment was in the clinical psychology wing of the department, and I was based in the Harvard Psychological Clinic, a large old wood-frame dwelling at 64 Plympton Street. By this time Robert White had become Director of the Clinic, and Murray had moved into a recently created "Annex," heavily involved in a new phase of his explorations in personality. The Annex was around the corner on Mt. Auburn Street, and the two buildings were joined at the rear by special hallways. The image that occurs to me is that of two whales with linked tails. This image comes, of course, from the Melvillean culture that Murray created at the Clinic and bequeathed to it. The Clinic was known informally as the Baleen, and it was permeated by artifacts and symbols of the whaling life. As you can imagine, coming to the Clinic I experienced myself as the aspiring knight who suddenly found himself transplanted in King Arthur's court, and, equally, as the long-lost son returning to the familial home at last. I was meeting Murray for the first time, yet I felt I knew him well. He was, after all, my symbolic mentor, and a primary mentor of my primary mentor. And others, such as White, Allport, and Parsons, who had been heroic figures in my mythic world, were also suddenly real-life colleagues.

Bob White has already painted a vivid picture of the architecture, culture, and collective psyche of the Clinic in the 1930s. During my time there, 1950–1955, the Clinic was more established and thus probably more restrained, but it was animated by much the same qualities. There was still the large rectangular room, measuring perhaps 50 by 20 feet, that formed the social and psychological center of our microcosm. This room was called the library, and indeed it functioned in part as library, lounge, and reading room. But the library served many other functions as well. It was the intellectual center of the Clinic: our seminars were held here, as well as informal discussions and meetings of all kinds. People could always arrange to meet in the library. By a wise tradition, it was also the lunchroom. Every weekday, an elegantly simple meal was prepared in an adjacent kitchen by a part-time cook, who was an important person to us in her own right, for the electively assembled staff, students, and guests. The atmosphere was not that of a restaurant or ordinary common room, but that of an aristocratic manor in which all of us were both "family" and workers. Although Murray was no longer the formal lord of the manor, and White was regarded as an eminently worthy successor, it was generally understood that the lunches, like so many other Clinic traditions, were an intrinsic part of our heritage from Murray.

Murray's continuing presence at the Clinic was evoked in diverse other ways. I have mentioned the many signs of Murray's attachment to Melville and the whaling tradition. In addition, the walls bore several letters of historic significance, written to him by assorted dignitaries. The one that impressed me the most was written by Morton Prince on the occasion of his retirement and Murray's appointment as his successor. It was a brief, loving, hair-raising note—the kind that a father might write on his deathbed, giving his ambivalent blessing to the eldest son who is taking over the family enterprise. After expressing joy that his legacy was in such good hands, Prince observed that he would be watching over Murray's shoulder from the skies. The tone of this comment somehow conveyed the impression that Prince would watch with high hopes, but that he was prepared to intervene from above if his protege were not quite up to the job. It was Murray's genius, as it seemed to this 30-year-old reader, that he posted the letter for all to see, that he dedicated his book to Prince (among others), and that he proceded blithely on his own, different, uniquely creative way.

Although psychologists such as Murray, White, and Allport were of great personal importance to me at this time, my strongest intellectual involvement was in sociology. Murray was in the midst of a long-term collaborative research project; it was not feasible for me to join his project, and at this point in my own development I needed to seek my own path on the boundary of psychology and sociology. For several years I taught a seminar with Gordon Allport on "Group Conflict and Prejudice"; this reflected my earlier work on authoritarianism, but it did not lie on the main route I had to traverse. Robert White was an unexpected treasure I discovered after getting to the Clinic. Initially my boss, he became also my friend and counselor. His first book, *Lives in Progress* (White, 1952), was published in 1952 and extended the biographical aspect of the tradition set by the earlier *Explorations*. I am still the fond owner of the copy he gave me. The inscription contains the words: "Be it ever so humble, there is no place like personality." White's main love was the personality, and his favorite activity was the study of the individual life in its manifold aspects. As compared to his work on competence, *Lives in Progress* did not create a great stir. This book is a fine example of a work that appeared ahead of its time. It is a landmark in the development of a biographical approach that is conjointly biological, psychological, and social. Although impressed and intrigued, I was not yet ready to venture far in this direction. I needed another ten years before I could take up the challenge presented by Murray's *Explorations* and White's *Lives* and deal with it in my own way.

The major new development during this time was my intellectual engagement with sociology and my relationships with sociologists such as Talcott Parsons and Alex Inkeles. Parsons was a towering figure in American sociology, to my mind its one great theoretician. He contributed to the mainstream of sociological theory and to the boundaries of sociology with other disciplines such as psychology, anthropology, and economics. I valued Parsons chiefly as a social psychologist whose ideas enabled me to enter sociology and make use of many viewpoints in addition to his own. He clarified the distinction between the social system and the personality, and he understood the myriad forms of "interpenetration" between them. Alex Inkeles was the collaborator who most helped me to live in the interstices between sociology and psychology. For over ten years we jointly taught a seminar on "Personality and Social Structure." We co-authored a theoretical statement on "National character: the study of modal personality and sociocultural systems" (Inkeles and Levinson, 1968), outlining a sociopsychological approach to the study of the individual and society. In these and countless other ways, a sociologically oriented psychologist and a psychologically oriented sociologist gave each other intellectual and emotional sustenance as they pursued interests beyond the usual confines of their disciplines. Gradually I began to form a conception of society, culture, class, social structure—the complex workings of collective life—as these interweave with the individual life.

In 1955 I moved to the Department of Psychiatry at Harvard, and was based at the Massachusetts Mental Health Center. I continued teaching the seminar with Inkeles, advising on doctoral dissertations in psychology and sociology, and maintaining various research ties with the Social Relations Department. But a basic change was getting underway: I was modifying my earlier identity as a psychologist and becoming a hybrid, situated at the margins of psychology, sociology, and psychiatry. With the support and collaboration of Milton Greenblatt (who was then Director of Research at the Massachusetts Mental Health Center), I began a program of research on the mental hospital as an organization. Over the next ten years I studied various aspects of the hospital social structure, as well as the relations among personality, role, and ideology in patients, staff, and student-professionals Gilbert and Levinson, 1956; Williams, 1957; (Greenblatt, Levinson, and Sharaf and Levinson, 1964; Levinson and Gallagher, 1964; Levinson, Merrifield, and Berg, 1967; Levinson and Klerman, 1967). With colleagues from the Harvard Business School, I examined the management of a mental health center, with emphasis on the "executive role constellation" (Hodgson, Levinson, and Zaleznik, 1965). While continuing to use structured research methods such as questionnaires and scales, I placed increasing emphasis upon the methods of field research, including semi-participant observation and extended interviewing.

A seemingly antithetical change was occurring at the same time: my thinking and research took on a more clinical aspect. Through personal psychoanalysis and experience as a psychotherapist, I came to appreciate more fully the subtle complexities of an individual life and an evolving intimate relationship (Levinson, 1977). I was influenced by the psychodynamic-clinical culture of the Massachusetts Mental Health Center case conferences, teaching and observation on inpatient wards, consulting with various management groups, intensive involvement in organizational life—these and other experiences heightened my awareness of the dense realities that our theories and research data barely begin to penetrate. Never primarily a clinician, I have always been more interested in normal functioning and development than in pathology. But I have come increasingly to believe that clinical experience and the intensive, experiential study of the individual life are of fundamental value in the education of personality researchers.

My move to Yale in 1966 marked the close of one chapter in my life and the start of another. As in all transitions, the work of terminating the outgoing phase went hand in hand with that of initiating the next. As an integral part of the effort to define new directions for the future, I had to review the past and come to a clearer sense of what it had given me as a basis for the emerging present. Looking back on the "Harvard years" from 1950 to 1966, I found that I had developed in two directions. I was becoming more sociological, moving *outward* from the personality to the sociocultural world in which it is so enmeshed. At the same time, I was moving *inward*, more deeply into the personality, learning through clinical experience and participant observation much more than I had previously by more formal research. These two directions are only apparently opposite. The study of institutions and groups showed me that psychological processes play a vital part in their formation and modes of functioning. Likewise, I learned from the intensive study of individual lives that the sociocultural world is reflected exquisitely within the personality.

The splitting of the "outward" and the "inward" views has created massive barriers between sociology and psychology. The field known as "social psychology" has led a double life, one as a specialty within psychology, the other within sociology. My own view, in contrast, is that social psychology must become a distinctive discipline on the boundary between psychology and the social sciences, linking the two parent disciplines yet having its own character. From this perspective, a conjointly social and psychological approach is needed for the study of society and collective life. Our traditional, unidisciplinary conceptions of social structure and of personality have to be modified. This realization opens new theoretical horizons for both sociology and psychology.

These changes in theoretical outlook were reflected in the evolution of my plans for a new research project. At first, staying close to my previous work, I thought about a study of occupational career, as shaped by personality and by various social contexts. I soon realized, however, that it was not enough simply to do another study of the occupational career. The next project would draw on my previous work, but a bold new beginning was required.

My dimly perceived goal was to study individual lives over time. But it was not clear how to study a person's life at a given time, let alone the course of life over a span of years. I turned for guidelines to the major concepts in my repertory: personality; social roles and careers in various settings (such as occupation, family, religion, community); the impact of these settings, by way of their culture, social structure, and social process, on individual personality and behavior. Although these concepts were still of great value, there was, I felt, something missing. Each of them dealt with an important segment of living but, taken together, they did not yield a picture of the individual life. The parts did not form a whole. I had a systematic basis for studying the occupational career, or the familial career, as it is influenced by personality and by various socializing influences. But I did not have an articulated theory or methodology for studying the individual life course.

In 1967 I resolved these issues just enough to apply for and receive a research grant from the National Institute of Mental Health. I decided to study a sample of forty men, currently in the age range 35–45 years old.

I conceived of this as the "mid-life decade," a time of transition from youth to middle age, though the meaning of these terms was still quite obscure. My ideas regarding this part of the life course were still quite intuitive and I was not ready to limit the research to a set of predetermined variables and hypotheses. I preferred to be more intensive and open-ended, and to accept the risks imposed by less structured methods. Each man would be interviewed for a total of about 15 hours. Gradually I came to identify this work as a form of *biography:* we were engaged in *biographical interviewing* (rather than, say, clinical or survey interviewing), and we utilized the interview material to produce a *biographical reconstruction,* a descriptive and interpretive account of a person's life course. Before going beyond the birth of this study, I want to consider briefly its relation to Murray's earlier work.

At first glance, there may seem little connection between my biographical exploration of the mid-life years and Murray's exploration of personality in the college years. Yet there are important similarities, in spirit and in content, between our two enterprises. Like Murray, I conceive of research primarily as exploration and only secondarily as hypothesis testing, hypothesis generating, or finding definitive answers. My work, like his, derives from multiple inspiring sources in various sciences and humanities. I seek the integration of "depth" psychology, "surface" psychology, and social science. I share with him the interest in combining clinical and other methods in the study of normal lives and normal development. If I start at a different place, it is because I have his and others' work to build on.

In addition to these general similarities, there is another, very specific connection: Murray explicitly characterized his approach as biographical. He identified his field of study as "personology," which is:

The branch of psychology which concerns itself with the study of human lives and the factors that influence their course, which investigates individual differences and types of personality . . . (Murray, 1938, p. 4.)

In short, *the study of personality was for him the study of lives.* His aim at a descriptive level was to write a life history or concrete biography; at an interpretive level, he sought to create an "abstract biography," a life presented in the terms of a conceptual scheme. Murray returned to this theme toward the end of his book, when he was trying both to summarize his accomplishments and to suggest important directions for the future. Let him speak for himself:

What are the necessary components and what is the best form for an abstract biography? Over and over again we have asked ourselves this question. In our minds it is not very different from the primary question, What is personality? since the proper conceptualization of a human life (abstract biography) *is* the personality in so far as it can be scientifically formulated.

We can think of no problem more important than this. Its adequate solution would provide a framework within which all more specific problems could be set. As Dollard has so pregnantly observed, it is the logical meeting ground of psychology and sociology. For the individual is always imbedded in his culture. He assimilates it, is changed by it, conserves it, represents it, conveys it, modifies it, creates it. The culture is expressed through personalities, and personalities are expressed in the culture.

Furthermore, if one takes the general drift of passionate preoccupation as a criterion, it becomes apparent that personality—the concrete, individual, human soul—is attracting the attention of creative genius as it never has before. Witness the rapid rise of biography, the prodigious increase of autobiographical literature and of autobiographical art in general. (Murray, 1938, p. 609.)

This statement conveys the rich substance and tangy flavor of Murray's views. It is pregnant with the issues that have excited—and divided—psychologists for over a hundred years. It also highlights an ambiguity in Murray's analysis, and a problem that became central to my own efforts. He begins by equating biography and personality: ". . . the proper conceptualization of a human life *is* the personality . . ." But he quickly goes on to say that biography is "the logical meeting ground of psychology and sociology," for it involves the transactions between personality and culture. This means, however, that personality is but one ingredient of biography. Other ingredients come from culture and social institutions, the external world that has traditionally been the province of the sociologist much more than the psychologist.

Murray thus ends his explorations with the position that *the study of lives requires more than a theory of personality.* It requires also a theory of society, *a sociological perspective as it bears upon the individual life.* This was not a sudden, fully formed insight. It evolved over the course of his work. Murray gradually developed a view of the environment, conceptualized as *press,* but he acknowledged that this conception "came to us rather late in the course of our explorations (and) was not suitably compounded with other concepts" (Murray, 1938, pp. 119–120).

Murray's slowness in conceptualizing the environment stemmed partly, I believe, from the nature of his sample. Limiting it to "college-age men," he had neither the burden nor the opportunity of examining the complexities of adult life in a complex sociocultural milieu. While taking account of gross demographic variables such as class, religion, and ethnicity (on which, however, Harvard students of the 1930s were not highly diverse), he could maintain his traditional psychoanalytic assumptions and focus chiefly on the subjects' relationships within the family as the chief influence upon pre-adult personality development.

This specific factor leads, however, to a much more basic reason for Murray's relative neglect of the environment. As we have learned, his guiding vision for the project was to create a new field, personology, through a joining and transformation of two previously disparate fields, academic psychology and depth psychology. The remarkable and largely unrecognized truth is that neither of the parent fields had then—nor do they have now—a serious theoretical interest in the nature of society and collective life. Academic psychology generally restricts itself to the study of physical "stimuli" and concrete situations that can be subjected to laboratory investigation. Even in academic social psychology, the assimilation of social science theory is still at a primitive level. In the depth psychologies there is reference to "objects" and "object relationships," but the emphasis is mainly on "internal representations" of the external world—on objects, relationships and events as subjectively experienced. It can be argued that the patient's inner life should be the main focus of therapeutic work, and that good clinicians make up for their theoretical deficiencies by an intuitive grasp of the realities and the actualities of their patients' lives. Whatever its advantages, however, the emphasis on internal processes has severely limited the intellectual scope and explanatory power of these viewpoints. Many of the theoretically creative depth psychologists devoted themselves increasingly, in middle and later life, to the interrelations of individual and society. This was certainly true of the first great depth psychologist, Freud, and of others such as Jung, Rank, Adler, Reich, Fromm, and Horney. Indeed, what might be called the problem of a psychoanalytic social psychology has been a root source of the major controversies and divisions in the history of this field. The importance of social-psychological issues in the intellectual struggles between Freud and Jung is dramatically portrayed in their correspondence during the two or three years before their irrevocable split (McGuire, 1974). Some progress is being made, but much more is necessary if depth psychology is to grow beyond its narrow clinical base and become a vital part of the human sciences. Without a sociological perspective, psychology can make only modest progress in the study of personality, and even less in the study of lives.

Thus if Murray's *Explorations* gave insufficient attention to the human environment, he was nonetheless ahead of his time. Murray's active engagement with the social sciences came a few years later, in the mid-1940s, as he took part in founding the Social Relations Department at Harvard. See, for example, his collaborative writing with the anthropologist Clyde Kluckhohn (Kluckhohn and Murray, 1949). The fascinating story of his long and creative career is beyond our scope here; I commend to the reader Murray's own account in Koch (1959).

EXPLORATIONS IN BIOGRAPHY

My own explorations in biography thus began, in guiding vision if not in concrete detail, where Murray's earlier explorations had left off. The results of our explorations are reported by Charlotte Darrow, Edward Klein, Maria Levinson, Braxton McKee, and myself in our book, *The Seasons of a Man's Life* (Levinson, 1978). A brief overview must suffice here.

My aim, stated in the most concrete, atheoretical terms, was to describe and illuminate the complexities of the adult life course. With regard to method, I needed a systematic means of doing biographical inquiry and studying lives over time. With regard to theory, I sought to develop a sociopsychological perspective on the life course, a perspective that gives equal weight to the personality, the sociocultural world, and the relationship of person and world. The key problem was to learn how to study the structure of a person's life (the engagement of self-in-world), the evolution of that life over a span of years, and the ways in which a life changes and remains the same. At a manifest level, individual lives show fantastic variability in pattern and sequence. Still, I wanted to know: is there an underlying order in the adult life course? Do our lives evolve in accord with basic universal principles? Can we speak of individual development in adulthood?

As I considered the gulf between these questions and the available research literature, I understood more deeply what Murray must have felt in the early 1930s when he began his explorations in personality. It was hard even to know where to begin. My previous research had often, I liked to believe, helped to open up a new frontier for study, but there was generally a solid base of relevant ideas and knowledge on which the new venture could be built. In the authoritarian personality research, for example, we could draw upon a body of relevant theory and could initially identify some key variables that provided a base on which to search for new concepts and variables.

Beginning a study of the adult life course in 1966 was a very different matter. I found evocative ideas and evidence scattered over a wide terrain: in the extensive writings of Erikson and Jung; in essays by Mannheim (1952) and van Gennep (1960); in the research of Buhler (1968a,b), Neugarten (1964) and a few others; and in the diverse literature of biography, autobiography, novels, plays, and poetry. However, the interesting ideas and insights did not form a coherent body of thoughts, and there was no empirical basis for committing oneself to a single theoretical approach.

The academic research had been done largely by psychologists, and in the years since 1950. It laid heavy emphasis on the measurement of predefined variables and the testing or generating of specific hypotheses concerning the relationships among the variables. This approach placed the investigators in a methodological straitjacket. Research of this kind is productive only when we know something about the empirically relevant variables, and when these variables have meaning within a larger body of concepts and theory. Other kinds of research are needed in order to gain some empirical grounding—a sense of the phenomena to be understood—and to create new theoretical constructions that provide a context for the derivation of appropriate variables. This point was made by Bernice Neugarten (1964), one of the most creative investigators of adult development, at the very end of her concluding chapter of *Personality in Middle and Late Life*. Her counsel is still of value to anyone entering this domain:

> Age-related phenomena will be better understood only as investigators isolate variables that they have reason to believe have particular relevance for a developmental psychology of adulthood. It cannot be taken for granted . . . that constructs useful in describing personality in the child, the adolescent or the young adult will therefore be useful in describing personality in the older adult.
>
> A developmental theory of adult personality is likely to emerge only after . . . more of the relevant dimensions have become measurable. In the meantime, the investigator will proceed patiently with the descriptive studies that must first be carried out, in the confidence that *both his theories and his more rigorous research designs must grow from, rather than precede, systematic observations on normal adults* (Neugarten, 1964, p. 200; italics added).

After much searching of the literature, and of myself, I settled upon a research strategy. First, I decided not to commit myself in advance to any specific hypotheses, variables, or measuring instruments. This was not an easy decision for someone like me, trained to believe that research is the study of relationships among measured variables. In addition to my own misgivings about working in so loose a structure, I had repeatedly to face the altruistic concern of friends and colleagues: "You are studying mid-life development? How interesting. What are your hypotheses? You have none? Then what are your variables? What measures are you using? That's hard to believe." By the time we settled what I was *not* doing, we were so far apart that it was hard to go further and discuss what I *was* doing, and why.

Second, in a spirit of exploration, I decided to cast as wide a net as possible, gathering rich material and then seeing what concepts, principles and specific findings might emerge. Theoretical considerations were of great importance in the planning, but they operated as broad guidelines rather than as a tight, explicit structure for data collection. The primary aim of the study was to produce new concepts and a theoretical framework within which specific variables and hypotheses could be derived.

All forty men in the sample were between 35 and 45 years old. Each man was seen in a series of six to ten biographical interviews, each lasting about 1½ hours (occasionally much longer), for a total of ten to twenty hours. Biographical interviews involve "telling lives," in Pachter's (1979) apt phrase. Our task, as we informed every participant, was "to tell the story of your life." Some attention was given to the childhood years, but our main emphasis was on the span from the late teens to the present.

Biographical Interviewing as a Research Method

The development of this mode of interviewing was one of our major research tasks, and it illustrates well the problem of generating research methods appropriate to the current state of theory.

We do not use a predetermined interview schedule, that is, a list of questions to be gone through serially in a standard order. Certain topics should be covered, but the sequence is variable and a product of the ongoing transactions. The interviewer's task is not simply to elicit specific information but to generate, maintain and terminate a relationship of significance to both parties. This relationship extends over at least two or three months. It is a vehicle by which an intensive (though not logically ordered) picture of the subject's life is produced. The interviewer does not ask a set of standard questions nor impassively probe for areas of difficulty. While maintaining some detachments, he or she is an engaged participant in a highly personal process.

The interviewer has to keep in mind, and to combine, several different requirements.

1. We have to cover various "areas of living" such as family of origin, education, occupation, love relationships, marriage and family of procreation, leisure, bodily health and illness, ethnicity, religion, politics, and relation to self.

2. Within each area, it is essential to trace the sequence over the adult years, being alert to major events, choices and turning points, as well as to the character of relatively stable periods.

3. We must learn about the "interpenetration" of the areas. Occupation and family life, for example, are often closely intertwined. A man

may talk at length about his work life without mentioning his family. When the interviewer asks, "How did your wife feel about that?" or "How did your family enter into your choice of jobs at that time?", new dimensions are added and a broader life pattern emerged.

4.   As a series of interviews progresses, the interviewer gets a sense of different "chapters" in the life story: three years in military service; four to five years of relatively transient living; the years of starting a family and getting settled in a new city and job. It is important to apprehend the overall character of life within each of these chapters, as well as the kinds of changes that occurred within it. Here, the emphasis is on the patterning among the many areas of living—the forms of integration as well as the contradictions, gaps, and fragments.

5.   In the lives of many persons, there are occasional periods, lasting a few months to a few years, that constitute dramatic "high points" or "rock bottom" periods. These times often mark the end of one life phase and the beginning of another. They must be examined from many vantage points. The person may initially identify only a single crucial event—a remarkable success or failure in work, a divorce, the death of a loved one—but on more careful reflection it often turns out that other important changes were going on before and after this one. When the subject focusses on a single dramatic event, the interviewer should try to broaden the story and to learn about a process going on over time and touching many aspects of living.

6.   We are interested in the participant's view of his life as a whole, and of the interrelations among various parts and times within it. A man of 50 may ask himself not simply how he feels about his present marriage or job, but also what he has done with his life until now. If he can allow himself to pursue this question (perhaps with the help of an empathic interviewer), the process by which he entered marriage or occupation twenty-five years ago becomes as vivid as his present reality. The past is, in this sense, part of the present, and the biographer must so represent it. Likewise, the person's defined plans and more shadowy imaginings of the future shape and are shaped by the present. The future, too, forms a part of the present that the biographer must explore.

Whatever the issue under discussion, the interviewer invites the subject to examine its many facets. A man is speaking, for example, of a difficult time when he was considering whether to remain in a secure but limited job, or to accept a more attractive but less secure job in the same occupation, or to make the risky change of entering a long-desired, new occupation. There is a great deal to be explored: the meaning of work in general, and of these jobs and occupations in particular; the man's feelings regarding security and risk-taking; the concrete realities of the various jobs and occupations being considered; the diverse influences, pressures, and inducements affecting the choice; what the man actually did during the period of generating, considering, and choosing among the several options (which may have lasted several months or years); and the immediate and long-term outcome of the choice, for him and for significant others. In his initial account, he may note in passing that his wife left the decision to him. At some point the interviewer should explore more fully the interaction of husband and wife around this choice, his feelings about her response at the time, and how it has affected their relationship since, for better or worse. Again, he may mention that his initial occupational choice was the one his father had always wanted for him, and the alternative was one he had secretly cherished since adolescence. This gives the interviewer an opportunity, at the appropriate time, to learn more about the father-son relationship as it influences occupational (and other) choices, and as it evolved over the adult years.

Every interviewer has preferences and aversions that affect his or her readiness to hear various facets of the life story. These dispositions stem partly from personality. We are likely to get involved in matters that hold a special interest or importance for ourselves, and to move away from a topic that evokes painful feelings or indifference. Occupational skills and deformations also affect the interviewer's work. A clinically trained interviewer may pursue the other's inner feelings and fantasies to the neglect of external events and actions. Training in survey research generally leads an interviewer to ask specific questions and follow a "logical," information-gathering sequence, rather than to listen for subtle meanings and take cues from them. A sociologically oriented interviewer is best equipped to explore the workings of the social environment (family, workplace, occupation, political scene), and may not attend sufficiently to their concrete meaning for the person and the inner-psychological aspects of his participation in them. Biographical interviewing requires an amalgam of the skills of clinician, survey researcher, and fieldwork sociologist—as well as bartender and friend. If any one or two of these predominate to the exclusion of others, the work will suffer.

In summary, I want to emphasize two essential features of the biographer's theory and art. One is the idea of the *life pattern* at a given time: particular events and relationships serve as vehicles for the story, but their full meaning and their function in the person's life can be seen only when they are placed in the context of the current life as a whole. The second is the idea of the *life course:* we must pay attention to sequence and temporal order; we must connect a given time of life to the recent and distant past and to the future; we must see how the past and future are selectively represented in the present. These ideas play an important part in biographical interviewing, as the biographer invites the subject to review his life and to explore the connections among its spatial and temporal parts. The same basic ideas, when translated into organizing concepts, are important when the biographer goes on to make an interpreted construction of the life, drawing upon the subject's personal account as well as other available evidence. I turn now to some specific concepts, and a way of thinking, that were products of our biographical labors.

The Structure of the Human Life Cycle

Rather than attempt a detailed summary of our findings, I want to focus on a few major theoretical issues, and to present our concepts and findings on each. One of the most basic theoretical issues, I believe, is the question of the human life cycle. This term is a metaphor, not a precisely defined concept. Its key idea is that the course of human life has an underlying order, though the manifest forms of individual lives show myriad variations. Is there an underlying order in the evolution of our lives from birth through old age, and, if so, can we study and conceptualize it?

Both in the popular culture and the human sciences, the prevailing answer to this question has been: no. We have no traditionally accepted and understood conception of the life cycle. Or, to put it more precisely, we have a rather simplified conception in which the life course is divided into three segments: childhood, adulthood, and old age. We are fairly clear about childhood, and we have a limited though rather distorted and frightening view of old age. But the intervening adult years are largely a blur. Terms such as youth, young adulthood, mid-life, maturity, and middle age do in fact distinguish a sequence of phases within adulthood. However, there has been a powerful reluctance to adopt a consistent, well-defined terminology about these phases; words such as "youth" and "middle age" are used more as symbols than as descriptive categories.

In my opinion, a conception of the life cycle is urgently needed both to guide our scientific research and to enrich our cultural wisdom. I believe that we now have empirical grounds on which to form a systematic conception of the life cycle.

My own conception has grown out of my research and is consistent with the ideas of other investigators such as Erikson (1950, 1968), Jung

(1964), Neugarten (1968), Buhler (1968a,b), and Frenkel (1936), and Ortega y Gasset (1958), as well as the ancient writings of Confucius, Solomon, and the Talmud (see Levinson et al., 1978, Chapters 2 and 20).

I conceive of the life cycle as a sequence of *eras*. Each era has its own bio-psycho-social character, and each makes its distinctive contribution to the whole. There are major changes in the nature of our lives from one era to the next, and lesser, though still crucially important changes within eras. They are partially overlapping: a new era begins as the previous one is approaching its end. The *cross-era transitions,* which generally last about five years, terminate the outgoing era and initiate the next. The eras and the cross-era transitional periods form the macrostructure of the life cycle, providing an underlying order in the flow of all human lives yet permitting exquisite variations in the individual life course.

We have found that each era and developmental period begins and ends at a well-defined modal age, with a range of about two years above and below this average. The idea of age-linked phases in adult life goes against conventional wisdom. Nevertheless, these age findings have been consistently obtained in our initial research and in subsequent studies. I offer the concept of age-linked eras and periods as a hypothesis that deserves extensive testing in various cultures.

The first era, *preadulthood,* extends from birth to roughly age 22. During these "formative years" the individual grows from highly dependent, undifferentiated infancy through childhood and adolescence to the beginnings of a more independent, responsible adult life. It is the era of most rapid bio-psycho-social growth. The first few years of life provide a transition into childhood, a period that Mahler, Pine, and Bergman (1975) have referred to as "the psychological birth of the child." During this time the neonate becomes biologically and psychologically separate from the mother, and establishes the initial distinction between the "me" and the "not-me"—the first step in a continuing process of individuation (Winnicott, 1965).

The years from about age 17 to age 22 constitute the Early Adult Transition, a developmental period in which preadulthood draws to a close and the era of early adulthood gets underway. It is thus part of both eras, and not fully a part of either. A new step in individuation is taken as the budding adult modifies her/his relationships with family and other components of the preadult world, and begins to form a place as an adult in the adult world. From a childhood-centered perspective, one can say that development is now largely completed and the child has gained maturity as an adult. Textbooks on developmental psychology commonly take this view. Taking the perspective of the life cycle as a whole, however, we recognize that the developmental attainments of the first era provide only a base, a starting point from which to begin the next. The Early Adult Transition is, so to speak, both the full maturity of preadulthood and the infancy of a new era. One is at best off to a shaky start, and new kinds of development are required over the course of the new era.

The second era, *early adulthood,* lasts from about age 17 to age 45. It begins, as I have said, with the Early Adult Transition. It is the adult era of greatest energy and abundance, and of greatest contradiction and stress. Biologically, the twenties and thirties are the peak years of the life cycle. In social and psychological terms, early adulthood is the season for forming and pursuing youthful aspirations, establishing a niche in society, raising a family, and, as the era ends, reaching a more "senior" position in the adult world. This can be a time of rich satisfactions in terms of love, sexuality, family life, occupational advancement, creativity, and realization of major life goals. But there can be crushing stresses, too: undertaking the burdens of parenthood and, at the same time, of forming an occupation; incurring heavy financial obligations when one's earning power is still relatively low; having to make crucially important choices regarding marriage, family, work, and life-style before one has the maturity or life experience to choose wisely. Early adulthood is the era in which we are most buffeted by our own passions and ambitions from within, and by the demands of family, community, and society from without. Under reasonably favorable conditions, the rewards as well as the costs of living are enormous.

The Mid-Life Transition, from roughly 40 to 45, brings about the termination of early adulthood and the start of the next era, middle adulthood. The distinction between these two eras, and the concept of the Mid-Life Transition as a developmental period that separates and connects them, are among the most controversial of our proposals. The theoretical rationale and findings are given in *The Seasons of a Man's Life* (Levinson, 1978, Chapters 2 and 13–20). When we study the individual life course during these years, we find that the character of living always changes appreciably between early and middle adulthood. The process of change begins in the Mid-Life Transition (though the forms and degrees of change very enormously) and may continue throughout the era. The developmental requirement of this transition is that one begin a new step in individuation. To the extent that this occurs, we can become more compassionate, more reflective and judicious, less tyrannized by inner conflicts and external demands, more genuinely loving of self and others. Without it, our lives become increasingly trivial and stagnant.

The third era, *middle adulthood,* lasts from about age 40 to age 65. During this era our biological capacities are below those of early adulthood, but normally still sufficient for an energetic, personally satisfying and socially valuable life. The great philosopher-historian Ortega y Gasset (1958) has suggested that people aged 45 to 60 form the "dominant generation" in every society. In politics, industry, science, and the arts—in all social institutions—the main leadership comes from this generation. Unless our lives are hampered in some special way, most of us during our forties and fifties become "senior members" in our own particular worlds, however grand or modest they may be. We are responsible not only for our own work, and perhaps the work of others, but also for the development of the current generation of young adults who will soon enter the dominant generation.

The next era, *late adulthood,* starts at about age 60. The Late Adult Transition, from 60 to 65, is a developmental period linking middle and late adulthood. I shall not attempt here to discuss late adulthood, nor my speculations regarding a subsequent era, late late adulthood. Rather I want to consider another theoretical issue, psychosocial development in early and middle adulthood.

Adult Development: The Evolution of the Individual Life Structure

If the idea of the life cycle suggests an underlying order and unifying character in the life course as a whole, the idea of adult development suggests a more specific order and unity within certain eras or phases of life. I want to conclude this account of my biographical explorations by highlighting the question of adult development: Does it make sense to speak of development in adulthood, and, if so, how can we best conceptualize it?

This has been a thorny question for the humanities and the sciences of human life. The prevailing view has been that development occurs only during the preadult years; they are followed by a plateau and then moderate decline between roughly ages 20 and 65, leading to an accelerating senescence in old age. This model has its origins in biology, and may be valid for biological growth and decline over the life cycle. We must ask, however, whether this model is necessarily true of psychosocial development, and what alternative possibilities there may be. Psychosocial theories must take account of the ways in which biological development facilitates and constrains psychosocial development, but the modes need not be isomorphic.

In academic psychology, most personality theories offer a conception of personality development in childhood and adolescence. They generally do not posit a developmental process intrinsic to adulthood. Their emphasis in adulthood is more on personality *change* than development. Adult personality change is thought to occur chiefly as an adaptation to, or under the stimulation of, massively impacting events such as the loss of a loved one, a drastic uprooting, a significant role transition, or psychotherapy. The personality change may be seen in part as a form of growth. However, the growth is usually understood as a resolution of childhood-based conflicts or as a reduction of childhood-based impairments, rather than as part of a specifically adult developmental process.

Jung and Erikson are major exceptions to this widely held view. Jung's conception of individuation in mid-life and beyond provides a rich mine of ideas (though not a formal theory) concerning adult development. Erikson has portrayed the life cycle as a sequence of stages in ego development. The last three stages encompass early, middle, and late adulthood (1968). Unfortunately, he has written less about the adult stages than the earlier ones, and thus far others have made little use of his seminal ideas about them.

It is time, I believe, to take the idea of adult development more seriously, and I have made it a central issue in my own biographical work. If we are to study development, we must first decide: *The development of what?* The "what" might be some aspect of personality, such as the ego, or cognition, or moral functioning. Alternatively, it might be some form of career development, such as occupation or family. As I have said, I decided at the start against both of these options. In taking a biographical approach, I chose to examine the life course in its full complexity. With regard to theory, this meant that I sought a conception of development that encompassed the process of living in its manifold aspects—a conception that included careers and multiple aspects of personality (as well as other things), rather than being limited to a single dimension.

Our definition of the "what" emerged only in fits and starts over the first few years of research. We formed the concept of the individual life structure, and came to conceive of adult development as the evolution of the life structure. The life structure is the pattern or design of a person's life at a given time. It stems from the engagement of self and world, and its intrinsic ingredients are aspects of the self and aspects of the world.

In terms of open system theory, life structure forms a boundary between personality structure and social structure, and governs the transactions between them. A boundary structure in this sense is not totally separate from the two adjacent systems it connects. It contains elements of both systems; it is part of both systems; and it can be understood only if we see it as a structure mediating the relationship between them. Thus the life structure mediates the relationship between individual and environment. It has to be understood as the cause, the vehicle, and the effect of that relationship. It is an effect in that its formation is governed by the transactions between self and world. As it gains in strength, the life structure acts as a causal or controlling influence on these transactions; it functions so as to maintain a stable structure. In time a life structure must give way, under the combined pressure of internal and external forces, to be replaced after a period of transition by a new structure.

Personality and social environment operate conjointly in the building, maintaining, modifying and rebuilding of the life structure, and they are conjointly represented within it. The process of building a new structure is conjointly shaped by self and world. A given life structure, once stabilized, facilitiates the living out of certain aspects of personality while limiting the expression of others, and facilities the person's use of certain aspects of the external world while limiting the use of others. The termination of a life structure is brought about conjointly by inner psychological forces and by external social forces. At any particular point, the influence of the self may be greater than that of the environment, or vice versa, but our point of view leads us always to examine both and to give them equal weight in our way of thinking about individual life.

In metaphorical terms, we seek to characterize the fabric of a person's life, showing in the process how it bears the stamp both of the individual personality and the environing culture. How can we move beyond this metaphor to a more systematic theory and mode of analysis? As a first step, we need to learn a great deal about the person's diverse interests, activities, roles, social involvements, and private concerns. However a mere listing of concrete items is not enough. Two interpretive tasks remain: to identify the major components of the life; and to place these within an overall structure that has a unifying character as well as deep divisions and contradictions.

My view of the components of the life structure stems from the theoretical approach indicated above: the primary components are the *person's relationships with various aspects of the external world*. One may have a relationship with another person, with a group, institution, or culture, and with a particular object or place. A significant relationship involves an investment of self (desires, values, commitment, energy, skill), a reciprocal investment by the other person or social entity, and one or more social contexts that contain the relationship, shaping it and becoming part of it in gross and subtle ways. Every relationship shows both stability and change as it evolves over time, and it has different functions in the person's life as the life structure itself changes.

The starting point for our analysis is the relationship itself, rather than the person or the external world. This requires a difficult shift in orientation from the ones customarily employed by psychologists and social scientists. In psychology, the term "relationship" is ordinarily understood to mean a relationship with another individual. Psychoanalysis speaks of "object relationships." This term takes account of the fact that we may have significant relationships with nonhuman objects as well as human beings. Unfortunately, our language provides no term other than object—which ordinarily refers to inanimate things and is degrading when applied to humans—that embraces all the entities with which one may have a relationship. I speak of the one whose life is being studied simply as "the person" or, when emphasis is needed, "the focal person," and I use the word "Other" to identify the other parties to the relationship, be they animate or inanimate, individual or collective, real or symbolic.

The term "object relations," as it is used in psychoanalysis and other dynamic psychologies, has at least two referents. On the one hand, it refers to a person's relationship with someone in the environment—a father, let us say. At the same time, it refers to the person's relationship with an "internal object"—with the figure of the father as it exists in one's own head. The concept of the internal figure is of great importance in personality theory and in clinical work; our unconscious representations of father, mother, and other significant figures, formed in childhood, are often more real for us as adults and operate with more force in our adult lives than do the actual persons from whom they are derived. A man's relationship with his internal father is a significant part of his personality. It influences his ongoing relationships with the current external father and assorted Others. The psychotherapist, committed to the task of discovering the unconscious and often childhood-based sources of the patient's difficulties, is likely to view the man's ongoing adult relationships with others primarily as reflections of his relationships with internal figures.

However, a man's relationship with his actual father does not exist merely in his head. Both parties help to maintain and modify the relationship, which involves a continuing transactional process of giving and receiving, influencing and being influenced, jointly participating in a variety of tasks and enterprises. The relationship is influenced by many aspects of each man's personality and by the social context in which it is embedded. Moreover, it does not remain static over the years; while some themes persist, others change, and there is an evolution in the character of the relationship. Although our main focus is on one party, we must attend as well to the other. The biographer's chief task is to grasp the character of the relationship and its place in the subject's life as it evolves over time.

Sociology has been interested chiefly in the individual as a participant in society and its component groups and institutions. Everyone belongs to and participates in numerous social units—class, ethnic, occupational, familial, religious, political, and the like. Indeed, our participation in social groups and enterprises occupies by far the greatest part of our lives. From a sociological perspective, individual participation in a social group is patterned through the mechanism of social roles, which are defined and maintained by the social structure of that group. Less attention is ordinarily given to the ways in which the individual personality enters into the formation, enactment, and change of social roles.

Again I want to bring together the sociological and psychological perspectives. An adequate conception of the lived life must include the individual's participation in society. However, it is essential to avoid a narrow sociological determinism which conceives of the individual life solely as a set of social roles governed almost entirely by social structure. This view makes the person a mere sponge, molded and filled by society. It is equally important to avoid a psychological reductionism which regards the individual's social participation as merely a derivative of inner fantasies, motives, cognitive functions, or habits. We can avoid both of these pitfalls by beginning with neither personality nor social role, but with the concept of the relationship between a person and the various social contexts that have significance in his or her life. Some of these relationships form primary components of the life structure. Personality and role enter and play an important part in such relationships, but they are not the starting point for our analysis.

It is difficult enough to study a person's relationship with another person. How can we begin to think about, conceptualize and study a person's relationships with and within a complex social system such as family, occupation, or ethnic world, as these evolve over the years? This is an enormously difficult question, and after some years I am still very much a novice at it. I shall give just a few examples, using myself as the illustrative case.

My family is a central component of my life structure. I have a complex set of relationships with and within it. In addition to dyadic relationships with my wife and my adult sons and their families, I have a relationship with my nuclear family as a system. I have significant relationships with my mother (now dying), father (who died almost twenty years ago), and brother, with my current extended family (in several countries), and with previous and future generations in history. These relationships have great private significance for me, although they find overt expression only occasionally—at family reunions, with the death of a loved one, or with the sudden appearance of long-lost relatives from my immigrant parents' homeland.

We begin by exploring each of these specific relationships and their interconnections. After getting clear about the meaning of each part, we can make an interpretive formulation of "the family" as a component of my life structure. In the process of learning about the family, moreover, we will also have learned a great deal about other components of the life structure, such as occupation and leisure, which are strongly "interpenetrated" with family in the patterning and temporal sequence of my life. And we will have learned much about the ways in which each component, and the life structure as a whole, are shaped both by my personality and by the social-historical context of my existence.

Occupation will serve as a second and last example. In the theoretical perspective presented here, we say that my relationship with occupation is an important component of my life structure. I have a particular *occupational title:* professor of psychology (though, as we have seen, the discipline has become increasingly hybrid); a *job* in a particular workplace, Yale University; and a primary involvement in particular kinds of *work,* research and teaching. However, these terms refer to complex aspects of an even more complex pattern. If we are to grasp the nature of my occupation and its place in my life, we have to begin by situating me within an occupational world. I have diverse relationships with many individuals, groups and institutions within this world, and with "occupation" in a broader and more symbolic sense. I have personally important relationships with Yale University and the several departments in which I am most engaged, and with the Connecticut Mental Health Center (the service, teaching, and research facility where I am based). These two overlapping organizations form my immediate occupational context. Beyond these, I have membership in and relationships with various scientific and professional disciplines, especially psychology, psychiatry, and sociology, and the organizations that represent and sustain them. I am involved with professional journals, publishing houses, and other parts of the international communications system through which ideas and information are disseminated (and reputations built or destroyed). In recent years I have stumbled into the world of the mass media (trade books, magazine articles, television, and radio), an experience that has altered my work life, my income, and my identity as a professor. I deal with the federal government, foundations, and other sources of research funds; and, as a lecturer and consultant, with many educational, industrial, religious, and other organizations.

As we explore the character of my relationships with these and other aspects of the occupational world, a pattern begins to emerge. Certain relationships occupy a more central place in my life, others are more peripheral or incidental. There are basic themes that characterize the pattern as a whole, cutting across the relationships with particular persons and places. The contemporary pattern is different from earlier ones; my experience of the present is colored by my sense of continuity and change in the past, and by hopes and fears regarding the future. In short, occupation as a component of the life structure is comprised of many specific relationships, the connections among them, the broader pattern of which each is a part, and the themes and meanings that give coherence, content, and color to the total design. And occupation is interpenetrated with other components of the life structure.

We have a great deal to learn regarding the nature and evolution of an adult's relationships with the many significant Others in his or her world, and with the patterning of these relationships in the life course. The Other may be an *actual person* in one's current life. We need to study interpersonal relationships between friends, lovers, and spouses; between parents and their adult offspring at different ages; between bosses and subordinates, teachers and students, mentors and proteges. The Other may be a *person from the past* (e.g., Ezra Pound's vital relationship with the figure of Dante). It may be a *symbolic or imagined figure* from religion, myth, fiction, or private fantasy. The Other may also be a *collective entity* such as a group, institution, or social movement; *nature* as a whole, or part of nature such as the ocean, mountains, wildlife, whales in general or Moby Dick in particular; or an *object or place,* such as a farm, a neighborhood, "a room of one's own," a book or painting.

These relationships are the stuff our lives are made of. They give shape and substance to the life course. They are the vehicle by which we live out—or bury—various aspects of our selves; and by which we participate, for better or worse, in the world around us. The biographer's goals are to determine the meaning of each relationship within the person's life, and to gain a sense of the meaning of this life for the person and his or her world.

Our study revealed that one or two components—rarely as many as three—have a central place in the life structure. The central components have the greatest significance for the self and the evolving life course. They receive the largest share of one's time and energy, and they strongly influence the choices made in other aspects of life. The peripheral components are easier to detach and change. They involve less investment of the self and can be modified with less effect on the fabric of one's life. We found that *occupation and marriage or family are usually the central components* of a man's life, though wide variations occur in their relative weight and in the importance of other components.

Periods in the Evolution of the Life Structure

The life structure may change in various ways. A component may shift from center to periphery or vice versa, as when a man who has been totally committed to work starts detaching himself from it and involves himself more in family life. A formerly important component may be eliminated altogether. Or the character of a man's relationships within a given component may change moderately or drastically. For example, a man may enrich and deepen his existing marital relationship; he may modify the nature and meaning of his work, without changing occupations; or he may leave his present marriage or occupation in search of a basic change.

When we used the concept of life structure in analyzing the biographies of our men, we found that *the life structure evolves through a relatively orderly sequence of periods during the adult years.* The essential character of the sequence was the same for all the men in our study and for the other men whose biographies we examined. These periods shape the adult life course.

The sequence consists of an alternating series of structure-building and structure-changing (transitional) periods. The primary task of a structure-building period is to form a life structure and enhance life within it: a person must make certain key choices; form a structure around them, and pursue his values and goals within this structure. Even when a person succeeds in creating a stable structure, life is not necessarily tranquil. The task of making major life choices and building a structure is often stressful indeed and may involve many kinds of change. A structure-building period ordinarily lasts six or seven years, ten at the most. Then the life structure that has formed the basis for stability comes into question and must be modified.

A transitional period terminates the existing life structure and creates the possibility for a new one. The primary tasks of every transitional period are to reappraise the existing structure, to explore the various possibilities for change in self and world, and to move toward commitment to the crucial choices that form the basis for a new life structure in the ensuing period. Transitional periods ordinarily last about five years. Much of our lives is taken up with separation and new beginnings, exits and entries, departures and arrivals. Transitions are an intrinsic part of development, but they are often painful.

As a transition comes to an end, a person starts making crucial choices, giving them meaning and commitment, and building a life structure around them. The choices are, in a sense, the major product of the transition. When all the efforts of the transition are done—the struggles to improve work or marriage, to explore alternative possibilities of living, to come more to terms with the self—choices must be made and bets must be placed. A person must decide "This I will settle for," and start creating a life structure that will serve as a vehicle for the next step in the journey.

It is worth emphasizing that the transitions are major periods in their own right. They have the same weight in the sequence as the structure-building periods, and they occupy almost as many years of our lives. The transitional periods are essential in the shift from one life structure to another, and the process of structural change is in urgent need of study.

It is important to distinguish between transitional periods in the evolution of the life structure and transitions of other kinds. A transition is a process of change from one structure or state to another. A career transition, for example, occurs when a person shifts from one occupational role to another. Following the death of a loved one, a person goes through a transition in which he or she grieves the loss and transforms the relationship to the Other, who now exists primarily as an internal figure. Various transitions may occur within a life-structure transition (as well as in other periods); it is important both to keep them analytically distinct and to study their interrelations.

The actual sequence of periods in early and middle adulthood is shown in Figure 1. This sequence is shaped by, and must be seen within, the sequence of eras described above. The first period is the Early Adult Transition, which deals with the cross-era shift between preadulthood and early adulthood. It is followed by Entering the Adult World (roughly age 22–28), in which the major developmental task is to explore the options and build a first adult life structure. In the Age Thirty Transition (age 28–33), the tasks are to question the first structure, to do some further developmental work on unresolved issues from the past, and to create the basis for a new structure. The Settling Down period (age 33–40) is devoted to building a second adult life structure and, within this framework, attempting to realize one's youthful aspirations. We have, in effect, two developmentally given chances within early adulthood to fashion a life structure that is viable in society and suitable for the self.

The Mid-Life Transition (age 40–45) is another of the cross-era transitions which mark a fundamental shift in the life cycle. It involves more than a questioning and change of the current life structure; the entire era of early adulthood must be terminated, while the initiation of middle adulthood gets underway. A first, tentative life structure is then built in

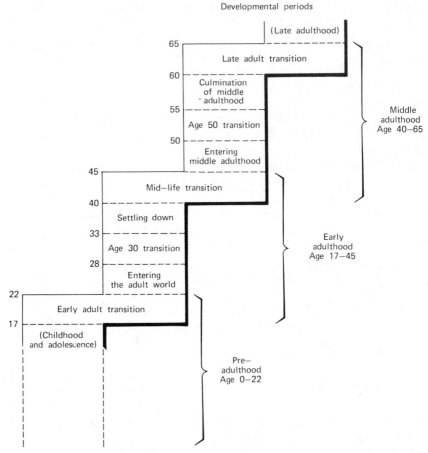

Figure 1. Eras and developmental periods in early and middle adulthood. (Adapted from Levinson et al., 1978.)

Entering Middle Adulthood (age 45–50). It is followed by the Age Fifty Transition (age 50–55), and then the building of a second life structure in the Culmination of Middle Adulthood (age 55–60). Finally, the Late Adult Transition (age 60–65) is devoted to the termination of middle adulthood and the start of the next era, late adulthood.

On what theoretical basis can this sequence be understood—what are its underlying sources or determinants? The sequence of life-structure periods cannot be derived simply from a maturationally given process of personality development in adulthood. It cannot be based on the socializing influence of any single social system such as occupation or family, nor on the interweaving of multiple systems (since the synchronization among them varies so widely). Nor does it follow directly from any known sequence of biological growth and decline. No one of the various human sciences holds the master key to the secrets of the life cycle, yet all are of major importance. The basic form of the adult life course, at this stage of human evolution, is conjointly determined by the maturational unfolding of the human psyche and the human body, and by the basic features of human society (as it has existed for, say, the last five or ten thousand years). In short, the order in the evolution of the individual life structure stems from multiple bio-psycho-social sources and not from any single source (Levinson et al., 1978). It cannot be described or explained by a unidisciplinary approach.

Conclusions

An exploration at best provides a map of a terrain and some insights regarding the nature of the landscape. Much additional research is needed to provide a more detailed picture and more conclusive findings. Certainly this is the case with these biographical explorations. Our conception of periods in the evolution of the adult life structure needs to be tested, modified, and extended. It will, I believe, provide a valuable framework for the systematic study of adult lives and for the writing of biographies.

I propose that there is an order in the adult life course. The order is not at the level of concrete events, actions, and experiences, nor is it derived from stages in personality development. The order is at a more underlying, interpreted level, which involves the building, modifying, and rebuilding of the life structure. The primary components of the life structure are the person's relationships with various aspects of the external world. The nature of the life structure, and the forces that lead to stability and change, have their sources conjointly in personality, biology, and the sociocultural world.

For those who are primarily investigators of personality, I am offering some bad news and some good news. The bad news is that if we are to understand the individual life course, it is not enough to focus narrowly on personality in our research. We must engage in biography, in the study of lives, of which personality is but one element. Psychologists must form a more genuinely sociological perspective. It is not enough merely to include "demographic variables" for purposes of statistical control or of explaining the residual variance. We will have to learn how to think about the nature of society and the individual's participation in it—via social roles and careers, family life, social class and social movements, generations and generational change. We must learn, in short, to study the individual life and not solely the personality.

The good news, I believe, is this: By taking a biographical approach and exploring "lives in progress," we can observe the personality more clearly as it permeates all aspects of living and as it evolves over the life course. By giving the concept of life structure a central place in our theoretical scaffolding, we don't reduce the importance of personality, we just give it a better home. The biographical study of lives enables us to study the personality in greater depth, complexity, and relevance for both individual and society. This is a crucial wisdom in the legacy Murray gave us forty years ago.

REFERENCES

Adorno, T., E. Frenkel-Brunswick, D. J. Levinson, and R. N. Sanford. *The Authoritarian Personality*. New York: Harper, 1950.

Allport, G. *Personality*. New York: Holt, 1937.

Buhler, C. M. *The Course of Human Life, a Study of Goals in the Humanistic Perspective*. New York: Springer, 1968(a).

Buhler, C. M. The course of human life as a psychological problem. *Human Development*, 1968(b), **11**, 184–200.

Dollard, J., L. W. Doob, N. E. Miller, O. H. Mower, and R. R. Sears. *Frustration and Aggression*. New Haven: Yale University Press, 1939.

Erikson, E. *Childhood and Society*. New York: Norton, 1950.

Erikson, E. *Identity Youth and Crisis*. New York: Norton, 1968.

Frenkel-Brunswik, E. Studies in Biographical Psychology. *Character and Personality*, 1936, **5**, 1–34.

Frenkel-Brunswik, E. and R. N. Sanford. The antisemitic personality: a research report. In E. Simmel (Ed.), *Anti-Semitism*. New York: International University Press, 1946.

Gilbert, D., and D. J. Levinson. Ideology, personality, and institutional policy. *Journal of Abnormal and Social Psychology*, 1956, **53**, 263–271.

Greenblatt N., D. J. Levinson, and R. Williams. *The Patient and the Mental Hospital; Continuations of Research in the Source of Social Behavior*. Glencoe, IL: Free Press, 1957.

Hodgson, R. C., D. J. Levinson, and A. Zalezik. *The Executive Role Constellation: An Analysis of Personality and Role Relations in Management*. Boston: Harvard Business School, 1965.

Inkeles, A., and D. J. Levinson. National character: The study of model personality and sociocultural systems. In G. Lindzey and E. Aronson (Eds.), *Handbook of Social Psychology*. Reading, MA: Addison-Wesley, 1968.

Jung, C. G. *Man and His Symbols*. Garden City: Doubleday, 1964.

Kluckhohn, C. and H. Murray. *Personality in Nature, Society, and Culture*. New York: Knopf, 1949.

Koch, S. *Psychology: A Study of a Science*, Vol. 3. New York: McGraw-Hill, 1959.

Levinson, D. J. *The Seasons of a Man's Life*. New York: Knopf, 1978.

Levinson, D. J. and E. B. Gallagher. *Patienthood in the Mental Hospital: Role, Personality, and Social Structure*. Boston: Houghton-Mifflin, 1964.

Levinson, D. J. and G. L. Klerman. The clinician-executive: Some problematic issues for the psychiatrist in mental health organizations. *Psychiatry*, 1967, **30**, 3–15.

Levinson, D. J., J. Merrifield, and K. Berg. Becoming a patient. *Archives of General Psychiatry*, 1967, **17** (4), 385–406.

Levinson, D. J., et al. Periods in the adult development of men: ages 18 to 45. *Counseling Psychologist* 1978, **6** (1), 21–25.

Lewin, K. *Dynamic Theory of Personality*. New York: McGraw-Hill, 1935.

Mahler, M., F. Pine, and A. Bergman. *The Psychological Birth of the Human Infant: Symbiosis and Individuation*. London: Hutchinson, 1975.

Mannheim, K. *Essays on Sociology and Social Psychology*. New York: Oxford University Press, 1953.

McGuire, W. (Ed.), *The Freud/Jung letters; The Correspondence Between Sigmund Freud and C. G. Jung*. Princeton, NJ: Princeton University Press, 1974.

Murray, H. A. *Explorations in Personality*. New York: Oxford University Press, 1938.

Murray, H. A. Morton Prince: A sketch of his life and work. *Journal of Abnormal and Social Psychology*, 1956, **52**, 291–295.

Neugarten, B. L. *Personality in Middle and Later Life*. New York: Athernon Press, 1964.

Neugarten, B. L. *Middle Age and Aging: a Reader in Social Psychology*. Chicago: University of Chicago Press, 1968.

Ortega Y Gasset, J. *Man and Crisis*. New York: Norton, 1958.

Pachter, L. *Telling Lives, the Biographic's Art*. Washington, DC: New Republic Books, 1979.

Sanford, N. Murray's clinic as a place to learn in. In C. Comstock (Ed.), *Learning After College*. Orinda: Montaigue, 1980.

Sharaf, M. R. and D. J. Levinson. The quest for omnipotence in professional training: The case of the psychiatric resident. *Psychiatry*, 1964, **27**, 135–149.

Van Gennep, A. *The Rites of Passage*. Chicago: University of Chicago Press, 1960.

White, R. *Lives in Progress*. Hinsdale, IL: Dryden Press, 1952.

Winnicott, D. *The Maturational Processes and the Facilitating Environment: Studies in the Theory of Emotional Development*. London: Hogarth, 1965.

PART THREE

Experimental Studies of the Person and the Situation: Toward a Comprehensive Theory of Personality and Behavior

As Levinson noted, Murray argued that the study of personality required a hybrid clinician-humanist-scientist; that personality was complex and needed an investigator whose scope could include highly disparate sets of variables, who wanted to see the whole person in a life context and who could also clearly identify and measure the characteristics that were interesting. An unfortunate result of Murray's typology was that the clarity of definitions and descriptions aided impatient, but psychometrically able, people. McClelland's chapter, the first in this section, is in large part, a response to the criticisms such as Mischel's (1968) that have been made of the work of these people. In his paper McClelland argues in clear concise strokes that conclusions based on inappropriately performed research should not define the field. The field of personality developed because there seemed to be a need for a construct that could account for the consistency that people show across widely varying circumstances. Much of modern empirical work in personality (as opposed to clinical work) selects a single internal variable and then attempts to demonstrate that it is real and important by calculating its level of association with apparently similar variables across situations. The measure of lawfulness, then, was taken to be consistency in measurement. McClelland argues, however, that consistency as a criterion was being handled in a very simple-minded fashion and that people such as Mischel "were looking for consistency in the wrong place."

In a relatively few pages, McClelland's response to this work really outlines the framework of a complex theory of personality and the most appropriate method for its study. As with other contributors to this volume, McClelland looks to the power of the inclusive strategy. Where so many psychologists in the field deal with single variables and are careless of the type of human experiences that underlies a measurement operation, McClelland asks how many dispositional variables are needed to explain behavior and how many different types of measurement operations are possible to measure them. To put his argument simply, McClelland argues that American psychologists have assumed that these types of variables (i.e., motives, beliefs, abilities) and their different types of measurement, are the same and so should be highly intercorrelated. When they are found not to be highly intercorrelated, the conclusion is that personality exists only in the mind of the psychologist. With a marvellous display of annoyance, McClelland crosses types of variables with types of measurements in a table that should be hung above every personality psychologist's desk. As McClelland argues, we should not be looking for consistency but rather for lawfulness. Only similar types of variables, measured in similar types of ways, should evidence consistency. Consistency within, and lack of consistency between types of variables indicates only the importance of recognizing that they are different.

It has been the mark of McClelland's theoretical writings that he usually concludes with a set of empirical results demonstrating the utility of his position. If there are all these classes of variables, what do we do with them? McClelland's basic position is that motives, beliefs, and abilities are all needed to account for behavior within a particular type of situation. He concludes his theoretical argument by presenting some recent work by his collaborators. McClelland's basic response to Mischel's argument that most relationships in personality studies hover around the .30 level is to say that Mischel is right, given that the research was done wrongly. The new approach that he demonstrates is to show that when appropriate measures are taken of a variable in all three classes, by itself each variable is associated with the criterion around the .30 level. However, when the variables are all entered into a step-wise multiple regression equation they combine to yield a multiple R of .68. Norman Endler, the contributor of the next chapter, concludes by citing Lewin's (1952) famous remark: "there is nothing as practical as a good theory." McClelland shows this statement to be as appropriate a keynote for his own chapter.

* * *

Murray's proposition that a need-press analysis is needed to explain behavior has held an honored place in psychology. It is successful as a maxim but unexamined as a principle. In the last decade, however, there has been a more serious commitment to investigating the potential power of that position. Not only have people been studying the joint effects of the two classes of variables on some dependent behavior but, more important, many have been examining seriously the logical, methodological, theoretical and metatheoretical details that such a position implies. The mathematical form of Murray's proposition is Lewin's equation that behavior is a function of the person and the environment $B = f(P, E)$. It may be a mark of the promise of this orienting point of view, as a model of human life, that when it begins to get examined seriously it becomes very complex. Two major anthologies (Endler and Magnusson, 1976; Magnusson and Endler, 1977) bring together the most serious and detailed work on this proposition. What began as an orienting formulation for Murray, resulted first in a cliché and then in a serious investigation. Ultimately, it may turn out to be a theory.

Norman Endler, the author of the second chapter of this section, has been at the forefront of this effort, both substantively and organizationally. In his paper he outlines the many facets of the complex theory of behavior proposed so simply by Murray. What is so exciting about this new integrative perspective is that most of the individual parts of the theory have been the subject of fairly intensive programs of work. The behavioral consequences of many individual variables, such as dominance, authoritarianism, or anxiety, have been studied in depth. Similarly, the psychological consequences of experiences with different situations, such as membership in democratic or hierarchical social structures, have been studied as well. A large stockpile of empirical results has been stored in our journals waiting broader theoretical use. One consequence of these efforts has been a sense of dissatisfaction with the level of control that has been attained in our experimental work. Usually, this dissatisfaction is expressed in the form of complaints about the failure of personality variables to yield correlations over the .30 level. Similarly low amounts of the variance are accounted for by experiments that manipulate situational variables. The promise of this new person by situation interaction perspective is that the low level of results produced by each of these conceptually plausible positions by themselves may be accurate. The isolated effects may simply be weak. Taken together, however, the positions may turn out to be very strong.

Endler outlines, in a unified presentation, the framework of an interactionist position, by blocking out the way to think about the different classes of variables jointly. As such, he provides us, for what Murray called the "short unit" (i.e., the relatively brief behavioral sequence), with a model similar to that attempted by Levinson for what Murray called the "long unit" (i.e., the life course). Both Levison and Endler are reaching toward a conception of how best to understand the need-press theme that Murray proposed and both of their chapters provide much of the material that may stimulate later work to reach beyond the fairly simple additive conceptions available at present.

An important contribution of Endler's chapter is the discussion of the alternative positions that might be utilized in each of the major sources of the interaction. For example, his discussion of the different models of personality leads to very different models of interaction effects than might be expected. A similar benefit can be drawn from his discussion of different models of the situation. What is exciting about the chapter is that Endler shows that there is much work that needs to be done and provides us with a very helpful framework within which to begin. In part, Endler is critical of much of the work on interaction that stays at the abstract level of analysis. He argues quite vigorously that this is the time to become specific about the nature of these variables. He, there-fore, provides an extended discussion of some of his more recent work on anxiety which shows that it is possible to move beyond the theoreti-cal stance of simply demonstrating that interactions occur. By specifi-cally examining alternative models of anxiety and their expected form of interaction with specific characteristics of the situation, Endler shows that a much more powerful model can be created that predicts and explains interesting patterns of interaction both in the laboratory and in the real world.

Endler's comments on method are equally germane. In fairly broad strokes he outlines a series of approaches and shows the correspondence of different measurement models to the different psychological models. As future work becomes more specific this discussion may prove quite helpful in directing the selection of the most appropriate research strategies that best fit the postulated nature of the variables.

Finally, Endler both begins and ends his chapter by calling for a more theoretical approach to the study of interactions. In particular, he calls for a theory of the organization of personality constructs within the person. Much of the advance in modern personality research came from those following the direction provided by Murray in his *Explorations* book. The typology of personality variables was a major advance in clarifying and defining the major motivational concerns of the individual. The weakness of the typology lay in a lack of clarity concerning the relationship among these variables. Thus while we possess, presently, a store of empirical information about the nature of these variables, Endler argues that most of the work has been piecemeal and atheoretical. Endler concludes that we now have a reasonable amount of information about personality variables and a way of thinking about the nature of their interaction with the situation. What is still needed to make the entire pattern coherent is a general theory of the person and the environment, phrased in specific terms; we also need a way of integrating the terminology of experimental personality research, derived from Murray, with that from the broader life span perspective, such as Levinson's.

REFERENCES

Endler, N. W. and D. Magnusson (Eds.), *Interactional Psychology and Personality*. Washington, DC: Hemisphere Publishing, 1976.

Lewin, K. Problems of research in social psychology. In D. Cartwright (Ed.), *Field Theory in Social Science*. London: Tavistock Publications, 1952.

Magnusson, D. and N. S. Endler (Eds.), *Personality at the Crossroads: Current Issues in Interactional Psychology*. Hillsdale: Erlbaum, 1977.

Mischel, W. *Personality Assessment*. New York: Wiley, 1968.

CHAPTER 4

Is Personality Consistent?

David C. McClelland

Many contemporary students of personality have concluded that there is very little empirical evidence for consistency in personality. According to current conventional wisdom, the person has practically speaking disappeared from personality theory except as a physical body or as a figment of the imagination of judges or of friends of the person who, since they are "trait theorists" persist in seeing consistency in his or her behavior even though it is not there. Mischel (1968), one of the most influential of these theorists, sums the matter up as follows:

> The results of trait-state assessments reviewed in this and the preceding chapters, taken collectively, lead to clear conclusions. With the possible exception of intelligence, highly generalized behavior consistencies have not been demonstrated, and the concept of personality traits as broad response dispositions is thus untenable (p. 146).

He goes on to say,

> It is not surprising that large scale applied efforts to predict behavior from personality inferences have been strikingly and consistently unsuccessful. . . . The initial assumptions of trait-state theory were logical, inherently plausible, and also consistent with common sense and intuitive impressions about personality. Their real limitation turned out to be empirical—they simply have not been supported adequately. (p. 147).

Since Mischel concludes that the evidence does not support the notion of broad internal personality dispositions, it is useless to think in terms of intrapsychic dynamics determining what the person does. Instead a person's responses are the product of specific external stimulus situations.

> Behavior depends on the exact stimulus conditions in the evoking situation and on the individual's history with similar stimuli. . . . Studies of the precise ways in which behavior comes to depend on stimulus conditions, and of how alterations in stimulus conditions are followed regularly and consistently by predictable behavior changes reveal basic lawfulness. (Mischel, 1968, p. 191)

In this view the person is like a chameleon whose coloration or response depends on precise changes in external stimulus conditions. Somehow this conclusion does not feel right—even to Mischel. For instance he says in another place: "It would be a complete misinterpretation, for instance, to conclude that individual differences are unimportant" (p. 38). But on closer examination it turns out that even these individual differences depend entirely on the concrete stimulus situation so that it is not possible to draw generalizations about the person across situations. He concludes somewhat wistfully that our enduring belief that people do remain the same is a result of the fact that we are trait theorists and find it too confusing to think of a person as changing all the time. Instead we stick labels on him or her to help process conflicting information more efficiently and then believe that the trait represents a consistency in the person rather than a product of our own need for consistency.

He is correct in reporting the evidence that we are all trait theorists in thinking about consistencies in ourselves or in others (see D'Andrade, 1965), but is this all there is to the notion of personality consistency? How did it come about that personality theorists lost the person in accumulating research evidence over the past thirty or forty years? To give my general answer in advance, they lost the person because they were looking for consistency in the wrong place and ignored the multivariate conception of personality so eloquently presented by Professor Henry Murray and his associates in *Explorations in Personality* (1938). A key element in Murray's approach was that he focused on trying to understand the concrete individual life. He understood the task of the theorist to be the explanation and understanding of the individual. He invented lots of different ways of measuring aspects of personality, he calculated correlation coefficients, and he theorized about personality, but he never allowed these abstractions to get too far from the reality of the concrete individual life or to falsify what could be more directly inferred by observation of a particular individual. In contrast many contemporary personality theorists appear to know nothing about individuals. They do not study lives in all their concrete details; they study symbolic responses on questionnaires. The person is typically asked to imagine what he would do in a hypothetical situation (see Endler and Hunt, 1966, or Dworkin and Kihlstrom, 1978), and from the responses made the most far reaching conclusions are drawn as to the relative importance of the person or the situation in producing a response. This is a very far cry from Murray's emphasis on real responses in real situations. One is tempted to conclude that if you search in an unreal place you get unreal results. The value of focusing on the live individual is that it brings abstract theories hard up against reality.

And my experience of individuals over time leads me firmly to the conclusion that they show quite an amazing amount of consistency even across wide variations in external circumstances. Furthermore a careful analysis of the reasons for my belief in consistency has convinced me that I am not just a victim of the labels I have pinned on people. Let me be specific and cite by way of illustration the case of a person with whom many psychologists will be familiar. Over twenty-five years ago by chance at an Eastern Psychological Association meeting, I met a charming young man named Richard Alpert. He had just graduated from college, wanted to go to graduate school in psychology but his father objected and was refusing to support him in this wish because he thought he should go to medical school. I took him on as a graduate research assistant at Wesleyan University and from there he went to Stanford where he got his Ph.D. working with Pauline and Robert Sears. Then he returned to Harvard where he was considered a very promising young assistant professor who would probably go far in the academic world. People liked him. He was energetic and ambitious and already able to attract the kind of research funds that almost guarantee success in the academic world. He came from a wealthy family, so he could fly his own plane, acquire other symbols of prestige, and hobnob with the great or the near great in the academic or business world. Although his success seemed assured, he got involved with Timothy Leary and the drug scene in the early 1960s and "tuned in, turned on, and dropped out." For several years he wandered around taking LSD, and advising other young people to do likewise on the grounds that it would lead to true enlightenment. Then he went to India where he fell under the influence of an Indian guru whose devotees called him Maharaj-ji, who seemed to have extraordinary psychic powers, although he was also referred to by at least one western-born guru as "that second-rate mind reader." Whatever Maharaj-ji was, he transformed Richard Alpert into Ram Dass—the servant of Ram or the Lord, who stayed for long periods of time in India worshiping in Maharaj-ji's ashram and elsewhere, and who eventually himself became a spiritual teacher writing up his experiences in two or three books that were very popular in the counterculture of the late 1960s and early 1970s (Be Here Now, The Only Dance There Is).

When I first saw Ram Dass again in the early 1970s he seemed like a completely transformed person. His appearance was totally different from what it had been. He was wearing long Indian style clothes with beads around his neck; he was nearly bald but had grown a long bushy beard. He had given away all his possessions, refused his father's inheritance, carried no money on his person, and for a time lived as a nomad in a van which was all he had in the world. He had given up drugs, abandoned his career as a psychologist, no longer wanted even to save the world, and talked all the time as if he were "nobody special," although previously it had been clear to himself and others that he was somebody special. From a behaviorally oriented Western scientist, he had shifted to a believer in supernatural powers, psychic influences at a distance, mind reading, and the power of God. His general philosophy of psychology had shifted from neo-Freudianism (he had been in psychoanalysis for five years or so) to an amalgam of Eastern psychologies drawing heavily on Theravadan Buddhism and Hinduism. And he certainly felt that he was a completely different person—that he had left behind his ego trip and was now spending his time "going to God."

At first glance then, Richard Alpert/Ram Dass seemed like a perfect illustration of Walter Mischel's thesis that there is very little consistency in personality. He appeared to have changed in almost every way—in his appearance, his attitudes, his career, and his purpose in life. Yet after spending some time with him, I found myself saying over and over again "it's the same old Dick," and I am convinced that Walter Mischel would have said the same thing to himself (unless his theory got in the way), since he had also known Richard Alpert in the early sixties before he took off on his drug and spiritual trips. But what exactly did I mean when I thought, "it's the same old Dick?" Was it just that I had a certain picture of him that I refused to give up in the face of the dramatic changes that had occurred in his life? Was the consistency in my mind and not in his personality? I don't think so because certain characteristics had so obviously remained the same. He was still very intelligent. The ingestion of large amounts of LSD over time had not destroyed his mind, as many assumed it would. I would wager that he would score as high on an intelligence test today as he would have twenty years ago. But perhaps Walter Mischel would grant that intelligence is a consistent personality trait, on the basis of the evidence? Alpert's expressive movements were also still the same because after all he still inhabited the same body. The length of his stride, the expansiveness of his gestures remained the same, demonstrating a consistency over time that Allport and Vernon had showed existed cross-sectionally years ago (1933). He was still verbally fluent. He continued to have a strong interest in internal psychic states: the difference here was not in what he spent his time talking and thinking about but in the terms he used to describe what was going on internally. And he was still charming. People liked to be with him and to talk to him just as they had twenty-five years earlier. I don't know what the research evidence on likeability is, but I would wager that over time it is a fairly consistent personality trait.

At a somewhat less obvious level, Alpert was very much involved in high drama, just as he had always been. While he had abandoned a successful career as an academic psychologist and could not hope for recognition in that area, he had remained a psychologist. His books have sold hundreds of thousands of copies, even though the most popular one was not even distributed by a regular publisher. When he comes to town, he can typically draw an audience of 3000 people to listen to him talk for 3–5 hours at a stretch. What academic psychologist can boast such a following? He is still very much involved in power games. It is only the nature of the power that has changed—from standard Western symbols of importance and influence to psychic or spiritual siddhis ("powers"). At a more genotypic level I would certainly conclude that he continues to have a strong interest in power (or need for Power in Murray's or Winter's sense, 1973). Furthermore he still feels guilty about being so interested in power. He describes his guilt over being so influential at such an early age when he became assistant to his father who was then president of the New Haven Railroad. Now he is paradoxically put off by the fact that he attracts so many followers and repeatedly tells them that he is "nobody special." Finally we can observe that he has consistently looked for a great teacher who will guide him. I played the role of an exemplar for a short period, then Robert and Pauline Sears, then Timothy Leary, then Maharaj-ji, and more recently Joya, a Brooklyn housewife guru. He has been alternately attracted and repelled by such exemplars throughout his life. But surely this is enough to make my point—namely that when one looks at a concrete life over time this way, one is bound to discover certain consistent themes that don't appear to be wholly imaginary, in the "eye of the beholder." And I am sure that each one of you can think of someone who has shown the same kind of consistency.

How then did personality theorists get into their current bind of seeming to prove empirically that there is no consistency in personality? The answer to me seems quite simple: they looked for consistency in the wrong way in the wrong place. They have behaved like the drunk who looked for the key to his house under the street lamp because "the light was better there". Personality theorists have looked for consistencies in the wrong place because it was easier to think of personality in a simplistic way and to make certain types of measurements that precluded their finding evidence of consistency. From the beginning trait theorists have ignored practically all of the key lessons that Murray and his associates had tried to teach them.

Let me just enumerate a few of the most important of these lessons to show how the recent theorists went astray.

1. Personality is complex. Many different kinds of variables are necessary to account for it. Murray was not a trait theorist as he makes

very clear in discussing Allport's book on personality which appeared at about the same time as *Explorations in Personality*.

According to my prejudice, trait psychology is over-concerned with recurrence, with consistency, with what is clearly manifested (the surface of personality), with what is conscious, orderly and rational. It minimizes the importance of physiological occurrences, irrational impulses and beliefs, infantile experiences, unconscious and inhibited drives as well as environmental (sociological) factors. (Murray, 1938, p. 715)

He recognized that there were consistencies particularly in style in the trait sense, but as a minimum two other major types of variables were needed to account for the bewildering variety of human experience and action—namely *needs* or motives and *press,* the apperceptive representation of environmental forces, as well as the forces themselves.

2.   These different types of variables were to be assessed in different ways—in concrete life situations, in interviews, in fantasy, in questionnaires, in the laboratory. But at no point did he make the assumption common to latter-day trait theorists that the information obtained about, let us say, a need in one way, such as a questionnaire, should be the same as that obtained in another way, say in fantasy. The reason for searching for motives in fantasy was precisely because one could not trust the information about motives obtained from questionnaires or interviews. Yet latter-day trait theorists assumed that these two sources of information must agree and if they do not, they infer that personality is inconsistent and that there is no evidence for stable internal dispositions.

3.   Thoughts and fantasies—the whole panoply of human experience—is just as important for the psychologist to understand and explain as the actions a person takes. Trait theorists have accepted the general American belief that "actions speak louder than words" and that therefore the purpose of studying thought or fantasy is to predict action. In fact Sears (1951) in presidential address before the American Psychological Association defined personality as the "sum of potentialities for action." Thus trait theorists have generally not often sought for consistencies in thought patterns or experiencing but have concentrated on trying to find consistencies between thought and action and when they have not found them they have concluded that personality is inconsistent.

4.   Do not trust self-reports because the person is unaware of unconscious needs or schemas that shape his or her behavior. It is astonishing how often this simple truism has been ignored by psychometrically oriented personality theorists wedded to their questionnaires. It is even

more amazing to some of us that it is only recently that some academic psychologists have gotten around to accepting the empirical evidence that people do not report accurately on their reasons for doing things (see Nisbett and Wilson, 1978). Ignoring this simple fact has led to great confusion in personality theory. The confusion was perpetuated by an article by Campbell and Fiske (1959) on the multitrait-multimethod matrix, an article that is cited with great favor by Mischel and regarded almost as Holy Writ by nearly every textbook writer on personality assessment. Campbell and Fiske were right in observing that consistencies are greatest within the same methods of measurement but wrong in arguing that theory requires that there be consistencies across methods of measurement. The point can be made quite simply in connection with the results reported by Burwen and Campbell (1957) on attitudes toward the father and general authority figures. They obtained conscious attitudes toward the father from interviews, correlated them with ideas about authority figures expressed in a Thematic Apperception Test (TAT), found no relationship and concluded that there is no evidence for a consistent generalizeed attitude toward authority. Wonder of wonders! The reason Murray had developed the TAT in the first place was precisely because he wanted to get behind conscious attitudes towards the father to more unconscious schemas. If these two sources of information were highly correlated, there would obviously be no need for a TAT. If Burwen and Campbell had wanted to examine the consistency of unconscious feelings towards authority they should have stayed in the unconscious realm, comparing let us say TAT responses to authority with responses to subliminal cues relating to father or authority figures using perhaps the method exploited recently by Silverman (1976). The fact is that many American personality psychologists have never really accepted the notion of the unconscious. They continually use conscious self-reports as means of "validating" measures obtained in other ways, when there is absolutely no basis in fact or in theory for proceeding in this way.

In my 1951 book on personality I attempted to develop Murray's ideas further in the direction of a systematic scheme for the analysis of personality. I started with the Lewinian formula that behavior is a function of both the personality and the environment, $B = f(p, E)$, and then asked, what are the minimum number of different types of person variables needed to explain behavior? I concluded that three or possibly four different types of dispositional variables were required—namely needs or motives, schemas, and traits, I was not sure then and I am not sure now whether self-schemas in the sense of what people say about themselves in questionnaires or interviews can be subsumed under the general schema heading or whether they should be treated as an independent type of disposition. My reasons for choosing these constructs were partly theoretical and partly methodological. I was impressed then as Campbell, Mischel and others have been since that different methods of personality measurement yield different results. I concluded not that personality was inconsistent since I was not a simple trait theorist, but rather that we needed *different types of constructs* to explain behavior. In this sense the lack of agreement between different methods of measurement was an advantage since they provided several independent determinants of behavior which could be put into a multivariate formula.

According to this theory *needs* or *motives* were to be measured largely in operant fantasies as obtained in the TAT. *Schemas* or internal representations of the way the world works were to be measured either through coding thought content or through self-report questionnaires. And *traits* were to be limited to observations of habitual stylistic ways of thinking or acting. To give a simple example, this meant that the *n* Achievement a person shows in fantasy (a motive) is not equivalent to the importance he places on hard work (a schema) which is not equivalent to the effort he typically puts out in work situations (a trait). Trait theorists and apparently most American psychologists have assumed that these different variables are one and the same so that measures of them should be highly intercorrelated. For Murray and for me this is far too simplistic an approach to the problem of accounting for human behavior. Apparently the notion that there are different *types* of personality constructs, measured in different ways, is too complex for most American personality psychologists to grasp, possibly because as Mischel points out we are all trait theorists and tend to oversimplify things. If proof is needed of this assertion, I cite as evidence that I have received an average of one or two communications a month for the past twenty-five years, proving triumphantly to me that the need for Achievement as measured in fantasy is invalid because it does not correlate with some questionnaire measure of interest in achievement, or with actual school achievement. Apparently I did not make the point clearly enough that in my theory these variables *should be independent*. So let me try once again to explain my theory and then demonstrate its utility for predicting behavior.

Table 1 lays out the three main types of personality variables in columns and illustrates different methods of measuring them in rows. For many reasons it is essential on the measurement side to distinguish between operant and respondent measures and between thought and action. Operants are spontaneous thoughts or actions, the stimulus for which cannot be readily identified. Respondents in contrast are responses to clearly identified stimuli—such as items in a questionnaire or some experimentally presented stimuli. The distinction is not hard and fast because obviously there is a stimulus picture in the TAT but it is ambiguous and the person is free to make any kind of response to it. In

Table 1. Types of Variables Needed for Personality Analysis as a Function of Method of Measurement, with Examples

Type of Measurement	Personality Variables		
	Motives	Schemas	Traits (Stylistic)
Thought Operants	TOM n Achievement n Power n Affiliation from TAT	TOS Rogerian summaries of client themes Stages of adaptation (Stewart, 1978)	TOT Perceptual (Rorschach) Speech characteristics (Sanford, 1942)
Respondents	TRM Questionnaire measures of interest, intentions v Achievement v Power v Affiliation Allport-Vernon Lindzey study of values	TRS Constructs in Kelly's REP Test Role constructs (as in sex, occu- pation, or race stereotype) Attributions Self-image	TRT Field independence (EFT) Questionnaire reports of habitual actions t Dominance t Extraversion t Extraversion Yea-saying
Action Operants	AOM Cannot be safely inferred from actions, but action correlates can be empirically established Examples: n Achievement: diagonals and S-shapes in expressive moments or entrepreneurship	AOS ?	AOT Expressive moments Working hard Extraversion Giving to others Success as military officer Competencies
Respondents	ARM n Achievement: moderate risk-taking Alternative manifestations	ASM Working harder when success is attributed to effort	ART Persistence Rigidity Reaction time Dominating Delay of reward Doing well on school tests Honesty

Source: After McClelland, 1951.

contrast if a person is asked about his interests or needs on a questionnaire, he is typically limited to agreeing or disagreeing on a scale, or saying yes or no. Similarly a person is relatively free in a nondirective interview to talk about anything so that summaries of the thematic content from such interviews are classified as operant thought measures (TOS, thought-operant-schema) in contrast to the attributions a subject is asked to make to explain success or failure where the alternatives are given him or her. Kelly's Rep test (1963) falls somewhere in between the operant and respondent ends of a continuum because the subject has to invent his own constructs in an operant way but is asked to do so in a fairly structured manner.

According to this method of classification the amount of white space a subject uses in responding to Rorschach ink blots is a TOT (thought-operant-trait) whereas perceptual skill in seeing embedded figures is a TRT (thought-respondent-trait). The operant-respondent distinction corresponds somewhat although not exactly with the unconscious-conscious distinction, because operants are less conscious and respondents more conscious. That is, people do not normally know how much achievement imagery they are injecting into TAT stories whereas they are very conscious of how much achievement striving they are attributing to themselves in a questionnaire about motives. In a vain effort to convince psychologists that these two kinds of measures of motives were separate and distinct, I introduced the letter v for value to precede the motive name, as in v Achievement (TRM) to distinguish it from n Achievement (thought-operant-motive, TOM, in Table 1). Similarly the letter s in front of Achievement was supposed to refer to constructs about achievement and the letter t to refer to achieving traits. All these distinctions may appear confusing, but they had the purpose of underlining the fact that measures obtained of personality constructs in different ways were essentially uncorrelated or independent.

The thought-action distinction is important if only because many personality theorists assume that the purpose of measuring thought is to predict action. Thus theorists are always trying to predict how dominant a person will actually behave in a series of situations from how he says he would behave in such situations in a questionnaire. So far they have had very little success in doing so, as Mischel correctly points out. The reason in my view is because they have been trying to fly on one wing so to speak—trying to predict behavior from only one of its main determinants, ignoring schemas and motives. But more of that in a moment. What is particularly worth noting in Table 1 is that it is extremely difficult to make accurate inferences about motives or schemas from actions. The problem is that most American psychologists are so oriented towards studying the behavior of animals and children who cannot talk very well that they keep trying to infer motives and schemas from actions. It is a little like trying to do personality analysis with one hand tied behind your back. Thus people have endlessly assumed that the action of doing well in school can be used to infer that the person has a high need to achieve. It cannot be used that way for the simple reason that there are obviously many motives for doing well in school and it takes a subtler analysis to discover which one is involved in a particular case. The reverse approach however does work. Thus repeated studies of individuals high in n Achievement, measured by the TOM method have shown that they are moderate risk-takers in certain work situations (see Korman, 1974). Once this has been established it may be possible to infer high n Achievement from moderate risk-taking actions. Similarly it has been found that individuals high in n Achievement are more apt to make diagonals and S-shapes in expressive movements (AOM in Table 1) and therefore it may be possible to infer n Achievement from these action characteristics.

In terms of the measures laid out in Table 1, where can we expect to find consistency in personality? To begin with we cannot expect to find it across the columns because the motive, schema, and trait variables were separated out primarily because measures of them do not correlate. Thus we do not expect the need for Power in thought to be correlated with personal constructs about hierarchies nor with explosive speech patterns. Nor do we expect conscious desires for power to be correlated with attitudes towards authority or with statements of how dominant a person would be in various situations. Much of the literature on the relative role of the person and the environment (Endler and Hunt, 1966, Argyle and Little, 1972, Dworkin and Kihlstrom, 1978) deals with symbolic respondent measures in the terminology of Table 1 and concludes that there is not a great deal of individual consistency across the person variables.

Nor can we expect much consistency between operant and respondent measures, because, as already noted, operants represent relatively unconscious behaviors and people do not observe very accurately their own characteristics. We need only recall that n Achievement is unrelated to v Achievement, that sexist patterns of thinking (operants) are unrelated to conscious attitudes toward sexual equality, and that operant responses to the Rorschach blots bear little relation to alternatives chosen in the multiple choice inkblot technique (see Holtzman, 1968).

Where then can one expect to find consistencies? For respondent measures, test-retest reliabilities are generally high within if not across boxes. That is, if a person is asked the same questions again on a second occasion, he or she will generally tend to give the same responses. Interests, stereotypes, self-images, yea-saying tendencies generally remain fairly stable, as even Mischel admits (1968). So far as operant thought measures are concerned however, conventional wisdom has it that they are extremely unstable. If you administer the TAT or the Rorschach a second time you are apt to get very different responses on all variables, which has convinced most theorists that there is little or no consistency in these measures. It is really extraordinary how firmly they have stuck to this conclusion despite two well-known facts: (1) the validities of, let us say some, TAT motive measures are often considerably higher than their reliabilities, which psychometrically is impossible if the reliabilities are true estimates; and (2) it has been well-known for nearly fifty years (see Telford, 1931) that when individuals are given free response instructions, they vary their responses. This used to be called "associative refractory phase." In common sense terms this means that if a person is instructed to "be creative"—the usual instruction for the TAT—he or she will normally tell a different story when presented with the same picture a second time, as I pointed out twenty years ago (in Atkinson, 1958). I concluded therefore that retesting for operant thought measures would not give a proper estimate of consistency and assumed that psychometricians would get the message, but they did not. Fortunately Winter and Stewart (1977) have finally conducted the obvious experiment in which they broke the set to vary the response on the second administration by telling the subjects that they should feel free either to tell the same or a different story. Without this instruction test-retest correlations were as usual low, but with it they rose to respectable heights (between .60 and .70). Furthermore Atkinson and Birch (1978) have built a model which shows that there can be consistency in such behavior even when test-retest reliability coefficients are low because of natural variations in underlying tendencies over time. So it is now reasonable to conclude that there is considerable consistency within operant thought measures of motives, when properly understood and measured, and within Stewart's measure of stages of adaptation (1978), which we have classified as a schema.

At the level of action the chief difficulty arises in the ART box since as Mischel correctly points out there is little consistency in such performance traits as persistence, rigidity, or delay of gratification across different situations. The chief exception to this rule has to do with performance on achievement tests and doing well in school. Here consistency is high across situations and over time. The reason seems obvious: in this domain the situation is held constant, meaning the nature of the test, the individual's understanding of the situation (his schema), his motives for performing on the test, and the skills he has learned from performing on similar tests. When we observe that a person who does well on academic achievement tests also tends to do well in school we are observing a consistency in response to two very similar situations. The same is not true with many other types of action traits that researchers have tried to investigate. It is not clear to the subject why he or she is being asked to perform in a lot of tests supposedly measuring rigidity. They are dissimilar in content and the demands they place on the individual. And they do not call for practiced skills. Thus we conclude the obvious: consistency can be found in the ART box only to the extent that the situation remains constant—which is exactly the conclusion that Mischel came to. But he erred by implying that the same generalization applied to all the other boxes in the Table.

Generally speaking, operant behaviors show more consistency across time and over situations because by definition they are less dependent on specific stimulus conditions. Thus we find a high consistency in expressive movements (Allport and Vernon, 1931), in the length of speech bursts (Takala, 1977), in the tendency to work long hours or give to charity, and so forth, so long as we do not test for these behaviors in specific situations. Years ago in a symposium discussion with Professor Guilford (1955) I made the same point in the following way. Suppose we were interested in an action characteristic like beer drinking. A psychometrician might set up a situation in which he or she tested how much beer different individuals *could* drink to get at individual differences in capacity. That would be what I am calling here a respondent measure, because people are asked to see how well they can do in a specific situation with strong demand characteristics. An operant measure would be simply a record of how much beer a person actually did drink over a period of time. My conviction is that how much beer a person can drink in a contrived experimental situation (1) will vary considerably depending on the specific demand characteristics of the situation, and (2) will not predict how much beer he or she does drink over time. Furthermore I believe the evidence shows that operant beer drinking patterns are fairly stable, at least among young men. That is, under normal conditions of social living, young men will either create situations or find themselves in situations that will evoke characteristically high or low levels of beer drinking. One of the great failures to my mind of contemporary personality measurement is that it seems almost totally to have failed to understand and utilize operant measures. I have done my best to popularize them for the past thirty years but only a glance at current journals and textbooks is enough to show that I have not been persuasive. If researchers had used operant measures more generally, I believe they would have been more impressed with the consistency of personality since the operant measures are not so dependent on particular stimulus conditions.

Certainly nearly all of the consistencies I observed in the personality of Richard Alpert/Ram Dass involved operant characteristics—his expressive movements, verbal fluency, interest in internal states, need for Power, guilt, and search for a great teacher. And I am convinced that if I had some respondent measures from him taken twenty-five years ago and now, they would show major inconsistencies. For certainly his attitudes towards many things and his conscious image of what he is like and what he is trying to do have changed.

What about consistency between the upper and lower portion of Table 1, between thought and action? For respondent measures again, the record is not good. It has proven very difficult if not impossible to go from questionnaire reports of dominant behavior for example to dominant actions in real life situations. Again the reason is simple: it is almost impossible to create symbolically, at least with a short verbal description, the precise situation in real life in which a person finds himself when the same action might be called for. It is possible to ask a person what he would do if a fire breaks out in his house, but there is little evidence that what he says he would do is consistently related to what he would actually do under such circumstances. For operants, as one might expect, the record is somewhat better. In my book on personality I noted some consistencies between my subject Karl's perceptual and expressive movement traits, although psychology since has shown relatively little interest in this area. More work has been done in the motive area. Thus an operant thought characteristic like n Achievement has been shown to lead over time to the operant risk-taking actions involved in entrepreneurship (McClelland, 1965). It is worth recalling here that an operant measure like n Achievement is not related to school achievement (a respondent measure) and that school achievement, as the model in Table 1 predicts, is not related to operant entrepreneurial achievement in later life. In fact school achievement does not appear to be strongly related to any operant measures of success in later life (Winter, McClelland, and Stewart, 1979). It is just one more illustration of the generalization that what one *can do* in a particular test situation is not strongly related to what one *does do* when the test situation does not exist. To cite another example of operant thought predicting operant action, it has been reported that the imperial motive pattern (high n Power, low n Affiliation, and high Activity Inhibition) is fairly strongly connected with high blood pressure twenty years later, probably through chronic overactivation of the sympathetic nervous system (McClelland, 1979). Here we have instances of a stable personality disposition leading to actions which over time produce a predictable or consistent effect.

Unfortunately the search for consistency between thought and action has been marred by the belief that they should have a one-to-one relationship. Trait theorists act as if they believed that thoughts about power should translate themselves into power actions—arguments, fist fights, watching and participating in competitive events, and so forth. When we discover that this is not so empirically, are we to conclude that personality is inconsistent? I think rather that we should conclude that the expectation of such simple isomorphic consistencies represents a very unsophisticated level of theorizing. What we are interested in is not consistency *per se* but in lawfulness, in understanding and predicting behavior. Thus we need a theory that explains inconsistencies as well as consistencies as Murray pointed out.

In the case of the power motive, or any motive, we have such a theory although trait theorists act as if they have never heard of it. It is the notion that motives express themselves in alternative ways—now in this symptom, now in that. Freud built his theory of the substitutability of symptoms on it and Elsa Frenkel-Brunswik (1942) provided empirical evidence for the alternative manifestations model nearly forty-five years ago. In fact one of the chief reasons for insisting that it is necessary to employ the motive construct in explaining individual behavior is precisely because it can lead to alternative rather than consistent types of actions. This may look like inconsistency at the manifest level, but at the genotypic level there is consistency. For example people high in the need for personalized power, as coded in thought samples, may engage in heavy drinking, gambling, accumulating prestige supplies, or in acting on aggressive impulses. None of these possible actions is by itself highly correlated with the personal power drive (suggesting a lack of consistency between thought and action), but the maximum manifestation of any one of them is (McClelland et al., 1972). In other words the theory says that if a man drinks heavily, he does not need to express his personal power drive in gambling or accumulating prestige supplies, or if he gambles he does not need to drink heavily. But if he has a strong personal power drive he will tend to go to extremes in one of these four typical outlets, and this is what turns out to be the case.

On an even more sophisticated level, I have demonstrated (McClelland, 1975) that the need for Power expresses itself differently depending on the stage of adaptation of the person, as determined by the Stewart measure of stages of adaptation. At Stage I or the intake stage, *n* Power is associated with power oriented reading (about sex and aggression), at Stage II or the stage of autonomy, it is associated with many controlled impulses to anger, at Stage III or the assertive stage, it is associated with expressing anger towards people, and at Stage IV or the stage of mutuality, it is associated with many organizational memberships. In a miscellaneous sample of adult males, the correlations between n Power and any one of these outlets tend to be low and insignificant—they actually vary between $-.01$ and $+.15$. Why? Because the men will be at varying stages of maturity and will tend to express their power drive in different ways as a consequence. But the alternative manifestation model predicts that every man high in n Power will tend to go to an extreme in one of these four outlets depending on his stage of maturity. The expectation is confirmed. The correlation between n Power and the maximum expression in standard score terms of one of these four action outlets is .32, $p < .05$. Furthermore the correlation of n Power with the *average* expression of all four outlets is only .19, confirming the action substitution notion. What is consistent is the man's search for a power outlet for his n Power and not the tendency to be assertive in every sort of way, as simplistic trait theory assumes. Rather he will pick the way that is consistent with his level of maturity.

The same reasoning applies to understanding the results obtained by Hartshorne and May (1928) in their *Studies of Deceit*. They found very little consistency from one situation to another in the extent to which school children were honest or lied and cheated. Trait theorists have seized on this finding with glee and concluded that it proves that the personality or character of the child contributes little to the determination of honest behavior whereas the concrete specific situation contributes everything. But once again their theory is very unsophisticated. What few people have noted in recent years is that Hartshorne and May also reported that children who were given special instruction in honesty and merit badges for good behavior actually cheated more. How are we to understand this behavior? Many psychologists I suspect were secretly delighted by the result since they did not like religious education anyway. It seemed to be just further proof that you could not mold character in ways that would affect behavior. But introducing the most elementary notions of developmental theory suggests another reason for the result. All theories of moral development—whether promulgated by Piaget, Erikson, Kohlberg or the highest religious authorities—distinguish between an earlier stage of conformity and a later stage of autonomy or choice. At the outset children are good—that is, honest or kindly—because they do not know any better (Piaget) or because they are rewarded for being good and punished for not being good. At this stage their behavior tends to be dependent on external sanctions. They exhibit good behavior if the authorities or sanctions are salient, but not if they are not. At a later stage of development internalization takes place.

Children break away from their complete dependency on external authority, become somewhat autonomous and make decisions on their own. But if this is so, by definition children will almost certainly make fewer conformist moral responses as they grow more mature, for the simple reason that more choice is involved. At a common sense level everyone knows that this is true—that 13- or 14-year-olds are beginning to think for themselves and show more signs of "adolescent rebellion" than say 10-year-olds who are still being good for external reasons. Yet this very elementary notion has apparently been overlooked by those interpreting the Hartshorne and May studies. Moral education if it makes children more mature may in fact make them *less* moral in action because they are becoming more autonomous and self-assertive. Elsewhere we have reported empirical evidence (McClelland et al., 1979) that adults who score at Stages II and III (the autonomous or self-assertive stages) on the Stewart scale actually show less conformist moral behavior than those at Stage I (dependence on external authority) or at Stage IV, the most highly developed stage in which the person is good out of genuine concern for others. Thus what appeared to be inconsistent behavior turns out to be lawfully related to an increase in maturity.

A DIFFERENT APPROACH

So far I have managed to be critical of trait theorists only in their mindless search for isomorphic consistencies, and their insistence that there is only one variable of importance in personality theory. But Mischel (1968) complains that even when we take into account many of the points I have made, the results are still discouraging. Most relationships in personality studies still appear to hover around the .30 level and those that I have cited above are no exception. He is right. Old theories never die no matter how severely criticized they are until they are replaced with new theories that account better for the known facts. Does my elaborate classification of types of personality variables and types of measures in Table 1 provide guidelines for a new and better type of personality study in which more of the variance of human behavior can be accounted for? I think so. Let me give some empirical examples.

The different approach starts not with the person but with the criterion, with the competencies shown by an individual in an important category of situations. Traditionally personality theory has started with the person. A lot of different measures are obtained, they are intercorrelated, and a scale for some personality dimension is derived from these correlations. Then we determine whether it gives a reliable estimate of the characteristic and finally we attempt to relate this personality dimension to some transactions with the environment, usually with poor success. Let us reverse the process, start with the transactions with the environment, try to identify the competencies involved and work backwards to the personality measures that will predict them. First one has to make a practical decision as to the range of transactions to be considered. My first example has to do with leadership behavior. The studies of characteristics of successful leaders are legion and the conclusions to be drawn from them quite disappointing. Mann (1959) reviewed hundreds of such studies and showed that very few individual characteristics have been regularly shown to be correlated with effective leadership, and then at very low levels. However, he included in his survey all types of leadership situations—from highly structured positions to leaderless group discussions. This ignores the importance of environmental determinants to a degree unwarranted in psychological science.

In the research to be reported here, the goal was more modest (Winter, 1978). It was to discover the competencies displayed by successful leaders in highly structured positions, that is, by officers in the Navy at different ranks. It seemed reasonable to assume that there was some consistency in the demands made by the Navy on an officer across situations, but also some room for individuals to behave quite differently in face of these demands. It also seemed likely that the situational demands made on a commanding or executive officer were not identical to those made on a petty officer. Thus we restricted the range of leadership situations to be considered first to a fairly consistent set of demands in a highly structured organization, and second made some further distinctions of situational demands within the organization. In this sense we were remaining true to the model that $B = f(P, E)$ and looking for personality dispositions that would predict behavior only for a fairly stable and consistent set of situational demands.

The method for determining the competencies needed for various Navy officer positions involved behavioral event analysis. Officers were interviewed not primarily to get their ideas as to what their jobs required, but to obtain concrete examples of how they had behaved on particular occasions. They were asked to describe occasions in which they had performed particularly well as an officer or in which they had not done as well as they would like to have done. The technique is similar to Flanagan's critical incident method (1954), but it differs in the degree to which a person is encouraged to tell in great detail exactly what led up to the situation, what he was thinking at the time, what he did and how it all turned out. As these events are accumulated from both outstanding and average officers, the observer uses them to form concepts as to the competencies shown by the successful officers. The approach is somewhat analogous to what a clinical psychologist does in identifying themes in a TAT. The goal is to derive a scoring system, or a method of coding the episodes that is objective and gives high intercoder reliability, and which also is valid in the sense that it distinguishes between the more and less successful officers.

The competencies identified in this way must also be potentially measurable or trainable, that is they must have behaviorally specific implications. In the study of Navy officers (Winter, 1978) some twenty-five such different competencies that distinguished between more or less successful officers in the Pacific fleet, and which were subsequently cross-validated by a similar set of interviews in the Atlantic fleet, were identified. They were grouped into five general categories by factor analysis according to whether they related to task achievement, skillful use of influence, management control, advising and counseling, coercion, or technical problem solving. Then nine different tests were chosen or devised to measure the competencies in a variety of ways. The objective was to sample behaviors so far as possible from all the different categories laid out in the matrix in Table 1. A picture story exercise (TAT) was administered to get operant thought measures of motives. At the other extreme, to get at a respondent trait in action (ART, in the terminology of Table 1), a special Navy planning exercise was devised that required the officer to figure out the most efficient order in which to carry out various steps to get a ship out of the harbor. An organizational climate questionnaire was included to get a respondent measure of the schemas officers had as to what the ideal working conditions should be. And to assess advising and counseling competencies, an exercise was devised in which they listened to a number of taped dialogues, observed pictures of the people talking, and then reported on what was going on and what they would do in response to the situations presented. This provided several measures both of operant and respondent traits in the counseling area. Note that in three of the four tests just named, behaviors were sampled in a Navy context (the planning exercise, the organizational measure of climate, and the listening and counseling test). This was because a healthy respect for the situational determinants of behavior requires sampling behaviors in situations as much as possible like those in which the competencies were displayed. Altogether measures of some fifty different personality type variables were obtained from these tests. So many were assessed because it was hard to know in advance just how a particular competency might show itself in a test variable, because it was desirable to have two or three measures of each competency, and because the objective was to sample to some extent from each of the twelve categories in Table 1.

Finally it was necessary to cast a broad enough net to come up with different patterns of competencies, if necessary, for different types of officer jobs—that is, commanding and executive officers versus petty officers.

The overall expectation was that if the test measures of the competencies known to be related to superior officer performance were any good, then at least some of them could be used to predict success as an officer. It was soon evident however that officer ratings could not be predicted successfully from any of the test variables, unless two further distinctions were made in the criterion. First those technical officers had to be put aside who have a given Navy rank but who have no responsibility for leadership and management. They are largely engineers and their rated performance depends largely on technical rather than management competencies. The Navy itself was much more interested in what characteristics lead to successful management of men. Second, three major levels of authority had to be distinguished—commanding and executive officers versus division heads and division officers versus all kinds of petty officers. The results for commanding and executive officers in leadership and management positions are shown in Table 2. Overall nine different test variables taken together contributed to predicting success as a commanding officer in a stepwise multiple regression equation. Two motive variables, four schema variables, and three trait variables combined to yield a multiple r of .68 which accounts for a very respectable amount of the variance—five times the amount that Walter Mischel complains is the best we can usually do in personality research. The last schema variable (understanding that the job does not require affiliation) does not contribute by itself significantly to the prediction equation although it does raise the multiple r by at least .01.

The competencies identified in the interviews do not always relate to the variables as one might expect or in a consistent way—which is a good reason to try to get at them through a variety of measures—but they do help explain how certain characteristics are related to superior officer performance. Better commanding officers not only have the power motive pattern which I have elsewhere shown (McClelland, 1975) is associated with successful management, they also see their job as requiring greater use of power and influence in a work analysis questionnaire (a schema variable). This involves them more often in policy formulation and planning. They also are not individualistic, entrepreneurial "hard chargers", since they show low entrepreneurial interests on the Strong-Campbell instrument (a respondent motive measure), infrequently report taking initiative or being concerned about achieving something on their own, describe the ideal climate as not demanding personal (as opposed to organizational) responsibility (a schema mea-

Table 2. Characteristics Related to Superior Performance among Commanding/Executive NAVY Officers ($n = 72$)

Compentency	r	Tested Variable	Unique Variance Contributed (%)	p Value
Motives				
Formulates policy	.39**	Leadership motive pattern	6	.01
Plans	.31*	(n Power $>$ n Affiliation,		
Monitors results	.46**	high Activity Inhibition)		
Takes initiatve (low)	.32*	Low entrepreneurial		
		interest[a]	10	<.01
Schemas				
Low concern for		Ideal climate: responsibility		
achievement	.28*	organizational not		
Low monitoring		personal	5	.02
results	.33*			
Low on coercion	.30*	Ideal climate: reactance		
		against bureaucratic		
		inertia	9	<.01
—		Use of power required		
		in job	10	<.01
		Use of affiliation not		
		required in job	2	.11
Traits				
Optimizes	.26*	Manages by optimizing	12	<.01
Disciplines	.32*			
Positive expectations				
(low)	.29*	Manages by helping (low)	5	.02
Formulates policy	.30*	Scheduling skill	7	<.01
Positive expections	.26*			
Low on coercion	.35**			

Multiple $r = .68$, $p < .001$, for all 9 variables. Regression stopped when additional variables added less than .01 to r.

	Motives Alone	Schemas Alone	Traits Alone	Motives Plus Schemas	Motives Plus Traits	Schemas Plus Traits
Multiple r	.24	.40	.30	.47	.39	.52
p value	.12	.02	.095	.01	.05	.001

*$p < .05$
**$p < .01$
[a]From Strong-Campbell Vocational Interest Blank.

107

sure), and do not see themselves as personally helping others (a managerial trait measure). Rather they see themselves as breaking through bureaucratic routines if necessary to get something done, although this is not accompanied by acting impulsively or coercing others. It is the organizational as opposed to the personal form of being innovative. Finally on the trait side they manage by optimizing—making the best of a situation, getting orders to work together—and they have superior scheduling skills in the specially designed Navy planning exercise. As the figures at the bottom of Table 2 show, relying exclusively on trait, or schema, or motive variables, or on a combination of any two of them does not yield multiple correlations nearly as high as the one based on all three types of variables. In fact they are at about the same low level of predictive consistency (multiple $r = .3$) that Mischel complains is characteristic of personality study. Thus my main thesis is supported: if you want to predict behavior successfully, be sure to include measures of motives, schemas, and traits—that is, of what people want to do, of what they understand the situation to be, and of traits or adaptive skills they can use in the situation. Also use operant measures. Two of them—the leadership motive pattern and the scheduling measure—contributed significantly as predicted to successful performance as a commanding officer.

The pattern of tested variables related to successful performance as a petty officer is the same in two respects and different in others. Better petty officers also are low in seeing the situation as requiring personal as opposed to institutional responsibility, and on managing by helping. But they see their work as oriented around getting things done (achieving) and affiliation (schema variables) and they show both greater accuracy and more attention to detail in the advising and counseling exercise, two operant trait measures which account uniquely for nearly 14% of the variance in the multiple regression. Although no motive variable surfaced as important in this analysis, the six variables together accounted for 58% of the variance in rated performance (multiple $r = .76$, $n = 35$), again a very respectable figure. And it certainly makes sense to conclude that neither power motivation nor the perception that their job involves exercise of power is particularly relevant to success as a petty officer in the way that it is for a commanding officer.

Such results need to be cross-validated, but as far as they go, they support the theoretical position I outlined in my personality book in 1951. We can account for a large portion of individual differences in behavior if we hold the external situation to which we are predicting reasonably constant, and if we sample motives, schemas, and traits. Furthermore we will often do better if some of our personality measures are operant rather than respondent because respondent variables are so readily influenced by extraneous situational variables such as the way the questions are worded, tendencies toward response bias, and so on.

Let me give one more illustration to show that this is not just a flash in the pan. Here the criterion to be predicted was even more circumscribed, although it was more objective than the officer ratings obtained in the previous study. The subjects were Navy alcoholism counselors. Boyatzis and Burruss (1977) obtained, for all the patients each counselor had seen in a given time period, the work performance record for the six months after treatment. That record was scored either 1 (for discharge with a recommendation against re-enlistment), 2 (for discharge without a recommendation against re-enlistment), or 3 (for person still on active duty six months after treatment with no recommendation against re-enlistment). An average of eighteen patients per counselor were rated in this way and the criterion was the average score a counselor's patients had received indicating the extent to which they were returned to active duty.

Boyatzis and Burruss interviewed the counselors, obtained behavioral episodes, analyzed them for competencies shown, chose or designed a number of tests to get at the competencies, and then attempted to use the measures to predict success as an alcoholism counselor. The results are shown in Table 3. Again they are quite encouraging. The multiple correlation for five variables accounts for some 63% of the variance in counsellor effectiveness. A motive pattern is an important determinant of success as are some four trait variables. The schema variable did not come out possibly because there was not enough variation from one counseling facility to another.

It is worth noting that the empathy competency which they identified was conceived to have both a trait and a motive aspect. At the trait level, it should lead counselors to be able to understand better what was going on in their patients. A programmed case was designed to test this skill following the method popularized by Dailey (1977). Subjects are given some information about a person and asked to predict what he would do in a given situation. They are then told what he did and asked to predict to a new situation, and so on for some twenty predictions. The test is scored for the overall number of correct predictions about what the person did and also for the improvement from the first to the second half of the test corrected for overall level of performance. Both of these measures of diagnostic skill or empathy were associated with effectiveness among Navy alcoholism counselors. But so also is what Boyatzis and Burruss (1977) call the caring motive pattern which consists of a higher need for Affiliation than need for Power plus high control (Activity

Table 3.   Alcohol Counselor Characteristics Associated with Effective Performance

Competencies	Tested Variable	Correlation with Average Work Performance Rating of all Patients Counseled $(N = 26)^a$
Related		
Motive		
Empathy	Caring motive pattern (*n* Affiliation > *n* Power, high Activity Inhibition)	.38*
Traits		
Empathy	Programmed case	
Diagnostic skill	Number correct	.33
	Improvement	.44*
Genuineness	Aware of own feelings (focussing)	.57**
Conceptual thinking	Test of thematic analysis	.38*

Multiple $r = .79, p < .001$, accounting for 63% of the variance in counselor effectiveness

Unrelated		$(N = .29)$
Traits		
Belief in people's ability to change	Scenarios test positive bias	.16
Sense of efficacy	Internal locus of control[b]	−.11
Schema		
Supportiveness of facility	Ward atmosphere scale of supportiveness[c]	−.11

$*p \sim .05$;
$**p < .01$
[a]Cases with missing observations omitted.
[b]Nowicki-Strickland Measure (1973).
[c]Moos (1974)

Inhibition). In other words empathy involves an interest and feeling for people as well as a skill in diagnosing their problems.

Boyatzis and Burruss (1977) also designed a special measure of genuineness which they felt would be displayed best by those counselors who were in good touch with their own feelings. The measure is based on a guided exercise in focusing on one's own feelings, patterned after some suggestions made by Gendlin et al., (1968). This kind of skill in keeping in touch with one's own inner states turned out to have the highest correlation with the criterion. Finally the conceptual thinking measure (Winter and McClelland, 1978) involved psychological content.

The task is to compare two sets of TAT stories and conceptualize the similarities and differences between them. Note once again that three of these five measures were operant, that is, the responses were not given to the subjects to choose among, but they had to invent or construct them. In contrast, many of the respondent measures such as the Nowicki-Strickland Locus of Control Test (1973) did not predict the criterion.

In this method the identification of competencies from interview data is clinical and involves considerable skill in psychological conceptualization. The translation of these competencies into measures of the various types laid out in Table 1 is necessarily somewhat loose. But the final test of the process is rigorous. If the work has been done correctly, it proves possible to identify variables which will account for a large amount of the variance in behavior in broadly equivalent situations. In this theoretical context a simplistic search for consistency appears misguided. There is more consistency in personality than trait theorists believe there is, which they would soon discover if they would shift their attention from their favorite respondent, situation-determined measures to operant measures. But far more importantly they should seek not consistency *per se,* but lawfulness in accounting for individual behavior, a lawfulness which can account for inconsistency as well as consistency, as Murray pointed out years ago. Such an approach involves a much more complex conception of personality structure than trait theorists usually entertain, as I hope I have made clear in many ways in this paper. But personality is not so complex that we must resign ourselves to hopelessness and confusion. On the contrary I hope I have demonstrated that by competency analysis one can identify the person variables—traits, schemas and motives—which account for a large part of how a person will behave in broadly equivalent situations, which is what I understand the science of personality to be all about.

REFERENCES

Allport, G.W. and P. E. Vernon. *Studies in Expressive Movement.* New York: Macmillan, 1933.

Argyle, M. and B. R. Little. Do personality traits apply to social behavior? *Journal of the Theory of Social Behaviour,* 1972, **2,** 1–35.

Atkinson, J. W. (Ed.) *Motives in fantasy, action, and society.* Princeton: Van Nostrand, 1958.

Atkinson, J. W., and D. Birch. *An Introduction to Motivation.* 2nd ed. New York: Van Nostrand, 1978.

Block, J. Advancing the psychology of personality. Paradigmatic shift or improving the quality of research? In D. Magnusson and N. S. Endler (Eds.), *Personality at the Crossroads. Current Issues in Interactional Psychology.* Hillsdale, NJ: Erlbaum, 1977.

Boyatzis, R. E. and J. A. Burruss. *Validation of a Competency Model for Alcoholism Counselors in the Navy.* Boston: McBer, 1977.

Burwen, L. S. and D. T. Campbell. The generality of attitudes toward authority and nonauthority figures. *Journal of Abnormal and Social Psychology,* 1957, **54,** 24–31.

Campbell, D. T. and D. Fiske. Convergent and discriminant validation by the multitrait-multimethod matrix. *Psychological Bulletin,* 1959, **56,** 81–105.

Dailey, C. *Assessment of Lives.* San Francisco: Jossey-Bass, 1977.

D'Andrade, R. G. Trait psychology and componential analysis. *American Anthropologist,* 1965, **67,** 215–228.

Dworkin, R. H. and J. F. Kihlstrom. An S-R inventory of dominance for research on the nature of person-situation interaction. *Journal of Personality,* 1978, **46,** 43–56.

Endler, N. S. and J. McV. Hunt. Sources of behavioral variance as measured by the S-R Inventory of Anxiousness. *Psychological Bulletin,* 1966, **65,** 336–346.

Epstein, S. Traits are alive and well. In D. Magnusson and N. S. Endler (Eds.), *Personality at the Crossroads. Current Issues in Interactional Psychology.* Hillsdale, NJ: Erlbaum, 1977.

Flanagan, J. C. The critical incident technique. *Psychological Bulletin,* 1954, **51,** 327–358.

Frenkel-Brunswik, E. Motivation and behavior. *Genetic Psychology Monographs,* 1942, **26,** 121–165.

Gendlin, E. T., J. Beebe, III, S. Cassens, M. Klein, and M. Oberlandes. Focusing ability in psychotherapy, personality and creativity. *Research in Psychotherapy,* 1968, **3,** 217–241.

Hartshorne, H. and M. May. *Studies in Deceit.* New York: Macmillan, 1928.

Holtzman, W. H. Holtzman Inkblot Technique. In A. I. Rabin (Ed.), *Projective Techniques in Personality Assessment.* New York: Springer, 1968.

Kelly, G. A. *A theory of Personality.* New York: Norton, 1963.

Korman, A. *The Psychology of Motivation.* New York: Prentice-Hall, 1974.

Mann, R. D. A review of the relationships between personality and performance in small groups. *Psychological Bulletin,* 1959, **56,** 241–270.

McClelland, D. C. *Personality.* New York: Sloane, 1951.

McClelland, D. C. Some social consequences of achievement motivation. In R. M. Jones (Ed.). *Nebraska Symposium on Motivation 1955.* Lincoln, NE: University of Nebraska Press, 1955.

McClelland, D. C. *n* Achievement and entrepreneurship: a longitudinal study.

Journal of Personality and Social Psychology, 1965, **1**, 389–392.

McClelland, D. C. *Power: The Inner Experience.* New York: Wiley, 1975.

McClelland, D. C. Inhibited power motivation and high blood pressure in men. *Journal of Abnormal Psychology,* 1979, (in press).

McClelland, D. C., W. N. Davids, R. Kalin, and E. Wanner. *The Drinking Man.* New York: Free Press, 1972.

McClelland, D. C., C. Constantian, D. Regalado, and C. Stone. Effects of child rearing practices on adult maturity. In D. C. McClelland (Ed.), *Education for Values.* New York: Irrington, 1979.

Mischel, W. *Personality and Assessment.* New York: Wiley, 1968.

Moos, R. *Evaluating Treatment Environments: a Social Ecological Approach.* New York: Wiley, 1974.

Murray, H. A. *Explorations in Personality.* New York: Oxford University Press, 1938.

Nisbett, R. E. and T. deC. Wilson. Telling more than we can know: verbal reports on mental processes. *Psychological Review,* 1977, **84**, 231–259.

Nowicki, S., and B. R. Strickland. A locus of control scale for children. *Journal of Consulting and Clinical Psychology,* 1973, **40**, 148–154.

Sears, R. R. A theoretical framework for personality and social behavior. *American Psychologist,* 1951, **6**, 476–483.

Silverman, L. H. Psychoanalytic theory: "the reports of my death are greatly exaggerated." *American Psychologist,* 1976, **31**, 621–637.

Stewart, A. J. *Scoring Manual for Stages of Psychological Adaptation.* Boston: Psychology Department, Boston University, 1978.

Takala, M. Consistencies and perception of consistencies in psychomotor behavior. In D. Magnusson and N. S. Endler (Eds.) *Personality at the Crossroads. Current Issues in Interactional Psychology.* Hillsdale, NJ: Erlbaum, 1977.

Telford, C. W. The refractory phase of voluntary and associative processes. *Journal of Experimental Psychology,* 1931, **14**, 1–36.

Winter, D. G. *The Power Motive.* New York: Free Press, 1973.

Winter, D. G. *Navy Leadership and Management Competencies: Convergence among Tests, Interviews, and Performance Ratings.* Boston: McBer, 1978.

Winter, D. G. and D. C. McClelland. Thematic analysis: an empirically derived measure of the effects of liberal arts education. *Journal of Educational Psychology,* 1978, **70**, 8–16.

Winter, D. G. and A. J. Stewart. Power motive reliability as a function of retest instructions. *Journal of Consulting and Clinical Psychology,* 1977, **45**, 436–440.

Winter D. G., D. C. McClelland, and A. J. Stewart. *Competence in College: Evaluating the Liberal University.* San Francisco: Jossey-Bass, 1979.

CHAPTER 5

Persons, Situations, and Their Interactions

Norman S. Endler

Where have all the people gone? What has happened to the person in personality research? Have we lost the human touch? With the technological advances of the last forty years engulfing almost all aspects of our lives, and with bigger becoming a synonym for better, is it possible that the individual person has become lost in the shuffle? Can this be the reason why many individuals feel alienated and why many individuals feel that they do not count; that they cannot have an impact? Does the research and theorizing of psychologists reflect or distort society at large? Does it mirror or distort their own predilections and interests?

Rae Carlson (1971) in reviewing all of the 1968 articles appearing in the *Journal of Personality* and in the *Journal of Personality and Social Psychology* noted that research in the area of personality focuses on undergraduates, relies heavily on experimental methods, collects data on a very limited sample of responses from each subject, and that the relationship between the subject and the experimenter is impersonal and artificial. She states that *"not a single published study attempted even minimal inquiry into the organization of personality variables within the individual"* (Carlson, 1971, p. 209). She wonders "where is the person?" in current personality research. Allport (1961) had the same concerns a decade earlier, and Bowers (1973) more recently has questioned the overemphasis on the environment and the situation, and the underemphasis on the person. The current state of affairs is indeed very different from that of the 1930s. At that time, Murray (1938) and his collaborators conducted their monumental research for *Explorations in Personality,* which focused on the person and person variables. They used the term *personology* to indicate their approach, rather than the more general term personality.

However, I believe that the person is again becoming our focus of attention. Mischel who has unfairly been accused of being a situationist has recently stated that "The person is what personality psychology must be about; no one really disputes that" (Mischel, 1976, p. 497). The work of Block (1971) focusing on longitudinal studies of personality, the work of Levinson (1978) focusing on the developmental crises of early, middle, and late adulthood, and the work of White (1966, 1976) focusing on in-depth cases studies readily attest to the re-emergence of the study of the person in personality research. The interactionists also do believe in people, but they believe that situations are important too (see Endler and Magnusson, 1978).

To what extent is personality research guided by objective, rational, and theoretical concerns and to what extent is it influenced by practical concerns, the personal interests, and the views of human nature espoused by the scientists? Where and how do scientists get their ideas? Perhaps it would be useful at this point for me to indicate how I became interested in interactional psychology.

For a number of years, in my late teens and early twenties, I was a counselor and head counselor at a summer camp. I was puzzled by the fact that various counselors discussed each camper in a different manner. For example, the waterfront counselor might have described Bill as a very anxious camper because Bill was afraid to jump into the water. However the nature-study counselor disagreed with the waterfront counselor and thought that Bill was very brave, because he was not afraid of handling snakes. A third counselor, the bunk counselor, might have described Bill as being afraid of the dark, but being very relaxed while playing baseball. I was puzzled by the fact that different counselors perceived the same camper differently and that the same counselor perceived Bill differently at different times. I respected all the counselors and at first thought they were not describing the same camper. However, they were. I tried to make some sense of this, but the answers did not come very readily.

When I started my Ph.D. graduate training in Clinical Psychology at the University of Illinois (after completing a master's degree in Social Psychology at McGill University) I again had the opportunity to be puzzled. Often times during a case conference, while I was involved in my practicum training and internship, I discovered that the psychiatrist, the psychologist, and the social worker, all described the patient differently from one another and differently from me. I had assessed the patients with the assistance of various psychological tests (including Henry Murray's Thematic Apperception Test). Because I respected the ability of the psychologist, the social worker, and the psychiatrist I was concerned when they described the patient differently from one another.

At about the same time, I took a graduate course in Personality from J. McV. Hunt in which he presented a logical analysis of what can be meant by saying that one individual manifests more than another individual of a given adjectively designated common trait (e.g., anxiety). One of the things that we discussed in class was that observers do not always agree about the extent to which any given trait or characteristic is exhibited in a person or sample of persons. One of the sources of disagreement among observers or raters is that they may observe subjects' responses in different situations or contexts. For example, Bill the camper may be anxious in the swimming situation, but not in the snake-handling situation. The disagreement between the two counselors, regarding Bill's anxiety, resides in the fact that they observed Bill in two different situations.

The S-R Inventory of Anxiousness (Endler, Hunt, and Rosenstein, 1962) was developed and grew out of the concerns discussed above. This inventory was distinctive because it separated *stimulus situation* from *response* in its format. The format of the inventory made it feasible, at least at the level of self-report, to determine the percent of variance due to persons, to situations, to modes of response, and to various interactions among these main effects. The intensity of the subjects' responses could also be assessed as well as the factor structure of the eleven situations (e.g., you are going to meet a new date; you are alone in the woods at night) and the fourteen modes of response (e.g., perspire; heart beats faster). We will return to the substantive findings shortly.

THE INFLUENCE OF PERSONAL AND SOCIOPOLITICAL FACTORS ON THEORY AND RESEARCH

Pervin (1978a) states that "the general public and many scientists have the view of science as a purely objective pursuit and the view of scientists as purely rational individuals. Yet, considerable evidence suggests that scientists are very much influenced by their personal histories and by the societal views of the time" (p. 269).

Because psychology is not an exact science like chemistry or physics, it is highly probable that personal factors and experiences have a greater role in psychological theory and research than in chemistry and physics research. This is especially true in the area of personality research where ambiguity in the field may be conducive to projection on the part of psychologists. There is probably an interaction between investigators and their fields of research that influences the content area of the research conducted.

Stolorow and Atwood (1978) believe that one source of influence for a theory of personality is the life experiences of the theorist proposing the theory. That is, subjective factors influence the nature of personality theories. Both the personal experiences and the sociopolitical climate play a role in the development of personality theories.

Ichheiser (1943) has suggested that the early work in personality research that overestimated the role of personal factors and underestimated situational factors has its roots in sociopolitical factors. According to Ichheiser, the emphasis on personal factors had its roots in the social system and ideology of nineteenth century liberalism. This ideology postulated that "our fate in social space depended exclusively, or at least predominantly, on our individual qualities—that we, as individuals, and not the prevailing social conditions shape our lives" (Ichheiser, 1943, p. 152). The sociopolitical and sociopsychological forces of the last five decades (e.g., the depression, unemployment, World War II, the Cold War, the revolution of rising expectations, Viet Nam) have probably tended to shift the emphasis in the direction of explaining behavior in terms of social conditions.

Pervin (1978a) points out that all "scientific pursuits have a historical context and a political aspect" (p. 280). For example, the political views regarding the nature-nurture issue are closely related to the scientific views regarding the relative importance of nature and nurture. Behaviorism is also closely linked to the american ideology of "doing and action" as opposed to "thinking and reflection" (see Buss, 1975; and Pervin, 1978a). Personality research is not value free but is, to some extent, influenced by personal, social and political considerations.

Not only are the contents of personality research and theory influenced by extrascientific considerations (e.g., personal and social factors) but so are the methodology and tactics of research. Should personality research be conducted in the laboratory, where we can hope to obtain "narrow band–high fidelity" information or should it be conducted in real-life situations, where we usually obtain "wide band–low fidelity" information? Is research in natural settings always more relevant than laboratory research? Should research be guided by practical concerns or by theory?

Lewin (1952) pointed out "that there is nothing so practical as a good theory" (p. 169). Theory and practice can mutually benefit one another. Work in an applied field (e.g., clinical psychology) can generate hypotheses which can often be tested under rigorous experimental methods. Similarly a theory can be tested in an applied setting and can suggest improved methods of assessment, for example. Often research stems from the need to solve a practical problem. One can call this type of research *action-oriented research*.

An excellent example of *action-oriented* personality research is that conducted by the *Office of Strategic Services* (OSS), under the leadership of Henry Murray during World War II. As you probably know, the task that confronted Murray and his colleagues concerned the assessment and selection of men for intelligence work as undercover agents, spies, and resistance leaders. The task of the OSS Assessment Staff (1948), as reported in the *Assessment of Men,* was to determine which individual would perform well in a variety of military intelligence situations. Each candidate was administered a battery of tests, questionnaires, projective techniques, was subjected to extensive and intensive interviews, and was placed in miniature real-life situations. In addition, the candidates were observed by a number of psychologists as they went through their daily routines. The unit of analysis was the person, who was studied intensively in a number of situations. These results provided evidence for situational specificity and seriously questioned the trait model. Unfortunately there was no systematic study of person by situation interactions. However, the OSS study was concerned with the intensive study of the individual, and the person was the unit of analysis as it was in Murray's *Explorations in Personality* (1938). It is rare today for personality research to involve the intensive study of the individual (refreshing exceptions are Daniel Levinson's *The Seasons of a Man's Life,* 1978, and Jack Block's *Lives through Time,* 1971).

Although Carlson (1971), as indicated earlier, is concerned about the underemphasis regarding intensive studies of the person, Sechrest (1976), in his recent *Annual Review of Psychology* paper on "Personality" suggests that emphasis on individual differences could be counterproductive to progress in personality research and theory. This issue of studying the individual versus groups of individuals, where the focus is on variables, is analogous to the debate regarding the merits of the idiographic (individual) approach as compared to the nomothetic (universal) approach to personality. Obviously, some combination of the two approaches would be most desirable. One should first isolate the crucial variables and then study their unique organization within the individual.

It should be noted that both Freud and Piaget, the two psychologists who have had the greatest impact on the field (see Endler, Rushton, and Roediger, 1978), both made their reputations primarily by studying individuals in great detail. During the 1930s, Henry Murray and his colleagues focused on individuals, in their intensive studies which resulted in *Explorations in Personality* (1938), and subsequently the *Assessment of Men* study (1948). The research conducted at the Berkeley Institute for Personality Assessment and Research also focused on studies of the individual.

One of the difficulties with respect to personality research in the

1950s, 1960s, and 1970s is that it has been primarily piecemeal rather than programmatic. Furthermore, as Block has indicated elsewhere (Block, 1977), much of the personality research has suffered from serious methodological flaws. I would add that a fair amount of it has been atheoretical and has focused on what is flashy and trendy rather than on what is substantive, meaningful and theoretical. The value system of many universities, where "publish or perish" is the norm, makes it difficult and impractical for students and faculty to become involved in longitudinal and intensive studies of persons.

MODELS OF PERSONALITY

As indicated elsewhere (Endler and Magnusson, 1976c; Endler, 1977), personality theory and research have been influenced by four basic models: trait psychology, psychodynamics, situationism, and interactionism. A fifth model, namely the phenomenological model, is concerned with the person's self-concept, personal constructs, and introspective and internal subjective experiences. It has also been influential, especially for humanistic and existential psychology, and for psychotherapy. However, because this model represents a diverse set of theories, all of which reject dynamic and motivational concepts, it is difficult to systematically compare phenomenology with the four basic models mentioned above. A sixth model, the *type* model (see Endler and Edwards, 1978), is a precursor of the trait model and proposes discrete categories of personality. The trait model postulates various continuous dimensions along which individuals differ.

The four models that will be discussed (namely trait, psychodynamic, situationism, and interactionism) all have relevance for a number of key issues in personality research (e.g., persons versus situations; consistency versus specificity; nativism versus empiricism; biological versus psychological emphasis).

The Trait Model

The trait model, which is the most influential of all the models, assumes that actual behavior is primarily determined by stable, latent dispositions. That is, the trait model proposes that behavior is basically determined by factors internal to the person. Traits serve as a predispositional basis for response-response (correlational) consistencies of behavior in a variety of different situations (e.g., Cattell, 1957; Guildford, 1959). The trait model recognizes the impact of situations because it does *not* suggest that individuals behave the same way in different situations. It does, however, assume that the rank order of persons with respect to a specified personality variable is the same across a variety of different situations. Allport (1937), for example, conceptualized traits as being general and enduring predispositions to respond, and not linked to specific stimuli or responses. The various trait theorists disagree as to the specific structures, numbers, and types of traits, but do agree that traits are the basic units of personality, and are dispositions, that account for cross-situational consistency. Trait theorists are becoming cognizant that traits interact with situations in eliciting behavior.

Psychodynamics

The psychodynamic models (especially psychoanalysis), like the trait models emphasize internal determinants of behavior. However, they differ from trait models in a number of ways. The psychodynamic models postulate a basic personality core which serves as a predispositional basis for behavior in different situations. Psychoanalysis pays special attention to personality structure (id, ego, and superego), dynamics, and development (Freud, 1959). Personality dynamics are concerned with the continuous interaction of and conflict among the id, ego, and superego. Anxiety is one of the consequences of this conflict, and the person develops defense mechanisms, which are motives, and which defend the self-concept against this anxiety. According to Freud, developmentally, *experiences* serve basically to modify the expression of instinctual impulses. However, the neo-Freudians (e.g., Erikson, 1963; Fromm, 1955; Horney, 1945; Sullivan, 1953) have de-emphasized the psychosexual stages and the role of instincts, and have focused instead on social factors, the ego, and psychosocial stages of development. Whereas the trait model assumes a one-to-one positive monotonic relationship between responses and underlying hypothetical constructs, the psychodynamic models suggest that there may not always be a one-to-one relationship between hypothetical constructs and overt behavior. For example, as a result of defense mechanisms consistency at the mediating level (e.g., the hypothetical construct of aggression) may not always lead to consistency at the response level (e.g., aggressive behavior).

Situationism

Classical social learning theory (Dewey and Humber, 1951; Dollard and Miller, 1950), a prime example of situationism, emphasizes external factors, especially stimulus situations, as the prime determinants of behavior. The various social learning theories do not provide a homogeneous viewpoint (Endler and Edwards, 1978). Dollard and Miller (1950), classical behavior theorists, emphasize learning and the importance of situations, but they also investigate organismic variables such as drives, motives, and conflict. The modern behavior theorists (Bandura, 1971; Mischel, 1973; and Rotter, 1975) are primarily concerned with the individual's behavior rather than with attributes, traits, and motives. However, despite the fact that they emphasize situations, they also incorporate person factors into their theories (e.g., see Mischel, 1973 on cognitive factors, and Rotter, 1975 on expectancy).

Interactionism

The interactional model of personality (see Bowers, 1973, Endler and Magnusson, 1976c; Magnusson and Endler, 1977) focuses on the role of person by situation interactions in personality. According to this model there is a continuous interaction between the person and the situations that he or she encounters. Furthermore, people select the situations in which they perform, and subsequently affect the character of these situations. We therefore have an ongoing process whereby situations affect persons, who in turn affect situations.

The question of persons versus situations or internal versus external determinants of behavior is primarily a pseudo-issue (Endler, 1973). The basic question is *how* do persons and situations interact in restricting or promoting behavior? Modern interactionism (Endler and Magnusson, 1976c) postulates that behavior is a function of a continuous process of person by situation interactions; that the person is an intentional active agent in this process; that cognitive, emotional, and motivational factors play essential roles on the person side; and that the psychological meaning of the situation for the person is the key determining factor with respect to behavior.

INTERACTIONAL PSYCHOLOGY: THEORY AND RESEARCH

Much of the empirical research on person by situation interactions started in the late 1950s and early 1960s. Surprisingly this research (see Endler, Hunt, and Rosenstein, 1962; Endler and Hunt, 1966; Raush, Dittmann, and Taylor, 1959a, 1959b) was conducted almost independently of the theoretical bases of interactional psychology formulated in the 1920s and 1930s, and to some extent was guided as much by practical considerations as by psychological issues.

Ekehammar (1974) discusses the early formulations of interactional psychology as espoused by Angyal (1941); Kantor (1924, 1926); Koffka (1935), Lewin (1935); Murphy (1947); and Murray (1938). Let us briefly discuss Murray's (1938) need-press theory. One of the basic characteristics of Murray's theory refers to the interaction between personal and situational factors.

"Since at every moment, an organism is within an environment which largely determines its behavior, and since the environment changes— sometimes with radical abruptness—the conduct of an individual cannot be formulated without a characterization of each confronting situation, physical and social" (Murray, 1938, p. 39). Murray was concerned with person factors, which he called needs, and environmental factors, which he called presses. Murray postulated two types of presses, alpha press which is concerned with the objective characteristics of the environment and beta press which is concerned with the psychological or subjective aspects of the situation. The need-press unit was called a thema. Because needs and presses are parallel constructs, it is possible to examine themas, which are person by situation interactions, in the context of Murray's theory. However, to the best of my knowledge no one has ever done this in a systematic fashion.

In addition to distinguishing between needs and presses, Murray (1938) made a distinction between psychologists whom he labelled as centralists and those he labelled as peripheralists. This distinction has relevance for the issue of internal versus external determinants of behavior. According to Murray the *centralists* emphasized active organisms whose behavior was primarily determined by *internal* factors, and the *peripheralists* emphasized passive organisms who responded primarily to *external* factors. Murray tried to combine the two viewpoints with respect to the discussion of need-press or individual-environment interaction. (This centralist versus peripheralist distinction has implications for trait or psychdynamic models versus the situationism model, and for the distinction between internal and external locus of control). "The peripheralists have an objectivistic inclination, that is, they are attracted to clearly observable things and qualities— simple deliverances of sense organs—and they usually wish to confine the data of personology to these" (Murray, 1938, p. 6). *Peripheralists,* according to Murray, define personality in terms of action rather than in terms of central processes. The *centralists* are a heterogeneous group of scientists who are concerned with subjective facts of purposive or emotional significance. "They are *centralists* because they are primarily concerned with the governing processes in the brain . . . Their terminology is subjectively derived" (Murray, 1938, p. 8).

Murray (1938) stated that "It is important to define the environment since two organisms may behave differently only because they are, by chance, encountering different conditions. It is considered that two organisms are dissimilar if they give the same response but only to different situations as well as if they give different responses to the same situation" (p. 39). Furthermore he states that "the organism and its milieu must be considered together, a single creature—environment interaction being a convenient short unit for psychology" (1938, p. 40). Murray was not the first of the interactionists. In fact, interactionism can be traced back to the time of Aristotle.

I must admit that although I had read Murray and Lewin, and although my master's thesis and doctoral dissertation were both in the area of conformity—an area that is concerned with both situational factors and individual differences—my interest in interactionism had much humbler beginnings. As indicated earlier, my interest in the S-R Inventory of Anxiousness grew out of my work as a camp counselor and my work as a psychological intern in a clinical setting. Maybe unconsciously it was related to the fact that I used the Edwards Personal Preference Schedule (1954), which measures the needs postulated by Murray's theory, in my Ph.D. dissertation on conformity. Although I found strong situational effects, there was no relationship between conformity and the needs (individual differences) measured by the Edwards Personal Preference Schedule. Nevertheless, I did not make the connection between my own empirical work, done in the 1960s, using the S-R Inventory of Anxiousness, on interactionism, and the theoretical formulations of Murray and Lewin (first postulated in the 1930s) until the 1970s. The empirical work of Raush, Dittmann, and Taylor, (1959a, b) on interactional psychology also seems to have developed independently of the theoretical formulations of Murray and Lewin.

Ekehammar (1974) in his historical review of interactionism states that "whereas the classical interactionist views were usually formulated within comprehensive personality theories, most often without empirical support, the more recent conceptualizations have usually been proposed in the absence of any elaborate theories, but often with some empirical support" (p. 1032). Nevertheless, as a result "of the first empirical studies on person-situation interactions during the early 1960s, the interest in the theoretical aspects of the issue redeveloped" (Endler and Magnusson, 1976c, p. 968). (For examples, see Bowers, 1973; Endler, 1977; Endler and Hunt, 1969; Endler and Magnusson, 1976c; Hunt, 1965; Magnusson and Endler, 1977; Magnusson, Gerzen, and Nyman, 1968; Mischel, 1973; Raush, 1965; Sells; 1963a,b).

ISSUES IN PERSONALITY RESEARCH

There are a number of key controversies in personality research, including the question of situational specificity versus cross-situational consistency, the issue of persons versus situation, the issue of reaction variables versus mediating variables, and the distinction between measurement models and psychological processes models.

Personality Theories and Their Measurement Models

There is often a failure to distinguish between personality theories that are *models of psychological processes* and the *measurement models* that are relevant to these theories (Endler, 1977; Magnusson, 1976; Magnusson and Endler, 1977). There is also frequently a failure to distinguish between the responses (or reactions) that one is investigating and the methods used for data collection (Magnusson and Endler, 1977). We can obtain measures of overt behavior by ratings, by self-reports, or by objective measures. The S-R Inventory of Anxiousness, (Endler, Hunt, and Rosenstein, 1962) assesses self-report of imagined situations. To what extent does this produce results that are different from actual behavior in situations that are actually encountered?

The assumption of the trait measurement model is that there is a *true* trait score for each person. This implies that individual positions on the trait dimension are *stable* across situations, and that therefore the behavior (test score) that is an indicator of this trait is also stable across situations. According to this measurement model the rank order of individuals with respect to behavior, indicating a trait dimension, is stable across situations.

In actual fact the empirical studies relevant to the person by situation issue have failed to provide evidence for trans-situational consistency (Endler, 1973, 1975a, 1975b; Mischel, 1968, 1969). The critics of traits, based on the empirical results, have directed their arguments against the *trait measurement* model, whereas the defenders of traits have focused on the *trait personality theory*.

Both the trait and psychodynamic models emphasize the importance of person factors as determinants of behavior. However, they differ in their measurement models. The trait measurement model assumes a positive monotonic relationship between mediating (hypothetical construct) variables and overt behavior whereas the psychodynamic measurement model does not. According to the psychodynamic model, an increase in the mediating variable of anxiety may, at a certain level of intensity, lead to a *decrease* in the overt anxious behavior (or reaction), because of defensiveness.

Reaction Variables versus Mediating Variables

It is necessary to distinguish between behavioral or reaction variables and mediating variables (hypothetical constructs) in personality research and theorizing (Magnusson and Endler, 1977). Consistency at the reaction level is not always related to consistency at the mediating level.

Reactions variables consist of at least four classes of responses; namely physiological reactions, covert reactions (feelings, etc.), overt behavior, and artificial behavior ("test" behavior, role playing). Mediating variables are usually inferred from phenomenological self-reports and from behavioral observations. The mediating variables (e.g., traits, motives) aid us in explaining, understanding, and predicting the processes whereby both concurrent stimuli and stored information are selected.

Magnusson and Endler (1977) discuss three types of mediating variables, namely structural, content, and motivational variables.

Structural variables would include intelligence, competence, and cognitive complexity and abilities. These variables are not basically influenced by situational factors, within a normal range of situational conditions. However, extreme situations, for example threatening situations, can and do modify the manifestation of these variables. Mischel (1968, 1969), and Rushton and Endler (1977) have provided evidence for the consistency of structural variables.

Content variables involve situationally determined or stored information, for example, the content of anxiety-arousing situations. The content that the mediating system processes in a particular situation is determined by the specific stimulus cues that are selected by (or imposed on) the person, and by the stored information activated by sensory stimulation. The content of the mediating process is influenced by situational factors.

Motivational variables include attitudes, drives, motives, needs, and values, and are involved in the arousal, maintenance, and direction of behavior. Why does a person select and treat certain information and why does the person react the way he or she does? Different contents (both situational and stored) evoke different motivational factors which are influenced by situational factors. The mediating system selects and processes a variety of content and motivational variables in a coherent (and consistent) manner, but the expression of content and motivational variables differ in various situations.

Persons versus Situations

One controversy in the field of personality refers to whether persons or situations are *the* major source of behavioral variance. This controversy or issue has also been conceptualized in terms of the relative importance of internal and external determinants of behavior. Endler (1973) in discussing this issue in detail, has pointed out that it is not really an issue. Personality trait theorists (e.g., Allport, 1966; Cattell, 1946; Guilford, 1959; McClelland, 1951) and clinicians (e.g., Freud, 1959; Rapaport, Gill, and Schafer, 1945) have assumed that traits and their dynamic sources within individuals are the major determinants of behavior. Sociologists, social psychologists, and social learning theorists (e.g., Cooley, 1902; Cottrell, 1942a,b; Dewey and Humber, 1951; Mead, 1934, Mischel, 1968; Rotter, 1954; Skinner, 1953) have assumed that situations and the meanings the situations have for persons are the major determinants of behavior. Obviously, behavior is a function of the interaction of person and situation variables.

Situational Specificity versus Trans-Situation Consistency

Related to the person versus situation controversy is the issue of whether behavior is consistent (stable) across situations or whether it is situationally specific. There is no necessary one-to-one relationship between consistency at the mediating variable level and consistency at the reaction variable level. Magnusson and Endler (1977) and Endler (1977) discuss three different meanings of "consistency" at the reaction variable level: (1) *absolute consistency* which implies that a person manifests a specified behavior (e.g., friendliness) to the same degree in various situations; (2) *relative consistency* which implies that the rank order of persons regarding a specified behavior (e.g., anxiousness) are stable across situations; and (3) *coherence* which implies that behavior is predictable and inherent without being stable in either relative or absolute terms. The individual's *pattern* of changing and stable behavior across a wide variety of situations is characteristic for that person (see Block, 1977; Endler, 1977; Magnusson, 1976; Magnusson and Endler, 1977). Endler (1977) states that coherence implies that "the *rank order* of a person's behavior in various situations with respect to a number of variables, is stable and predictable, but his (or her) rank order may differ from another person's rank order of the situations" (p. 348).

Magnusson and Endler (1977) point out that while it is possible to classify behavioral consistency on the basis of temporal (longitudinal) versus spatial (cross-sectional) variables, it is more useful to distinguish consistency in terms of reactions to similar and dissimilar situations. This is because spatial and temporal factors are *not* independent of one another. Cross-sectional investigations have been primarily concerned with consistency across *dissimilar* situations (usually over a short time span). Longitudinal studies on the other hand have focused on consistency of individuals across *similar* situations, ontogenetically over time. Longitudinal investigators have studied the correlation for a specific personality variable (e.g., nurturance) over two time periods (e.g., youth and adulthood) and have frequently ignored specific situational variables. Block (1977) has empirically demonstrated longitudinal consistency. Investigators conducting cross-sectional research have studied the correlation for a specific personality variable (e.g., dominance) in two different situations (e.g., at work and at home), frequently occurring over a very short time span. The empirical evidence for cross-sectional consistency with respect to personality and social variables is *neither* encouraging *nor* impressive, with correlations averaging about .30 (e.g., see Endler, 1973, 1975a, Mischel 1968, 1971). (McClelland, in Chapter 4 of this volume, suggests that there may be more consistency with respect to *operants* than with respect to *respondents*).

Consistency of mediating factors refers to the consistency of structural, content, and motivational variables. Magnusson and Endler (1977) have pointed out that with respect to information processing, structural variables are consistent and coherent in the *manner* in which they process (and select) content and motivational variables. However, the manifestation of the content and motivational variables may differ from one situation to another. The consistent or coherent style of *processing* both content and motivational variables is a function of social learning processes.

Empirically, the issue of cross-situational consistency versus situational specificity has been tested in at least three ways: (1) using a multidimensional variance components research strategy; (2) using a correlational research strategy; and (3) using a personality by treatment analysis-of-variance, experimental design.

There have been a number of reviews of the empirical literature with respect to the consistency versus specificity issue (Argyle and Little, 1972; Bowers, 1973; Endler, 1973, 1977; Magnusson, 1976). There is some evidence for trans-situational consistency and stability *over time* for structural variables (cognitive and intellectual factors). There is, however, little evidence for cross-situational consistency with respect to social (content) and motivational variables.

Multidimensional Variance-Components

The initial studies using the variance-components strategy were those conducted by Raush, Dittmann, and Taylor (1959a,b) and by Endler and Hunt (1966, 1969). Raush and his co-workers, utilizing ratings of the observed behavior of delinquent boys in six different situations, found that the person by situation interaction accounted for more behavioral variance than either persons or situations *per se*. Endler and Hunt analyzed subjects' responses nested in various situations, for twenty-one samples of females, and twenty-two samples of males who had completed the self-report S-R Inventory of Anxiousness (Endler, Hunt, and Rosenstein, 1962). On the average, persons accounted for 4.44% of the variance for males and 4.56% of the variance for females; situations, 3.95% for males, and 7.78% for females; and person by situation interactions about 10%. The three simple two-way interactions accounted for about 30% of the variance. Bowers (1973), summarizing the results of eleven relevant studies published since 1959, found that person by situation interactions accounted for more variance than either persons or situations on fourteen out of eighteen comparisons. The results of these studies demonstrate interactions, but they do not explain them.

Correlations

The correlations research strategy of persons across situations provides a more direct test of the assumption of relative consistency or cross-situational stability. An examination of the research using this approach indicates that there is no evidence for cross-situational consistency with respect to personality and social variables. There is, however, evidence for moderate consistency for: (1) intellectual and cognitive (structural) variables (Mischel, 1968, 1969; Rushton and Endler, 1977); (2) various situations that are similar (Magnusson, Gerzén, and Nyman, 1968; Magnusson and Heffler, 1969; Magnusson, Heffler, and Nyman, 1968); and (3) stability over time (longitudinal studies) across similar situations (Block, 1971, 1977). The degree of situational specificity or cross-situational consistency is, however, related to the variable being investigated.

Personality by Treatment Designs

Both the correlational and variance-components approaches indicate that interactions are important but do not provide information as to *why* (Sarason, Smith, and Diener, 1975) or *how* persons and situations interact in evoking behavior (Endler, 1973). Experimental studies, that incorporate both personality and situational variables in their designs, enable us to predict the nature of the interactions, especially if the studies are guided by theory. Fiedler (1971, 1977) found that situational variables interact with leadership style (a person variable) in influencing group effectiveness. Berkowitz (1977), and Moyer (1973) have demonstrated an interaction of person and situation variables, with respect to aggression. Endler and Magnusson (1977), Hodges (1968), Flood and Endler (1976), and Diveky and Endler (1977) have all demonstrated an interaction between trait anxiety (a person variable) and situational stress, with respect to state-anxiety arousal (We will discuss these anxiety studies in more detail when we discuss the interaction model of anxiety).

The results of the various studies, using three different research methods, seriously question the assumption of the trait model of personality, that the rank order of individuals is stable and consistent across various situations.

THE ROLE OF SITUATIONS IN PERSONALITY RESEARCH

The two fundamental tasks for an interactional psychology of personality are answering: (1) how persons and situations interact in eliciting behavior (which was discussed above and will be discussed later with respect to the interaction model of anxiety, and (2) the description, classification, and systematic analyses of stimuli, situations, and environments. (For a detailed discussion of the issues pertinent to the definition, measurement, and classification of stimuli, situations, and environments, the reader is referred to Pervin, 1978b.)

As indicated earlier, sociologists and social learning theorists have emphasized situation factors as the prime determinants of behavior. Ecological psychologists (e.g., Barker, 1965) have been concerned with environmental factors. There have, however, been very few attempts at studying situations *psychologically* (Endler, 1975a). Pervin (1978b) bemoans the fact that there have been definitional problems, including the failure to define and adequately differentiate the terms stimuli, situations, and environments. Frederiksen (1972) has stated that "we need a systematic way of conceptualizing the domain of situations and situation variables before we can make rapid progress in studying the role of situations in determining behavior" (p. 115).

Ekehammar (1974) states that there are five major ways of investigating the problem of situational description and classification. One can have "description of situations based on (a) a priori defined variables of *physical* and *social* character, (b) *need* concepts, (c) some *single reaction* elicited by the situations, (d) individuals' *reaction patterns* elicited by the situations, and (e) individuals' *perceptions (cognitions)* of situations" (pp. 1041–1042). Moos (1973) has suggested six major methods whereby "characteristics of environments have been related to indexes of human functioning" (p. 652): (1) ecological dimensions (e.g., architectural-physical variables, geographical-meteorological variables; (2) behavior settings involving both ecological and behavioral properties (3) parameters of organizational structure; (4) personal and behavioral parameters of the environment inhabitants; (5) organizational climate and psychosocial variables; and (6) variables related to reinforcement or functional analyses of environments. "The six categories of dimensions are non-exclusive, overlapping and mutually interrelated" (Moss, 1973, p. 652).

Feshbach (1978) discusses two levels of a dimension he defines as the environment of personality: (1) the *situational* level of environment, and (2) the *sociocultural* environment. "The situational level refers to the immediate social and physical environmental stimuli to which the organism responds and adapts" (Feshbach, 1978, p. 447). Feshbach notes that this level of analysis provides the empirical basis for issues such as the trait versus the situation specificity controversy. "The second category of environmental influence relates to the broader social and physical context that provides situations their meaning and their continuity" (Feshbach, 1978, p. 447). Examples of variables at this level are cultural ideologies, social norms, and population density. Feshbach (1978) also discusses a third class of variables that are part of the environment of personality and a distinct subset of our culture (or sociocultural environment). This refers to the perspectives and theories that determine our research. We would venture to call this a sociopolitical factor or even an ideology.

Ekehammar (1974), Endler and Magnusson (1976b,c) and Pervin (1978b) have all emphasized the important distinction between the objective aspects and the subjective or psychological aspects of situations and environments. This distinction is analogous to the one made by Murray (1938) between *alpha press* (objective) and *beta press* (subjective). Endler and Magnusson (1976b) point out that the subset of the "outer world" with which the individual interacts (including both physical and social environmental factors) can be conceptualized as the *ecology* (see Brunswick, 1952, 1956). Behavior *per se* occurs in a *situation*, or that part of the ecology that a person can perceive and react to immediately (Murray, 1938, p. 40), or the "momentary situation," according to Lewin (1936, p. 217).

Both the objective "outer world," that is, the environment as it is, independent of the person's interpretation, and the subjective world, that is, the psychological significance of the environment to the person, can be discussed at different levels of generality (Endler and Magnusson, 1976b). That is, we can describe macro- and micro-environments. With respect to the "outer world" we can describe the environment in terms of social factors, physical factors or a combination of the two. Buildings, cities, lakes, and parks would be examples of the physical *macro-environment* whereas single stimulus variables or objects would be examples of the physical *micro-environment*. Norms, roles and values, common to a whole culture or society, would be examples of the *social macro-environment* (that which is common to most members of a society), whereas attitudes, norms, habits and values of the specific groups and individuals with whom a person interacts directly at home or at school (e.g. that which is to some degree unique to the person) would be examples of the *social micro-environment*.

There have been at least two systematic strategies of investigating situations from a psychological perspective, namely situation *perception* and situation *reaction* studies (see Endler and Magnusson, 1976b,c; and Magnusson and Ekehammar, 1975a,b). These refer to categories *d* and *e* in Ekehammar's (1974) classification scheme for investigating situations. That is, "The psychological significance of the environment can be investigated by studying the individual's *perception* of the situation (the meaning he assigns to a situation) and *reaction* to a situation (a specific situation or the general environment)" (Endler and Magnusson, 1976b, p. 15).

Magnusson (1971) has pointed out that "individuals differ not mainly with regard to certain stable characteristics of behavior but particularly regarding their specific characteristic ways of adjusting to the varying characteristics of different situations" (p. 851). He has emphasized the importance of the meaning of situations and has developed an empirical psychophysical method for investigating the perception of situations (Magnusson, 1971, 1976). Using this method, Magnusson and Ekehammar (1973) found two bipolar situational dimensions: positive versus negative, and active versus passive, which are similar to the semantic differential factors. They also found one unipolar dimension, a social factor. These dimensions are relevant for the domain of situations that they examined, that is, those common to the university students in their studies. When Ekehammar and Magnusson (1973) extended their research to stressful situations, they found essentially the same results as in their previous studies. The *perception* (meaning) of the situation seems to be an influential and essential factor affecting an individual's behavior.

The studies of *reaction to situations* have been based on persons's responses to situations. Rotter (1954) pointed out that situations could be classified in terms of the similarity of behavior they evoke in persons. Frederiksen (1972) has also discussed the same strategy. Using this approach, the aim is to develop taxonomies of situations. The reaction studies, for the most part, have been conducted on data from inventories originally constructed for research purposes (e.g., the S-R Inventory of Anxiousness, Endler, Hunt, and Rosenstein, 1962, the Interactional Reactions Questionnaire, Ekehammar, Magnusson, and Ricklander, 1974; and the Stressful Situations Questionnaire, Hodges and Felling, 1970). Endler and his co-workers (1962), using the S-R Inventory of Anxiousness, performed a factor analysis of subjects' responses to various situations, and found three situational factors: interpersonal, inanimate physical danger, and ambiguous. Using the S-R Inventory of General Trait Anxiousness, Endler and Okada (1975) found similar situational factors. These studies have examined the dimensionality of situations on the basis of individuals' reactions to situations as wholes.

Magnusson and Ekehammar (1975b, 1978), and Ekehammar, Schalling, and Magnusson (1975) have investigated the relationship between the *perception* of situations and the *reaction* to situations. Since reactions to a situation are to some degree a function of the person's perceptions of the situation, the relationship between perceptions and reactions have implications for an interactional model of personality. Using data on situation perception and situation reaction, Magnusson and his colleagues compared the two strategies, within a single study, in order to assess the psychological significance of situations, and to investigate person by situation interactions.

Magnusson and Ekehammar (1975b) collected situation perception and situation reaction data on forty subjects for twelve situations, covering four different types of stressful situations. For three of the four *a priori* groupings of situations the coefficient of congruence between perceptions and reactions ranged from .89 to .92; for the fourth group of situations the coefficient of congruence was .69. Ekehammar, Schalling, and Magnusson (1975) in a similar study obtained, basically, the same results. These two studies used group data. Magnusson and Ekehammar (1978) analyzed individual data and also obtained results congruent with an interactional model of personality. It is important to differentiate situation *perception* dimensions and situation *reaction* dimensions when exploring the psychological significance of situations. Note that while two persons may *perceive* the same situation as threatening, one person may react by attacking the situation, and another individual may react by withdrawing from the situation. The studies by Magnusson and his colleagues provide a promising approach for determining how reactions are influenced by perceptual factors in situations.

In addition to distinguishing between perceptions of, and reactions to situations, a useful distinction is between objective and subjective (or psychological) characteristics of situations, as mentioned above. An analysis of the environment in objective terms has infrequently been advocated by researchers (see Gibson, 1960; Sells, 1963a; Tolman, 1951). Murray (1938) using the terms alpha press and beta press, Kantor (1924, 1926) using the terms biological and psychological environment, and Koffka (1935) using the terms geographical and behavioral environment, have all made useful distinctions between objective and subjective (psychological) environments.

Magnusson and Endler (1977) and Magnusson (1976) have discussed the important distinction between the various elements or situational cues *within* a situation and the situation as a *whole*. Most of the research on situations has focused on the situation as a *whole*, and has compared the effects *between* different situations. This research has examined how each situation is interpreted or experienced in its total context (see Magnusson, 1971). However, it is important to investigate the various situational cues *within* a situation and examine how they continuously interact with one another and thereby change in the process. For example in a social situation, John's reaction to Bill is influenced by Bill's reaction to John, and this is a continuous and ongoing process (see Endler, 1977; Magnusson, 1976). "One can construe a situation as a dynamic process in which a person selects certain elements or events (primarily other persons) and is in turn affected by these other elements" (Endler, 1977, p. 356). Future investigations of situations should focus on the interaction of elements (e.g., person by situation interactions, person by person interactions *within* situations).

It is essential, however, that we have representative samplings of all aspects of situations (Brunswik, 1952, 1956). We are usually quite careful with respect to sampling persons, but rarely do we obtain representative samples of situations or environments. This may well bias our conclusions. There are a number of unresolved conceptual and definitional problems. How large is a situation? When does it end? What are the differences between situations and events? When does a person respond directly to a situation; when does he or she respond independently of the situation? Skinner's (1938) distinction between respondents (direct reactions to stimuli) and operants (reactions independent of observable stimuli) may be useful with respect to the consistency versus the specificity issue (see McClelland, Chapter 4 of this volume). One would predict greater consistency of operant reactions than of respondent reactions. For the former (operants), the person may select his situations, and seek situations similar to those that he or she has found rewarding in the past. For the latter (respondents), the individual may have situations imposed on him or her and may well have to respond primarily to the demands of the situations rather than on the basis of his or her own proclivities.

Frederiksen (1972) and Pervin (1978b) have discussed taxonomies or classifications of situations. However, there is an inherent danger of overemphasizing taxonomies of situations, because different investigators will produce different taxonomies, in the same way that different trait theorists have produced different taxonomies or classifications of traits. A taxonomy or classification of situations or environments, or both, should not be arbitrary but should fit into a theoretical context. Furthermore such a taxonomy should probably be based on situations that people encounter and the perception or meaning that the situations have for them. Pervin (1977) has developed a useful approach whereby he samples situations ecologically, in terms of natural habitats. Pervin examines free responses of people on the basis of their perceptions and affective and behavioral responses to the situations they encounter daily. He does a factor analysis of his data (classifies variables) and proposes that one should focus on the person-situation interaction as the unit of analysis.

DYNAMIC VERSUS MECHANISTIC INTERACTION

Magnusson and Endler (1977) discuss two basic meanings of the construct of interaction as it applies to interactional psychology: namely mechanistic (structure) interaction and dynamic (process or organismic) interaction (see also Endler 1975a, Endler and Edwards 1978; Magnusson, 1976; Overton and Reese, 1973).

Mechanistic Interaction (Structure)

This refers to the interaction of independent variables. The mechanistic model of interaction uses analysis of variance procedures in its measurement model. This model makes a clear distinction between independent and dependent variables, and furthermore assumes an additive and linear relation between situation and person factors (both independent variables) in determining behavior (a dependent variable). For this model, interaction is concerned with the interdependency of determinants of behavior. The "interaction is not between cause and effect, but between causes" (Overton and Reese, 1973, p. 78). It is concerned with the structure of the interaction and not with the process (e.g., persons by situations, persons by modes of response, situations by modes of response, and persons by situations by modes of response).

This reflects a mechanistic model of human beings and is inadequate for studying the dynamic interaction process within the interactional model of personality.

Dynamic Interaction (Process)

This refers to the interaction of independent and dependent variables. The dynamic or organismic model of interaction emphasizes the reciprocal interaction between behavior and environment (or situational) events. "*Reciprocal causation* means that not only do events affect the behavior of organisms, but the organism is also an active agent influencing environmental events" (Endler and Magnusson, 1976c, p. 969). Pervin (1968) suggests that this type of reciprocal interaction should be called *transaction*.

"*Dynamic interaction* refers to a model of behavior in which person mediating variables, person reaction variables, and situations (environments) are integrated in order to describe and explain the *process* whereby individual behavior develops and maintains itself" (Magnusson and Endler, 1977, p. 19). There are at least two different kinds of dynamic interaction: *within-situations interaction,* and *between (across) - situations interaction* (see Magnusson, 1976). The dynamic model of behavior implies that the traditional distinction between dependent and independent variables may not be very useful (Raush, 1977). People influence situations and situations influence people. People, to a certain extent, select the situations (some are required or imposed) within which they interact and are in turn influenced by these situations. It is a continuing and ongoing process.

Units of Analysis

What *kind* of unit should be used in scientific investigations of personality and what *size* units should be used? In terms of *kinds* of units, the most frequently ones used in personality research have been traits. Traits are inferred from response-response consistencies. Psychoanalytic theorists have used motives, defenses, and instincts as their units of analysis. Perhaps the person by situation interaction unit should be used as the unit of analysis (see Pervin, 1977; Raush, 1977). As noted earlier, Murray (1938) suggested that need-press units or themas were most appropriate. Murray (1938) stated that

much of what is now *inside* the organism was once *outside*. For these reasons, the organism and its milieu must be considered together, a single creature-environment interaction being a convenient short unit for psychology. A long unit—an individual life—can be most clearly formulated as a successor of related short units or episodes (p. 40).

To the best of my knowledge no one has conducted systematic investigations of *themas* although there have been systematic longitudinal and intensive studies of persons (e.g., Block, 1977; Levinson, 1978; White, 1966, 1976). With respect to *size* of units it is often difficult to determine when a situation or event begins or ends. Do we focus on a total situation or do we emphasize elements within situations? Do we focus on a specific event or on a family of events? Do we focus on person by person interactions (Patterson and Moore, 1978)? Pervin (1978b) has discussed the importance of clearly defining our units, and clearly differentiating among stimuli, situations, and environments.

ANXIETY FROM AN INTERACTIONAL PERSPECTIVE

The interactional model of personality has both practical and theoretical implications for anxiety. The construct of anxiety has been involved in a number of comprehensive theoretical formulations, and has been defined in various ways. It has also been assessed by various methodologies, and has generated voluminous research. At different times anxiety has been defined as a learned drive, as a stimulus for behavior, as a complex response and as a personality variable. Lewis (1970) has defined anxiety as ''an emotional state, with the subjectively experienced quality of fear or a closely related emotion (terror, horror, alarm, fright, panic, trepidation, dread, scare)'' (p. 77). Anxiety is unpleasant, directed toward the future, is out of proportion to the threat and includes both subjective and manifest bodily disturbances. Let us compare and contrast Spielberger's (1966, 1972) state-trait theory of anxiety and Endler's (1975b) interaction model of anxiety.

A Conceptual Distinction between State and Trait Anxiety

Cicero (Lewis, 1970) originally distinguished between *anxietas*, as a predisposition and *angor* as a transitory state. Cattell and Scheier (1958, 1961), Spielberger (1966, 1972), and Zuckerman (1960) have all amplified this distinction between chronic or *trait* anxiety (A-trait), a relatively stable personality variable, and *state* anxiety (A-state), a transitory emotional condition.

Individuals high on A-trait are self-deprecatory and are concerned with "fear of failure." High A-trait persons (i.e., those high on anxiety proneness) are more likely to perceive ego-involving situations as threating than would low A-trait persons. Therefore, high A-trait individuals would manifest greater A-state arousal in ego-threatening situations than low A-trait individuals. When the situation is nonthreatening or neutral, the differences between high and low A-trait persons, with respect to A-state, should be minimal.

Spielberger's (1972) theory can be recast as an interaction between A-trait (persons) and ego-threatening situations, in elevating A-state arousal. Spielberger's state-trait theory, however, is somewhat restrictive because the instrument used to assess A-trait, namely the State-Trait Anxiety Inventory (STAI) (Spielberger, Gorsuch, and Lushene, 1970) focuses on ego-threatening trait anxiety, and ignores the other dimensions (e.g., physical danger and ambiguity) of the multidimensional A-trait. Recently, Spielberger (1977) has discussed both situation-specific and general measures of A-trait.

Endler and Okada (1975), and Endler and Magnusson (1976a) have determined that both A-trait and A-state are multidimensional. Sarason (1975a,b) and Wine (1971) have proposed two components of A-state, namely a *cognitive worry* component and an *emotional arousal* component. Anxiety is related to self-evaluation, and the highly anxious person is self-centered and focuses on self-evaluation (self-worry), rather than on the situational task (Sarason, 1975b). Since cognitive components have a more negative influence on performance, than do autonomic factors, it is proposed that the cognitive worry components of A-state may be more changeable. It suggests that an alleviation of cognitive worry through cognitive appraisal therapy (see Meichenbaum, 1975) might well improve academic achievement. Emotional arousal may be reduced by relaxation therapy and counterconditioning. An interaction model of anxiety must take into account the multidimensionality of both A-state and A-trait.

State-Trait Anxiety and Person by Situation Interactions

The interaction model of anxiety (Endler, 1975b) postulates that both A-state and A-trait are multidimensional. A second basic postulate is that for the trait (person) by situational stress interaction to be effective in inducing A-state arousal, it is necessary for the particular facet of the A-trait to be cogruent to the threatening situation. The S-R Inventory of General Trait Anxiousness (S-R GTA) developed by Endler and Okada (1975) assesses four facets of A-trait, namely interpersonal ego-threat, physical danger, ambiguous, and innocuous or daily routines. Recently a fifth facet, namely, social evaluation threat was added. The facets were primarily derived from the factor structure of the situations of the original S-R Inventory of Anxiousness (Endler *et al*, 1962). The interaction model of anxiety predicts that interpersonal ego-threat A-trait interacts with a congruent interpersonal ego-threatening situation in evoking A-State arousal changes, but does not interact with a noncongruent physically dangerous situation in eliciting changes in A-State arousal. Physical danger A-trait, however, interacts with a congruent physically dangerous situation in eliciting A-state arousal changes. A derivative of this model is the *differential hypothesis*, which predicts significant interactions when facets of A-trait and situational threats are congruent, and no interactions when they are not congruent. The interaction model of anxiety allows us to predict rather than merely describe, both the nature and direction of the interaction between situational factors and (anxiety) traits; and to examine their joint effects on behavior, such as anxiety states.

The Interaction Model of Anxiety: Empirical Tests of the Theory

We have conducted a number of experiments in our laboratory and in real-life situations that have direct relevance for the interaction model of anxiety. In one of our laboratory studies (reported in Endler and Okada, 1975) we investigated the joint effects of a physically threatening situation and physical danger A-trait (as assessed by the S-R GTA). The subjects were male and female university students, in an experiment where threat of shock was the physical danger situation. For female subjects, there was an interaction between the situation (nonstress versus physical danger stress) and physical danger A-trait in evoking A-state arousal as measured by the Behavioral Reactions Questionnaire (BRQ) (Hoy and Endler, 1969; Endler and Okada, 1975). However, there was no interaction between physical danger, situational stress and noncongruent interpersonal A-trait, when subjects were classified as high or low interpersonal A-trait. The differential hypothesis was, therefore, confirmed for the female students. (It was not, however, confirmed for the male students.) Endler and Magnusson (1977) studied the interaction model of anxiety in a real-life psychology course examination situation. The A-trait of Swedish college students was measured via the multidimensional S-R GTA, prior to an important psychology exam, and A-state was assessed both by the self-report BRQ and by pulse rate, just prior to the psychology examination (stress) and again two weeks later (nonstress). When pulse rate was used as the measure of A-state (the dependent variable), the interaction between interpersonal A-trait and the examination situation was significant ($p < .01$). When the BRQ was used as the measure of A-state (the dependent variable), the interaction was in the right direction and approached significance ($p < .086$). The interaction between the examination situation and physical danger A-trait, for the BRQ scores, was also significant ($p < .05$). However, none of the remaining six (noncongruent) interactions were significant. The differential hypothesis (significant interactions for facets of traits congruent with situations; no interactions for noncongruent facets of traits and situations) was partially confirmed. The Endler and Magnusson (1977) investigation also provided evidence for the multidimensionality of A-trait.

Flood and Endler (1976) have examined the person by situation interaction anxiety model in the field setting of a major track and field meet in Toronto. In this real-life athletic competition situation, Flood and Endler postulated that there would be a significant interaction between an ego-threatening (social evaluation) track and field meet situation and the congruent social evaluation A-trait, in inducing changes in A-state arousal. On the basis of the differential hypothesis, they postulated that there would be no significant interactions between the other noncongruent facets of A-trait (e.g., ambiguous, physical danger, and innocuous) and the track and field ego-threat situation. Two weeks prior to competition, male athletes ($N = 41$), aged 15 to 30, competing in short-, middle- and long- distance track events completed a modified form of the Endler and Okada (1975) S-R GTA (which included interpersonal, social evaluation, physical danger, ambiguous, and innocuous situations), and the BRQ measure of A-state. This constituted the nonstress condition. The BRQ, which was the measure of A-state, was completed again prior to a major competition that the athletes considered important (the stress condition). All the athletes perceived the track and field event as a social evaluation situation. Flood and Endler (1976) found a significant interaction between social evaluation A-trait and the stressful track and field situation. That is, high social evaluation A-trait athletes showed greater increases in A-state between the nonstress and stress situations, than did low A-trait athletes. There were no significant interactions between the track and field situation and the physical danger, ambiguous, or interpersonal facets of A-trait. (The high and low innocuous A-trait groups did not differ on A-state for the stressful condition, but did differ on the nonstressful condition). This study essentially supports the interaction model of anxiety.

In a recent study, Diveky and Endler (1977) examined middle management male bankers in both nonstressful "off the job" situations (as reported by the bankers) and stressful (social evaluation) "on the job" situations (as reported by the bankers). We found a significant social evaluation A-trait by congruent social evaluation situational stress interaction in evoking changes (increases) in A-state. There were no significant interactions between the social evaluation situations and the noncongruent facets of A-trait. (We had originally planned to also include females in our study. Unfortunately there were very few female bankers in middle management positions. Therefore, we limited our study to male bankers.)

Philip Kendall (1978) conducted a study at an urban Virginia university, where he compared and contrasted the Spielberger (1972) state-trait anxiety model with the Endler (1975b) interaction model of anxiety. Kendall tested male university students in both social evaluation and physical danger situations. Basically, his results support the interaction model of anxiety. Kendall notes that "high-trait-anxious subjects responded with greater state reactions when the trait measure corresponded with the type of stress. The results are discussed as support for the interaction model of anxiety and for the need to measure situational components of trait anxiety" (p. 280).

Note that in all of the studies discussed above, both low and high A-trait persons report greater A-state under stressful conditions than under nonstressful conditions. Stress is effective in producing increases in A-state. One of the implications is that A-state can be reduced by decreasing actual threat, or by altering the person's perception of the threat (via cognitive reappraisal techniques) so that he or she now perceives a situation as less threatening than previously. We are currently testing this proposition in a psychotherapeutic situation, where we are predicting that high ego-threat A-trait people will show a greater decrease in A-state as a function of psychotherapy than low ego-threat A-trait people.

WHERE DO WE GO FROM HERE?

As we look towards the future of personality research and theory we should ask ourselves the question, "Where do we go from here?" Let us put this first in the context of the goals of science.

These goals have at least three components: (1) to isolate the effective and predictive variables; (2) to examine the functional relationships between antecedent conditions (independent variables) and the behavior they influence or control (dependent variables); and (3) to examine behavioral processes so that we can both explain and predict behavior.

We have undoubtedly made progress in isolating some theoretically important and relevant variables. However we are only beginning to understand the effective functional relationships. Therefore, it may be premature to limit ourselves to an intensive investigation of behavioral processes. The ideal approach would be to take simultaneous cognizance of all three goals. Although "it is important to study dynamic interaction and to develop appropriate techniques for doing this, we have still not fully explored the nature of mechanistic interactions" (Endler, 1975a, p. 18).

Strategies for Studying Interactions

Most of the studies on interactionism have been conducted in the context of the mechanistic model (e.g., see the research on literature on anxiety, locus of control, and conformity, reviewed by Endler and Edwards, 1978) and have indicated the existence of strong person by situation interactions. As the research suggests, we have made progress towards predicting *how* persons and situations interact. The various person by treatment (situation) experimental designs do not investigate the dynamic (multidirectional) or *process* views (i.e., transactions; see Pervin, 1968) of interaction. However, this person by treatment research may serve as a focal point toward developing an interactional psychology of personality. The ultimate goals, however, should be a description, explanation, and understanding of the process of dynamic interaction.

Situations

As discussed earlier, it is important to distinguish objective and subjective (psychological) situations (Endler 1977; Endler and Magnusson, 1976b), and between perceptions of and reactions to situations (Magnusson and Ekehammar, 1975a). However another distinction, and one which is rarely made, is that between specific elements *within* a situation, and differences between more global situations or situations as *wholes* (see Magnusson and Endler, 1977). The mechanistic interaction studies on anxiety, discussed above, have primarily examined the macro-aspects of situations (e.g., an interpersonal situation) and have focused on differences *between* situations (e.g., social evaluation versus physical danger). They have not investigated the process of the various elements *within* a situation (e.g., the effect of person *B* on person *A*, and the subsequent effect of person *A* on person *B* within the interpersonal situation; or, the mutual effects of the person on the situation and vice versa).

It is important to examine the multidirectional and multicausal *ele-*

ments within the situation. The elements within a situation encompass both person by situation interactions and person by person interactions. Other persons constitute important elements of the situations we encounter. We serve as a situational cue for other persons with whom we interact, and in turn we are influenced by these other persons.

Methods for Studying Situations Intensively

In order to conduct intensive studies of persons and of situations we should ask persons to keep daily logs of the situations they encounter (see Pervin, 1977). We usually do not observe individuals in a representative sample of situations. It might be useful to conduct longitudinal investigations where we ask individuals to keep logs or diaries over a three, four, or five year period. Although self-reports are subject to some distortion because of defenses or inaccuracies of perceptions, we must attempt to minimize these distortions. It should be noted that the observations of psychologists are also subject to distortion because of sociopolitical factors and other biases. Another method which can be cast in both a longitudinal and cross-cultural framework involves asking children of different ages and from different countries the situations (including other people) that make them anxious or the situations that make them angry or hostile.

Dynamic and Static Approaches

We are usually inclined to arbitrarily select a subsample of behavior, at a particular period of time and in a very static fashion. We rarely investigate the dynamic ongoing chain of events. While it is true that situations have an impact on us, it is also true that we actively seek and select the situations and persons with whom we interact. The person is an active, intentional, stimulus-seeking organism, and not a passive victim of situational encounters. The process is important!

Rules and Strategies

Endler and Edwards (1978) suggest that one reason for the lack of progress, with respect to personality research and theorizing, may be because we have been seeking the wrong thing in the wrong place. Perhaps we should concentrate on the rules and strategies of interaction rather than concentrating on the content. Argyle (1977), for example, has suggested that we investigate and analyze the generative rules of social interaction, in preference to making predictions about the content of social interaction. The rules of grammar with respect to language behavior provide us with an excellent analogy. Although we are usually not very successful at predicting the exact content of what someone will say, we are usually quite successful in predicting the rules of grammar that the individual will use (e.g., each sentence will have a subject and a predicate). Mischel (1973) has suggested that we should examine the decoding and encoding strategies a person uses. Perhaps a useful approach for studying person by situation or person by person interactions is to infer the rules and strategies that people use in interacting with one another, in different situations.

Dynamic or Process Interaction Systems

A number of methods, techniques, and strategies have recently been used by various psychologists for investigating the dynamic process and for studying persons intensively. For examples, see Block (1977) on longitudinal studies of personality, Pervin (1977) on methods for having subjects generate their own situations, Peterson (1977) on person by person interaction process in married couples, Raush (1977) on Markov chains, and the previously mentioned studies by Argyle (1977) on rules for social interaction, and by Mischel (1973) on encoding and decoding strategies.

Content, Theory, and Methodology

There are intricate and intimate relationships among content (subject matter), methodology (or technology), and theory. Theory, method, and content all feed upon one another, and enhance one another's development. To some extent we are limited by the lack of appropriate methodologies (or technologies) for examining interactions and dynamic processes. However, recent developments in causal modeling (see Asher, 1976), including path analysis and cross-lagged panel, and the use of Markov chains in psychological research can greatly aid us in examining interaction processes.

Science is hard work and does not proceed by leaps and bounds. Rather it usually proceeds and progresses one small step at a time. Perhaps we should use person by situation interactions (or themas) as the units of analysis rather than using persons or traits as the key units requiring analysis. We need more longitudinal studies (see Block, 1971, and Block, Chapter 2 in this volume), and more studies on how traits develop and the contexts in which they develop.

Pervin (1978c) has suggested that, when we conduct research in the personality area, we should perhaps use a general systems theory in which we are aware that persons are open systems rather than closed systems. It is essential that we develop new research strategies and new methods for studying interaction processes, and new ways of conceptualizing the complex problems involved. "Until and unless this occurs we will continue working within our own mythological framework—a convenient and satisfying illusion to some, but frustrating to many" (Endler, 1976, p. 179).

To Discover the Future Look to the Past!

Although intensive and longitudinal personality studies take time, and are difficult and expensive, the potential payoff may be worth the effort. The model of intensive and multimethod personality research pioneered by Henry Murray and his colleagues in the 1930s seems appropriate for interactional psychology in the 1970s and 1980s. Unfortunately sociopolitical factors, both within and without the groves of academe (e.g., the overemphasis on applied and relevant research, the publish or perish syndrome), produce an environmental context where we may be studying more and more about less and less, and we may wind up by knowing everything about nothing. Personality is complex, and to study it adequately involves the difficult and intensive work of the type conducted by Murray and his colleagues in connection with *Explorations in Personality* (1938). Unfortunately the current social mileu and social values do not support this (see Chapters 1 and 2). To make progress in the future we may have to return to the values and methods of the past.

Hunt (1965) in his paper on traditional personality theory in the light of recent evidence states: "In the words of a Vermont farmer once quoted by Henry A. Murray, 'people is mostly alike, but what differences they is can be powerful important' " (p. 83)—and these differences are due to both personal and situational factors, and to their interactions!

REFERENCES

Allport, G. W. *Personality*. New York: Holt, 1937.

Allport, G. W. *Pattern and Growth in Personality*. New York: Holt, Rinehart Winston, 1961.

Allport, G. W. Traits revisited. *American Psychologist*, 1966, **21**, 1–10.

Angyal, A. *Foundations for a Science of Personality*. Cambridge, MA: Harvard University Press, 1941.

Argyle, M. Predictive and generative rules models of P X S interaction. In D. Magnusson and N. S. Endler (Eds.), *Personality at the Crossroads: Current Issues in Interactional Psychology*. Hillsdale, NJ: Erlbaum, 1977.

Argyle, M. and B. R. Little. Do personality traits apply to social behavior? *Journal for the Theory of Social Behavior*, 1972, **2**, 1–35.

Asher, H. B. *Causal Modeling*. Sage University Paper Series on Quantitative Applications in the Social Sciences, series no. 07-003. Beverly Hills and London: Sage Publications, 1976.

Bandura, A. *Psychological modeling: Conflicting Theories*. New York: Aldine-Atherton, 1971.

Barker, R. G. Explorations in ecological psychology. *American Psychologist*, 1965, **20**, 1–14.

Berkowitz, L. Situational and personal conditions governing reactions to aggressive cues. In D. Magnusson and N. S. Endler (Eds.), *Personality at the Crossroads: Current Issues in Interactional Psychology*. Hillsdale, NJ: Erlbaum, 1977.

Block, J. *Lives through Time*. Berkley, CA: Bancroft, 1971.

Block, J. Advancing the psychology of personality: Paradigmatic shift or improving the quality of research. In D. Magnusson and N. S. Endler (Eds.), *Personality at the Crossroads: Current Issues in Interactional Psychology*, Hillsdale, NJ: Erlbaum, 1977.

Bowers, K. S. Situationism in psychology: An analysis and a critique. *Psychological Review*, 1973, **80**, 307–336.

Brunswik, E. *The Conceptual Framework of Psychology*. Chicago: University of Chicago Press, 1952.

Brunswik, E. *Perception and the Representative Design of Psychological Experiments*. Berkeley, CA: University of California Press, 1956.

Buss, A. R. Emerging field of the sociology of psychological knowledge. *American Psychologist*, 1975, **30**, 988–1002.

Carlson, R. Where is the person in personality research? *Psychological Bulletin*, 1971, **75**, 203–219.

Cattell, R. B. *The description and measurement of personality*. New York: World Books, 1946.

Cattell, R. B. *Personality and Motivation Structure and Measurement*. Yonkers-on-Hudson, NY: World Books, 1957.

Cattell, R. B. and I. H. Scheier. The nature of anxiety: A review of 13 multivariate analyses comparing 814 variables. *Psychological Reports*, Monograph Supplement, 1958, **5**, 351–388.

Cattell, R. B. and I. H. Scheier. *The Meaning and Measurement of Neuroticism and Anxiety*. New York: Ronald, 1961.

Cooley, C. H. *Human Nature and the Social Order*. New York: Scribner's, 1902.

Cottrell, L. S., Jr. The analysis of situational fields. *American Sociological Review,* 1942(a), **7,** 370–382.

Cottrell, L. S., Jr. The adjustment of the individual to his age and sex roles. *American Sociological Review,* 1942(b), **7,** 618–625.

Dewey, R. and W. J. Humber. *The Development of Human Behavior.* New York: Macmillan, 1951.

Diveky, S. and N. S. Endler. *The Interaction Model of Anxiety: State and Trait Anxiety for Banking Executives in Normal Working Conditions.* Unpublished manuscript, York University, Toronto, 1977.

Dollard, J. and N. E. Miller. *Personality and Psychotherapy: An Analysis in Terms of Learning, Thinking and Culture.* New York: McGraw-Hill, 1950.

Edwards, A. L. *Manual of the Personal Preference Schedule.* New York: Psychological Corporation, 1954.

Ekehammar, B. Interactionism in personality from a historical perspective. *Psychological Bulletin,* 1974, **81,** 1026–1048.

Ekehammar, B. & D. Magnusson. A method to study stressful situations. *Journal of Personality and Social Psychology,* 1973, **27,** 176–179.

Ekehammar, B., D. Magnusson, and L. Ricklander. An interactionist approach to the study of anxiety: An analysis of an S-R Inventory applied to an adolescent sample. *Scandinavian Journal of Psychology,* 1974, **15,** 4–14.

Ekehammar, B., D. Schalling, and D. Magnusson. Dimensions of stressful situations: A comparison between a response analytical and a stimulus analytical approach. *Multivariate Behavioral Research,* 1975, **10,** 155–164.

Endler, N. S. The person versus the situation—A pseudo issue? A response to Alker. *Journal of Personality,* 1973, **31,** 287–303.

Endler, N. S. The case for person-situation interactions. *Canadian Psychological Review,* 1975(a), **16,** 12–21.

Endler, N. S. A person-situation interaction model for anxiety. In C. D. Spielberger and I. G. Sarason (Eds.), *Stress and Anxiety,* (Vol. 1). Washington, DC: Hemisphere Publishing Corporation, 1975(b).

Endler, N. S. Grand illusions: Traits or interactions? *Canadian Psychological Review,* 1976, **17,** 174–181.

Endler, N. S. The role of person by situation interactions in personality theory. In I. C. Uzgiris and F. Weizmann (Eds.), *The Structuring of Experience.* New York: Plenum Press, 1977.

Endler, N. S. and J. Edwards. Person by treatment interactions in personality research. In L. A. Pervin and M. Lewis (Eds.), *Perspectives in Interactional Psychology.* New York: Plenum Press, 1978.

Endler, N. S. and J. McV. Hunt. Generalizability of contributions from sources of variance in the S-R Inventories of Anxiousness. *Journal of Personality,* 1960, **37,** 1–24.

Endler, N. S. and J. McV. Hunt. Sources of behavioral variance as measured by the S-R Inventory of Anxiousness. *Psychological Bulletin,* 1966, **65,** 336–346.

Endler, N. S. and J. McV. Hunt. Generalizability of contributions from sources of variance in the S-R Inventories of Anxiousness. *Journal of Personality,* 1969, **37,** 1–24.

Endler, N. S. and D. Magnusson. Multidimensional aspects of state and trait anxiety: A cross-cultural study of Canadian and Swedish students. In C. D. Spielberger and R. Diaz-Guerrero (Eds.), *Cross-Cultural Research on Anxiety.* Washington, DC: Hemisphere Publishing Corporation, 1976(a).

Endler, N. S. and D. Magnusson. Personality and person by situation interactions. In N. S. Endler and D. Magnusson (Eds.), *Interactional Psychology and Personality.* Washington, DC: Hemisphere Publishing Corporation, 1976(b).

Endler, N. S. and D. Magnusson. Toward an interactional psychology of personality. *Psychological Bulletin,* 1976, **83,** 956–974(c).

Endler, N. S. and D. Magnusson. But interactionists do believe in people! A response to Krauskopf. *Psychological Bulletin,* 1978, **85,** 590–592.

Endler, N. S. and M. Okada. A multidimensional measure of trait anxiety: The S-R Inventory of General Trait Anxiousness. *Journal of Consulting and Clinical Psychology,* 1975, **43,** 319–329.

Endler, N. S., J. McV. Hunt, and A. J. Rosenstein. An S-R Inventory of Anxiousness. *Psychological Monographs,* 1962. **76** (17, Whole No. 536), 1–33.

Endler, N. S., J. P. Rushton, and H. L. Roediger, III. Productivity and scholarly impact (citations) of British, Canadian and U.S. Departments of Psychology (1975). *American Psychologist,* 1978, (in press).

Erikson, E. *Childhood and Society,* (2nd ed.) New York: Norton, 1963.

Feshbach, S. The environment of personality. *American Psychologist,* 1978, **33,** 447–455.

Fiedler, F. E. Validation and extension of the contingency model of leadership effectiveness: A review of empirical findings. *Psychological Bulletin,* 1971, **76,** 128–148.

Fiedler, F. E. What triggers the person situation interaction in leadership? In D. Magnusson and N. S. Endler (Eds.), *Personality at the Crossroads: Current Issues in Interactional Psychology.* Hillsdale, NJ: Erlbaum, 1977.

Flood, M. and N. S. Endler. *The Interaction Model of Anxiety: An Empirical Test in an Athletic Competion Situation.* (Department of Psychology Reports, York University, Toronto, 1976, No. 28). Unpublished manuscript, 1976.

Frederiksen, N. Toward a taxonomy of situations. *American Psychologist,* 1972, **27,** 114–123.

Freud, S. *Collected Papers,* (Vol. I–V). New York: Basic Books, 1959.

Fromm, E. *The Sane Society.* New York: Rinehart, 1955.

Gibson, J. T. The concept of the stimulus in psychology. *American Psychologist,* 1960, **15,** 694–703.

Guilford, J. P. *Personality.* New York: McGraw-Hill, 1959.

Hodges, W. F. Effects of ego threat and threat of pain on state anxiety. *Journal of Personality and Social Psychology,* 1968, **8,** 364–372.

Hodges, W. F. and J. P. Felling. Types of stressful situations and their relation to trait anxiety and sex. *Journal of Consulting and Clinical Psychology,* 1970, **34,** 333–337.

Horney, K. *Our Inner Conflicts.* New York: Norton, 1945.

Hoy, E. and N. S. Endler. Reported anxiousness and two types of stimulus incongruity. *Canadian Journal of Behavioural Science,* 1969, **1,** 207–214.

Hunt, J. McV. Traditional personality theory in the light of recent evidence. *American Scientist,* 1965, **53,** 80–96.

Ichheiser, G. Misinterpretations of personality in everyday life and the psychologist's frame of reference. *Character and Personality,* 1943, **12,** 145–160.

Kantor, J. R. *Principles of Psychology,* (Vol. 1), Bloomington, IL: Principia Press, 1924.

Kantor, J. R. *Principles of Psychology,* (Vol. 2), Bloomington, IL: Principia Press, 1926.

Kendall, P. C. Anxiety: States, traits—situations? *Journal of Consulting and Clinical Psychology,* 1978, **46,** 280–287.

Koffka, K. *Principles of Gestalt Psychology.* New York: Harcourt, 1935.

Levinson, D. J. *The Seasons of a Man's Life.* New York: Knopf, 1978.

Lewin, K. *A dynamic Theory of Personality: Selected Papers.* New York: McGraw-Hill, 1935.

Lewin, K. Problems of research in social psychology. In D. Cartwright (Ed.), *Field Theory in Social Science.* London: Tavistock Publications, 1952.

Lewis, A. The ambiguous word "Anxiety". *International Journal of Psychiatry,* 1970, **9,** 62–79.

Magnusson, D. An analysis of situational dimensions. *Perceptual and Motor Skills,* 1971, **32,** 851–967.

Magnusson, D. The person and the situation in an interactional model of behavior. *Scandinavian Journal of Psychology,* 1976, **17,** 253–271.

Magnusson, D. and B. Ekehammar. An analysis of situational dimensions: A replication. *Multivariate Behavioral Research,* 1973, **8,** 331–339.

Magnusson, D. and B. Ekehammar. Anxiety profiles based on both situational and response factors. *Multivarate Behavioral Research,* 1975(a), **10,** 27–43.

Magnusson, D. and B. Ekehammar. Perceptions of and reactions to stressful situations. *Journal of Personality and Social Psychology*, 1975(b), **31**, 1147–1154.

Magnusson, D. and B. Ekehammar. Similar situations—similar behaviors? *Journal of Research in Personality*, 1978, **12**, 41–48.

Magnusson, D. and N. S. Endler. Interactional psychology: Present status and future prospects. In D. Magnusson and N. S. Endler (Eds.), *Personality at the Crossroads: Current Issues in Interactional Psychology*. Hillsdale, NJ: Erlbaum, 1977.

Magnusson, D. and B. Heffler. The generality of behavioral data: III. Generalization potential as a function of the number of observation instances. *Multivariate Behavioral Research*, 1969, **4**, 29–42.

Magnusson, D., M. Gerzen, and B. Nyman. The generality of behavioral data: I. Generalization from observations on one occasion. *Multivariate Behavioral Research*, 1968, **3**, 295–320.

Magnusson, D., B. Heffler, and B. Nyman. The generality of behavioral data: II. Replication of an experiment on generalization from observation on one occasion. *Multivariate Behavioral Research*, 1968, **3**, 415–422.

McClelland, D. C. *Personality*. New York: Sloane, 1951.

Mead, G. H. *Mind, Self, and Society*. Chicago: University of Chicago Press, 1934.

Meichenbaum, D. H. A self-instructional approach to stress management. A proposal for stress innoculation training. In C. D. Spielberger and I. G. Sarason (Eds.), *Stress and Anxiety*, (Vol. 1). Washington, DC: Hemisphere Publishing Corporation, 1975.

Mischel, W. *Personality and Assessment*. New York: Wiley, 1968.

Mischel, W. Continuity and change in personality. *American Psychologist*, 1969, **24**, 1012–1018.

Mischel, W. *Introduction to Personality*. New York: Holt, Rinehart and Winston, 1971.

Mischel, W. Toward a cognitive social learning reconceptualization of personality. *Psychological Review*, 1973, **80**, 252–283.

Mischel, W. *Introduction to Personality*, (2nd ed.) New York: Holt, Rinehart and Winston, 1976.

Moos, R. H. Conceptualizations of human environments. *American Psychologist*, 1973, **28**, 652–665.

Moyer, K. E. The physiology of violence. *Psychology Today*, August 1973, **7**, 35–38.

Murphy, G. *Personality: A Biosocial Approach to Origins and Structure*. New York: Harper, 1947.

Murray, H. A. *Explorations in Personality*. New York: Oxford University Press, 1938.

OSS Assessment Staff. *Assessment of Men.* New York: Rinehart, 1948.

Overton, W. F. and H. W. Reese. Models of development: Methodological implications. In J. R. Nesselroade and H. W. Reese (Eds.), *Life Span Developmental Psychology: Methodological Issues.* New York: Academic Press, 1973.

Patterson, G. R. and D. R. Moore. Interactive patterns as units. In S. J. Suomi, M. E. Lamb and G. R. Stevenson (Eds.), *The study of Social Interaction: Methodological issues.* Madison, WI: University of Wisconsin Press, 1978.

Pervin, L. A. Performance and satisfaction as a function of individual-environment fit. *Psychological Bulletin,* 1968, **69,** 56–68.

Pervin, L. A. The representative design of person-situation research. In D. Magnusson and N. S. Endler (Eds.), *Personality at the Crossroads: Current Issues in Interactional Psychology.* Hillsdale, NJ: Erlbaum, 1977.

Pervin, L. A. Alternative models for the analysis of interactional processes. In L A. Pervin and M. Lewis (Eds.), *Perspectives in Interactional Psychology.* New York: Plenum Press, 1978(a).

Pervin, L. A. *Current Controversies and Issues in Personality.* New York: Wiley, 1978(b).

Pervin, L. A. Definitions, measurements, and classifications of stimuli, situations, and environments. *Human Ecology,* 1978(c), **6,** 71–105.

Rapaport, D., M. Gill, and R. Schafer. *Diagnostic Psychological Testing,* 2 Vols. Chicago: Year Book, 1945.

Raush, H. L. Interaction sequences. *Journal of Personality and Social Psychology,* 1965, **2,** 487–499.

Raush, H. L. Paradox, levels and junctures in person-situation systems. In D. Magnusson and N. S. Endler (Eds.), *Personality at the Crossroads: Current issues in Interactional Psychology.* Hillsdale, NJ: Erlbaum, 1977.

Raush, H. L., A. T. Dittmann, and T. J. Taylor. The interpersonal behavior of children in residential treatment. *Journal of Abnormal and Social Psychology,* 1959(a), **58,** 9–26.

Raush, H. L., A. T. Dittmann, and T. J. Taylor. Person, setting and change in social interaction. *Human Relations,* 1959(b), **12,** 361–378.

Rotter, J. B. *Social learning and Clinical Psychology.* Englewood Cliffs, NJ: Prentice-Hall, 1954.

Rotter, J. B. Some problems and misconceptions related to the construct of internal versus external control of reinforcement. *Journal of Consulting and Clinical Psychology,* 1975, **43,** 56–67.

Rushton, J. P. and N. S. Endler. Person by situation interactions in academic achievement. *Journal of Personality,* 1977, **45,** 297–309.

Sarason, I. G. Test anxiety, attention and the general problem of anxiety. In C. D. Spielberger and I. G. Sarason (Eds.) *Stress and Anxiety,* Vol. 1. New York: Hemisphere Publ. 1975a.

Sarason, I. G. Anxiety and self preoccupation. In I. G. Sarason and C. D.

Spielberger (Eds.) *Stress and Anxiety,* Vol. 2. Washington, D.C.: Hemisphere Publ. 1975b.

Sarason, I. G., R. E. Smith, and E. Diener. Personality research: Components of variance attributable to the person and the situation. *Journal of Personality and Social Psychology,* 1975, **32,** 199–204.

Sechrest, L. Personality. *Annual Review of Psychology,* 1976, **27,** 1–28.

Sells, S. B. Dimensions of stimulus situations which account for behavior variances. In S. B. Sells (Ed.), *Stimulus Determinants of Behavior.* New York: Ronald Press, 1963(a).

Sells, S. B. An interactionist looks at the environment. *American Psychologist,* 1963(b), **18,** 696–702.

Skinner, B. F. *The Behavior of Organisms.* New York: Appleton-Century Crofts, 1938.

Skinner, B. F. *Science and Human Behavior.* New York: Macmillan, 1953.

Spielberger, C. D. The effects of anxiety on complex learning and academic achievement. In C. D. Spielberger (Ed.), *Anxiety and Behavior.* New York: Academic Press, 1966.

Spielberger, C. D. Anxiety as an emotional state. In C. D. Spielberger (Ed.), *Anxiety: Current Trends in Theory and Research,* (Vol. 1). New York: Academic Press, 1972.

Spielberger, C. D. State-trait anxiety and interactional psychology. In D. Magnusson and N. S. Endler (Eds.), *Personality at the Crossroads: Current issues in Interactional Psychology.* Hillsdale, NJ: Erlbaum, 1977.

Spielberger, C. D., R. L. Gorsuch, and R. E. Lushene. *Manual for the State-Trait Anxiety Inventory.* Palo Alto, CA: Consulting Psychologist Press, 1970.

Stolorow, R. D., and G. E. Atwood. *Faces in a cloud: The Subjective World in Personality Theory.* New York: Jason Aaronson, 1978.

Sullivan, H. S. *The Interpersonal Theory of Psychiatry.* New York: Norton, 1953.

Tolman, E. C. Psychology versus immediate experience. In E. C. Tolman, *Collected Papers in Psychology.* Berkeley, CA: University of California Press, 1951.

White, R. W. *Lives in Progress,* (2nd ed.) New York: Holt, Rinehart and Winston, 1966.

White, R. W. *The Enterprise of Living: A View of Personal Growth,* 2nd ed. New York: Holt, Rinehart and Winston, 1976.

Wine, J. Text anxiety and direction of attention. *Psychological Bulletin,* 1971, **76,** 92–105.

Zuckerman, M. The development of an affective adjective check list for the measurement of anxiety. *Journal of Consulting and Clinical Psychology,* 1960, **24,** 457–462.

PART FOUR

Coping and
Its Failures

The earlier parts of this book have been concerned primarily with the structure of personality, the need to take process into account in following structure over time, the importance of internal and situational factors in explaining individual behavior, as well as the larger question of the conceptual space needed to account adequate for stability and for variation. In contrast, the authors in this section were invited to deal with those aspects of personality that were concerned with coping and failure. Given this assignment they appropriately, and to a greater degree, assume structure as a given, focusing instead on process aspects of individual functioning and on the mechanisms necessary to explain them. Like George Kelly (1955), they see process as primary and make the assumption that "the organism is delivered . . . into the psychological world alive and struggling" (p. 37). Their efforts thus are concerned with explaining this life and struggle. Like Kelly, as well, they focus on the positive aspects of this process—as it involves coping and mastery—as much as they do on the evidence of failure that we call distress, or when it persists, psychopathology. They also are concerned to a considerable degree with the cognitive elements involved in the structuring of environment and self, and they utilize cognitive personality constructs as organizing, intermediary mechanisms in their efforts to articulate the relationship between history and environment on the one hand, and behavior on the other.

At the same time both of these authors share a common perspective that differentiates them from Kelly's more purely American psychology. They, like Murray, hold a theory of personality that attempts to explain how process and individual differences (of either presumed or demonstrated biological origin) together with significant environmental influences, at developmentally significant time periods, account for the

153

variations we observe in childhood and adult behavior. Despite these similarities, one question we need to address is the degree to which they have either moved beyond or away from earlier concepts of personality as they embrace process conceptions of personality. We will return to this issue after a brief foretaste of some of the major issues for personality, as theory and as empirical science, raised by Dr. Murphy's and Professor Garmezy's chapters.

Murphy's exposition is set within an organismic framework. Personality exists at least at birth and probably before. It can be identified both by consistency and individuality of behavior, and by the infant organism's active and, to a considerable degree already differentiated efforts to engage with its environment. What are traditionally called process concepts, such as coping and defense, are involved along with structural characteristics (self-image, stage-related achievements, etc.) to account for both variation and consistency.

At another level, Murphy indicates that the conceptualization of personality must encompass both the mastery (competence) and the failure (distress, disturbance, defense) end of the continuum of coping, and preferably within the same conceptual structure. Her work, both here and in much of her earlier writing, attests to the success of that effort.

The chapter also clearly embraces a stage-specific view of structural and process variables; changes in the hierarchy of systems are to be expected as development progresses. In these respects Murphy's position is an interactionist one, with process leading to evolution of structure and hierarchy, which itself leads to a change in process, and so forth. Such a position implies that both the variables that we use in prediction and their relative efficacy will probably change as a function of developmental stage.

Finally, we should note briefly Murphy's conception of process, as she defines it in the latter portion of her paper. "Process may be seen as continuation through time of behavior which has aspects both of continuity and of change" (p. 189). We might just as easily substitute the word personality for process because Murphy visualizes personality as process. Within this definition both structure and function can be viewed as action oriented interactive systems. And although Murphy is not explicit about this, there is a teleologic flavor to her conceptualization that is rather close to modern systems theory (see Miller, Galanter, and Pribram, 1960; Urban, 1978).

* * *

An experimental psychopathologist interested in developmental issues—even such an eminent one as Professor Garmezy, the author of the last chapter—might at first blush appear to be far, in his work and his thinking, from personality research in the traditional ways it has been constructed, and even further removed from personality theorizing in its more formal aspects. There is some truth to these observations, and there also is a paradox—that the arena in which Garmezy operates so well is, in a very practical sense, far more concerned with the day to day (and year to year) issues of personality functioning, stability, and change, than is true of the bulk of traditional, academically based research and theorizing. From this latter vantage point what he has to say both explicitly and implicitly about current conceptualizations of personality and the ability to predict complex human functioning is highly germane.

Within this framework, it is not surprising that Garmezy turns to a later Murray for his linkages to the work of *Explorations,* a Murray who was preoccupied with conceptualization and personality theory only as they would render the task of predicting human behavior under conditions of life and death more workable. Such a task, for investigators brave enough to attempt it in the social sciences, has a slightly but importantly different focus from that of the more academically preoccupied scholar-scientist. Here the primary concern is to do the job first, and to build a conceptual structure only as is needed to do that work well. The evolution of theory is in the service of predictability. Under these circumstances we might anticipate the development of a different—more implicit—theoretical structure than is true in the more self-conscious circumstances of the hypothetico-deductive personality laboratory. Given these differences, the significance of Garmezy's paper needs to be understood not only at a manifest level, but also in terms of the implicit network he constructs of the elements necessary to adequately understand vulnerability and adaptation.

The work reviewed here—on vulnerability to schizophrenia, susceptibility to stress and its antipode, stress resistance and adaptation—clearly fits the model of that rarer breed of investigation referred to by White in Chapter 1. All of these scientists are studying personality the long way. Their problems, as far as the field of personality is concerned, are of several types: one is the extraordinary methodological difficulty of pursuing any viable yet at the same time scientifically worthwhile program in this area. These difficulties are amply documented by Garmezy.

At a conceptual metalevel, the review points to two major classes of variables that currently appear to be most productive in selecting for risk for later schizophrenia: those that measure attributes associated with adult psychopathology (attentional, cognitive, social, and psychophysiological deficits), and those that are associated with developmental lags (see p. 203). Garmezy suggests that the variables with the greatest promise for prediction of risk are of two types: first, "those that tap deficits or retardations in maturation in the earliest years . . ." and second, those that in later childhood and adolescence repeat "a failure to meet anticipated stages of cognitive, emotional, and social development, or the absence of those that reflect the growth of competencies." While these variables emerge out of empirical research, they are reminiscent at a theoretical level of both Maslovian (1954) and Allportian (1961) notions of the differentiation of deprivation from growth motivations. Potentially viable markers of risk appear to be those associated with deficits, that in less vulnerable children are either absent or quickly mastered at the earliest developmental stages, but that persist and make it continually difficult for individuals to meet developmental challenges in the at risk subjects. The other half of the picture, only briefly touched on in the early part of Garmezy's review, is the part played by environmental influences of a variety of different kinds in tempering or exacerbating the morbid potential.

An interesting sidelight to the overview of vulnerability presented here is Garmezy's emphasis upon a far from naive optimism about the diversity of outcomes that can occur, even from a background that predisposes toward schizophrenic breakdown. When contrasted with the picture presented by Block, both in 1971 and in later follow-up data reported on in Chapter 2, one is struck by the more cautious yet, at the same time, more positive view of the possibilities of successful coping that emerge out of some of the risk studies. Block (1971) emphasizes the psychological damage wrought by earlier inadequate parenting; Garmezy's review takes note of stylistic consistency over developmental time, but also places more importance on diversity of outcome. Perhaps this is only a matter of perspective and context; the issue still needs attention. More generally, from a conceptual perspective the review indicates that there are two problems which are not yet ready for solution. The risk literature although heavily predictor oriented, is by no means atheoretical; but the existing data are not yet sufficient to construct a comprehensive model of how schizophrenia develops and when it does not. Related to this is the difficult question of how to integrate behavioral and biological data in a model that will do justice to both. At some point risk researchers will need to deal more clearly with this, given the partially biological nature of the disorder. The problem is a broader one, however, that is only beginning to be addressed by contemporary personality researchers and theorists (Dworkin, Burke, Maher, and Gottesman, 1976; Murphy, this volume; Pervin, 1978; Prentky, 1979).

In the latter part of the chapter we are allowed to look over the shoulders of Garmezy and his Minnesota co-workers as they elaborate the scaffolding and then proceed to build the apparatus for a comprehensive but highly workable and innovative attack on the problems of invulnerability and stress resistance in childhood. With this blueprint before us, and after the tough work has been done, we take the liberty of asking: what are the nature of the variables dealt with here, from the perspective of personality theory? What also is implied about the nature of personality as a conceptual structure, as Garmezy discusses it in the work of others and within his own research program?

As was noted earlier, process aspects of behavior are clearly emphasized here also; in fact Murphy's work is one of the acknowledged predecessors of the formulations made by the Minnesota group. But insofar as Garmezy's research focuses on adaptations, he is ostensibly dealing with steady-state phenomena that are an *outcome* of styles of coping and/or defending. To the extent that this outcome is an achievement that persists over time, it also is suggestive of a structural, possibly traitlike view of personality; to the extent that it demonstrates variability over time, it is perhaps better understood as a dynamic conception that implies central organizing elements as the core structure. The Minnesota data should shed light on this issues.

The nature of the data being collected also imply a clearly interactionist view of personality; consequent behaviors are examined in the light of both central processing abilities (e.g. cognitive measures; impulse control capacity, creativity) and environmental experiences (e.g. recent environmental stressors, parental caretaking practices, school experiences).

We also see a distinctly developmental conception of personality advanced that is in some ways strikingly different from that found among researchers more preoccupied with the normal range of developmental process. The formulations contained in both the literature review and in the Minnesota research program imply a conception of developmental unfolding that allows for the possibility of more than one generic process being present. This is evident in a number of places: in the openness to across time outcomes of both continuity *and* discontinuity discussed in the review of issues concerning the competence literature, and in the design of the Minnesota study itself. In these formulations, maturational context is all important. There may be phenotypic similarity of competency behavior that in fact marks underlying process diversity. Garmezy suggests that this is an especially important issue when we look at behaviors at the extremes of intensity. Finally, adaptation itself is implied to be contextual, and possibly differing in its nature in different environments; the Minnesota group allows for this by their examination of the potentially varying antecedents and consequences among those who adapt, and do not, in high and low stress environments. Without the data, it would be premature to speculate about the types of models these investigators will construct, but the plan of their information gathering allows for it.

* * *

One last point: the reader might well ask: how has the work of these investigators shown change—if any—in our conceptualizations and activity as personologists over the forty years since Murray's seminal work was written? The broad guidelines laid out in *Explorations* still seem remarkably clear and appropriate forty years later. Nonetheless, a close reading of the text of these contributors indicates, at a pragmatic level, that there has been considerable reformulation and a great deal more in the way of empirical grounding to theory in the intervening years. Both of these investigators utilize theory only to the extent that it clarifies and helps to establish the lawfulness that underlies both consistency and change. In these respects, their formulations are theories of the middle ground, which dictate the nature of variables to be explored and organize the observations, once collected. They deal with a datum of facts, some now well established, many still to be discovered, which is the foundation for a science of personality that Murray could only hope for in 1938. This clearly is a part of the heritage of *Explorations*.

REFERENCES

Allport, G. W. *Pattern and Growth in Personality.* New York: Holt, Rinehart and Winston, 1961.

Dworkin, R. H., B. W. Burke, B. A. Maher, and I. I. Gottesman. A longitudinal study of the genetics of personality. *Journal of Personality and Social Psychology,* 1976, **34,** 510–518.

Kelly, G. A. *The Psychology of Personal Constructs,* Vol. 1. New York: Norton, 1955.

Maslow, A. H. *Motivation and Personality.* New York: Harper, 1954.

Miller, G. A., E. Galanter, and K. H. Pribram. *Plans and the Structure of Behavior.* New York: Holt, 1960.

Pervin, L. A. *Current Controversies and Issues in Personality.* New York: Wiley, 1978.

Prentky, R. A. (Ed.) *Biological Aspects of Normal Personality.* Baltimore: University Park Press, 1979.

Urban, H. B. The concept of development from a systems perspective. In P. B. Baltes (Ed.) *Life-Span Development and Behavior,* Vol. I. New York: Academic Press, 1978.

CHAPTER 6

Explorations in Child Personality

Lois Barclay Murphy

A PERSONAL INTRODUCTION AND SOME INTELLECTUAL INFLUENCES

Before I embark on this excursion into explorations of child personality, I want to retrace some milestones of my personal trail which preceded the intensive pursuit of beginnings, continuity, and change in personality development.

As the eldest of five very different children, and the granddaughter of two very contrasting grandmothers—one "fancy" with lace and embroideries, the other often Quakerish "plain," the first endlessly sweet, the latter full of sharp, pithy wisdom—I was early impressed by personality differences. Because my father was a minister, I was exposed to scores of people in his congregations and developed great sensitivity to the affected, sugary-sweet ladies who talked down to the minister's little girl, contrasted with those who made sense.

With thirteen moves in my first sixteen years, to one community after another, from heavenly countryside to smelly city, from North to South, and Middle West to East, I was alerted to differences in subcultural settings, although I didn't yet have the words for them. In addition, my California mother talked much about the mountains and gardens of her Pasadena childhood—neither of which existed then in the Middle West.

Along with this rich background of awareness of differences, I was impressed by change in personality. First, my busy, active grandfather, who I knew up to the age of five, became sad and silent after the crash of 1907, when he lost his wealth in the collapse of farm prices. My mother played Schubert and opera arias to us on her Steinway piano when I was a small child, but was no longer able to play the piano as vicious rheumatoid arthritis distorted her hands. My father was companionable and spent much time with us as long as he was the pastor of a church. When he became an executive in the church he was busier and less accessible, with less leisure for our former jaunts.

One of the first articles I wrote, with Gardner, was on variations in social behavior in different situations. My early experiences had clear impact on my professional life. More on differences and change when I come to our Topeka research. In the meantime, I present some of the background of my preoccupation with personality dynamics.

Both at Vassar and at Teacher's College, Columbia, psychoanalysis was taboo in the 1920s and 1930s. However, at Vassar, library stacks were open; Freud's books, *The Ego and Id* (1921), and *Group Psychology and the Analysis of the Ego* (1923), were on the shelves. As I read them despite the taboo, I thought they made sense, and I also thought my revered and often inspiring professor, Margaret Floy Washburn, president of the American Psychological Association, must be prejudiced and/or have some problems. Later in the twenties I took a course with Marian Kenworthy which gave me a start in thinking about ego and libido. My college friend and graduate school roommate, Ruth Munroe, was in the process of getting engaged to a psychoanalyst, John Levy; they introduced me to some of the analysts who escaped Hitler—notably Heinz and Dora Hartmann and Bela Mittelmann.

In the early 1930s Sarah Lawrence College was involved in adolescent research, collaborating with the analyst Carolyn Zachry, who included us in seminars with Erik Erikson and Erich Fromm. When we started the Sarah Lawrence Nursery School in 1937, Benjamin Spock, the pediatrician, recently out of psychoanalytic training, became our pediatric advisor. Dr. Spock met with us once a week; he was followed by Milton Senn, who was deeply committed to a dynamic approach to understanding personality. I was touched by the fact that Susan Isaacs in London quickly picked up on my study of *Social Behavior and Child Personality* (1937), and discussed it in one of her articles. This was before Americans began to pay attention to it, so I was impressed by the openness and receptivity of analysts and their creative, dynamic approach. We had a little correspondence, chiefly about Dan, one little boy in her study of social behavior (Isaacs, 1933) that preceded mine. Her extensive records on him included observations of both sympathetic and aggressive behavior; this further demonstrated to me the need to watch for variations in behavior in different situations—that is, in response to different stimuli and pressures.

One special reason why I was deeply impressed by Henry Murray's work on the Thematic Apperception Test (TAT) in the mid-1930s was that I had discovered preschool children had very idiosyncratic reactions to pictures in my study of sympathy (1937). For instance, I showed a picture of a child holding a rabbit very tightly; it happened to have a dark background. One child commented, "He is afraid of the dark." A few other children found aspects of some pictures to reflect anxiety. This, along with my excitement at the *Psychodiagnostik* of Rorschach (1921), which I read to Gardner, and my fascination with Erikson's reports on miniature toy play of small disturbed children led to my joint article with Ruth Horowitz on projective techniques for studying child personality (1938). A marvelous new world of study of young children's personality loomed up before me. This led, of course, to the monograph *Methods for the Study of Personality in Young Children* (1941) and later to the two-volume *Personality in Young Children* (1956). This was a world too wide to encompass completely then, and there is still much to be done.

Since I was a mother, a daughter, a sister, a wife, and a daughter-in-law as well as a teacher, I did not have time for more than limited part-time research until we went to the Menninger Foundation. At that time research on young children was the focus of my work, which did include, however, some psychotherapy with children and psychoanalytic training with a brilliant faculty of the Topeka Psychoanalytic Institute. A major contribution of my psychoanalytic training was the emergence of courage to explore the beginnings of personality in infancy—an exploration I think I would not have dared to undertake earlier, in spite of my awareness of the vivid differences in personality in our own two babies.

THE BEGINNINGS OF PERSONALITY

At what point in development can we speak about infant personality? Does that three-month-old baby who smiled at me when I sang "Polly Wolly Doodle" to her, have personality? To me she does; so does the three-month-old baby who refused to put up with being held in a supine position, but wanted to be held sitting up where she could see. So does the two-month-old baby who pushed the new solid food out of his mouth and would have none of it, and the one-month-old baby who frowned when the nipple of a bottle was put into her mouth—she was accustomed to the different feel, smell, and taste of her mother's breast.

What about babies at birth? The easily born baby—unwrinkled and wide-eyed twenty minutes after birth, also had personality, especially when she made ten determined efforts to get her thumb into her mouth before she succeeded. And what about before birth? Sontag and Wallace (1935) quoted the report of a pregnant mother who said she could not go to concerts because her unborn baby kicked in such excitement at the sound that it disturbed people sitting next to her.

In reviewing these examples I have been implying that social responsiveness, coping efforts, reactions to newness, and to stimulation are all aspects of personality. Gesell and Ames (1937) commented on the great alacrity of some babies. Babies cannot use our language, but if we look and listen, we can figure out some of their innovative symbols.

At eight months our baby "Arthur" made repeated blowing sounds to convey his wish that his mother would put a record on the phonograph. (She was in the habit of blowing any dust off the record before she put it on. When she got the point and complied, he responded with beaming smiles.) Similarly, Escalona and Leitch's records include the account of baby Teddy's bouncing on his mother's lap to stimulate her to bounce him. Baby Arthur in my own records later was a singer, actor, and director of light opera while baby Teddy grew up to be a musician in the Marine Band.[1]

These examples of early coping and of innovation clearly lead to a discussion of individuality, continuity, and change in the development of personality. Before discussing the evidence as it has mounted up today, we should pay our respects to important early efforts in this area.

EARLIER WORK ON PERSONALITY DEVELOPMENT

Mary Shirley of Minnesota, working in the 1920s, was one of the early pioneers in the study of infant personality. She was inadequately appreciated, as happens with many a pioneer blazing a new trail off the beaten path. She concluded that differences in behavior could be observed within the first twenty-four hours of life, that personality differences are pervasive and can be observed in different situations with consistent results, and that a behavioral item that is given up with increasing age is replaced by another that is consistent with it (Shirley, 1930). During the same early period, Nancy Bayley focused on mental and physical development. Being closer to the mainstream, her work in those areas was recognized although her contributions to personality development, mentioned incidentally (Bayley, 1949), were not noticed at the time. At about the same time, Macfarlane began her study (1963) of a larger representative sample of infants with interviews with mothers. This study continued into the preschool years and subsequently, using observations, intelligence and personality tests of the growing children. Eventually this study followed the same group into adulthood.

[1]These accounts are taken from Escalona's unpublished records of infant behavior, 1948–1952. The research undertaking, from which the data described here and at some later points in the chapter are drawn, is described in Escalona and Leitch's (1952) book.

Gesell's major emphasis was on general principles of genetic control of sequences in growth, yet an important paper on personality, "Early evidence of individuality in the human infant," was published in September 1937 (Gesell and Ames, 1937).

Ruth Washburn's study of smiling and laughing in the first year of life was published in 1929 and, again, attracted little attention. She found that some babies both smiled and cried much, others smiled or laughed but rarely cried, and another group were sober or high in crying. Finally, there was a fourth group who neither cried nor smiled much. These patterns later were discussed by other investigators under the heading of expressiveness, obviously of basic importance to personality. Other studies of very young children, toddlers, and two-year-olds were also seen in the 1930s with questions regarding infancy precursors not adequately followed up. These include *Social Behavior and Child Personality* (Murphy, 1937), and the many studies reviewed in Murphy, Murphy, and Newcomb (1937).

Piaget's exciting studies of the development of his own children stimulated a fascinating variety of investigations of infants. Methods ranged from technically elaborate experimental approaches (Rheingold and Eckerman, 1969) to the endlessly patient, meticulous observations of Peter Woolf in the natural setting of the home (1966). Meanwhile, Bernfeld's (1929) sensitive observations of the infant's efforts toward mastery and Melanie Klein's (1932) bold theories about the paranoid and depressive positions stimulated still other efforts to understand what contributes to personality as contrasted to purely physical aspects of a baby's development. Margaret Fries (Fries and Woolf, 1953) was a pioneer in the exploration of constitutional differences with cinema records of differences in activity level, while Spitz (1946) and Bowlby (1958) laid foundations for study of the meanings of the infant's relation to the mother and the effects of separation on personality development.

Beginning in 1948, Escalona and Leitch (1952), with a team of psychologists, undertook an historic naturalistic study of behavior of sixteen infants at each four-week stage of development, from four to thirty-two weeks (128 babies altogether). Grace Heider, Alice Moriarty, and I have analyzed the records of about half of these babies, who, as preschool children, were still available in Topeka. These analyses focused on coping and vulnerability in relation to an extensive list of behavior and personality characteristics observed as the children grew (Murphy and Moriarty, 1976). Escalona and Heider (1959) predicted personalities at the preschool level from the infancy observations with considerable success for some aspects of personality.

This incomplete sketch of the emergence of studies relevant to infant personality cannot do justice to the multitude of investigations, especially of the 1960s. These latter studies were partly stimulated by work with rats, dogs, and monkeys, and partly inspired by the wish to learn more about early tendencies important for later delinquency, emotional disturbance, or deviant personality patterns, such as autism. L. J. Stone, Henrietta Smith, and I made a large sample of this infant research available in our book, *The Competent Infant* (1973).

Other influences contributing to personality development include varieties of maternal relationship with infants interacting with individuality in babies. Certain monumental studies of interaction of mothers and babies include David M. Levy's study of overprotective mothers (1943, 1966), Sylvia Brody's volume on *Patterns of Mothering* (1956), Escalona's study of mother-infant interaction in *Roots of Individuality* (1968), and Grace Heider's 1966 monograph, *Vulnerability in Infants and Preschool Children,* which included a detailed analysis of mother's handling in relation to the infant's style.

THE COMPLEXITY OF EXPERIENCES CONTRIBUTING TO COMPETENCE

I believe we have to guard against overly simple explanations of differences in young children's competence. Sroufe, in the October 1978 *Human Nature,* has an attractive article attributing the two-year-old's competence to the quality of attachment between mother and baby, and attributing this, in turn, to the mother's sensitivity in handling her baby. But when we see mothers with more than one child, we find differences in the competence of the children hardly attributable to the mother's sensitivity. Constitutional factors in the children, the child's growth pattern, differences in family stress during the child's early years and the child's illnesses or accidents all contribute to the developmental adaptation. There are also differences in the mother's availability owing to her illness, or increasing household pressures, or overstimulation by excessive pressure from other members of the family. These and multiple other factors contribute to the child's level of equilibrium and responsiveness to new situations, demands, and new people.

Of course, not all modern-day psychologists take Sroufe's simplistic position. In the very same issue of *Human Nature,* Ira Gordon (1978), outstanding child psychologist, takes Papousek to task for claiming the discovery of organism/environment interaction thirty-odd years after Gardner Murphy's (1947) classic *Personality: A Biosocial Approach,* and some years after Ira Gordon's own statement (1970). It is a disservice to the science of child development, not to say irresponsible and potentially dangerous to attribute a child's competence solely to the mother's sensitivity in dealing with him. This is one important factor and only one. We need to respect the complexity and richness of an infant or young child's interplay with his total environment.

For example, Craig was a serene baby, born after a comfortable pregnancy, to an unusually sensitive mother; he continued equable and sociable and became a resourceful, competent child. His younger brother was born several years later during a period of acute financial stress in the family, and the inevitable anxiety which accompanied it. This probably contributed to a more difficult pregnancy and birth. He was a vulnerable baby and child who could not tolerate separation from his mother. She was still a sensitive mother, but was now hard-pressed and much busier, as was her husband.[2]

I am emphasizing this issue because we are in danger of misjudging the sources of a child's personality with destructive results. The 1930s were years of blaming mothers for their children's problems as if the genes and basic equipment of the organism had nothing to do with the child's behavior. We don't want to repeat that era of oversimplification.

It is certainly valid to delineate what goes on between a sensitive mother and baby—in particular, her capacity to give relevant and sufficient but not excessive support; her respect for the baby's autonomy, his likes and dislikes, his fatigue level and limits; his thresholds for overstimulation or, by contrast, for boredom; her healthy capacity to take his angers and upsets in stride, her freedom from excessive loving or libidinization. But this is not to say that she is the sole determinant of his developmental achievements, or his comfort in the world.

I have heard very intelligent child psychologists complain that Escalona's *Roots of Individuality* (1968) is too complex, too hard to absorb. I think this is a disgrace to our profession. Of course, it is easier to assimilate one concept like attachment than to absorb complex formulations of interactions between differentiated babies and mothers. But we are shortchanging our science if we settle for simplistic formulations of complex developmental processes. Escalona's analysis of mother-baby interactions is uniquely alert to variations in consequences of similar maternal behavior: "Identical environmental conditions or events generate quite different patterns of experience for different infants . . ."; "diverse constellations of organismic and environmental factors may produce similar patterns of concrete experience" (Escalona, 1968, p.

[2]The unreferenced observations of Craig and of other children described throughout the chapter come from my own records on individual children, kept from 1930 on, and from the data of the Escalona and Leitch infancy project, part of which later became the Topeka study. In some instances the data extend all the way into adulthood.

64). Working with syndromes of simultaneous or parallel behavior and somatic proclivities, Escalona found that a given characteristic such as high activity level "may increase or decrease the occurrence of distress . . . and how the same characteristic may facilitate or retard developmental progress" depending both on environmental circumstances and on other and independent reaction tendencies. (Escalona, 1968, p. 76).

Babies differ in their signaling resourcefulness. A quiet baby may demand little, and if the mother's handling is limited to cues from the baby he may not receive as much stimulation as he needs in order to evoke his latent potentialities. The matter of sensitivity of the mother to the baby's communication needs to be supplemented by awareness of differences in babies' deeper needs for stimulation from the environment. "The fairly impassive and perceptually robust infant, if stimulated seldom and very gently, would experience a minimum of arousal in contact with the mother and, in fact, be understimulated" (Escalona, 1968, p. 65).

We saw interesting examples of misfit and fit between mothers and babies in the Escalona-Leitch sample:

> Mrs. Rogers was an energetic, intelligent, devoted mother who did well with her energetic, active baby, Malcolm; but with the next baby, Vernon who was extremely sensitive and not as responsive, the fit was not as good. Tommy's mother, by contrast, was a sensitive little lady who was not up to the demands of her very vigorous, lively, energetic baby.

Mother Nature does not always distribute babies very appropriately and babies' mothers are not always infinitely adaptable to their babies' tempos, activity, and drive levels.

Misfit between mother and baby does not always show itself so directly in the baby's behavioral repertoire and in the mother's caretaking. Sometimes colic and gastric distress reflects tension between mother and baby. But other causes of colic are to be directly found in the baby's constitution, such as differences in the functioning of the gastrointestinal system and allergies, intolerance of certain foods, and other factors known to skillful pediatricians. Where gastric discomfort persists through the months when perception and cognitive functioning are becoming organized, the pressure of tension, pain, and emotional disturbance can interfere with normal development. Melanie Klein's (1932) "paranoid position," at about four months, calls attention to a critical period for differentiation of the external world. Distress and misery at this time, projected to the outside world, can interfere with the development of differentiation as biochemical products of stress flood the brain under these conditions. Differentiation and integration processes need a serene condition for optimal development; these are basic requisites for a healthy personality.

EXPERIENCES CONTRIBUTING TO PERSONALITY CHANGE

As I mentioned earlier, as a child I was intrigued by observations of *change* in personalities I came to know. This led to a later professional interest in forces contributing to change. This issue of continuity and change in personality was addressed by several members of our team for the coping study in Topeka. With naturalistic observations at parties and on trips to the park and zoo, pediatric and psychiatric examinations, psychological tests, interviews with the children and their mothers, thirty-two children were studied in depth at the preschool, latency, and prepuberty stages.

Thirty-one of these had previously been subjects of Escalona and Leitch's study of infants aged four to thirty-six weeks (1952). Two psychologists and a psychiatrist simultaneously recorded observations of these infants during four hours of normal infant experience, including feeding, sleeping, play, and also basic physical and mental tests. Home visits and interviews with the mothers extended information on the environment. On the basis of this extensive information, Escalona wrote descriptions of the children as she expected them to be seen at the preschool stage. Grace Heider and Escalona independently analyzed and rated the infancy and the preschool data, then reported the percentage of correct predictions on the children and on separate areas of development (see Escalona and Heider, 1959, p. 50).

Some of the prediction data, relevant to the present discussion, are shown in Tables 1, 2, and 3.

In *Personality: A Biosocial Approach to Origins and Structure* (1947), Gardner Murphy developed his field theory: personality is not contained within the skin of the individual; it "is . . . expressed by the interaction of the living system with the outer world" (Murphy, 1947, p. 881). Our Topeka studies of child development provide much documentation for this thesis. At the same time we need to recognize certain qualifications: certain areas of functioning were more correctly predicted by Escalona than others: motor coordination and development, attention, expressiveness, perceptual sensitivity, affect (complexity, intensity), and goal striving. These we could expect; these functions are primarily controlled by genes and are less easily modified. But sex role acceptance, sex role

Table 1.   Areas of Functioning Well Predicted by Escalona; Predictions of Preschool Behavior Made in Infancy

Prediction Area	Percentage of Correct Predictions
Motor coordination (pattern)	86
Motor development (maturation)	83
Attention, concentration, involvement	81
Activity pattern and range	78
Expressive behavior	74
Perceptual sensitivity (intake)	70
Intelligence level, pattern	70
Affects (complexity, intensity, history)	69
Decisiveness, goal-striving	68
Activity level	67

Source: Data from Escalona and Heider, 1959.

conflicts, relationship to siblings, reaction of staff to child, imaginativeness, were also among the areas well predicted (see Table 2). To be sure, the major aspects of the child-environment interaction were relatively stable in this midwestern community of stable families in a relatively stable culture.

Areas that were not predicted well (Table 3) included, among others, shyness and response to strangers, response to the unfamiliar, basic attitudes and feelings about self and the world, response to frustration. These and some other items are evidently more vulnerable to specific experiences in the environment than are such characteristics as motor

Table 2.   Additional Areas Surprisingly Well Predicted by Escalona; Predictions of Preschool Behavior Made in Infancy

Prediction Area	Percentage of Correct Predictions
Sex role acceptance	95
Sex role conflicts (internal)	75
Oedipal conflict, resolution, and so on	82
Relationship to siblings	75
Reaction of staff to child	80
Interest pattern in play	74
Interest pattern (excluding play)	86
Fantasy, imaginativeness (intensity)	73
Fantasy (quality, use of)	67
Use of space (freedom in structuring of)	67

Source: Data from Escalona and Heider, 1959.

Table 3. Areas of Functioning Less Well Predicted by Escalona: Predictions of Preschool Behavior Made in Infancy

Prediction Area	Percent of Correct Prediction
Response to the unfamiliar (new situations)	38
Shyness, response to strangers	47
Relationship with mother	47
Basic attitudes and feelings regarding self and the world	50
Achievement needs, competitiveness	43
Response to frustration (internal)	50
Play style (thematic)	48

Source: Data from Escalona and Heider, 1959.

coordination. If first encounters with strangers are experienced as threatening (as when well-meaning visitors approach the baby suddenly or roughly, teasing or pinching the baby's chin, or when a stranger is a doctor who gives a painful shot) a baby may early become fearful of strangers. By contrast, babies who have had comfortable or pleasurable encounters with strangers are more at ease with them. "Relationship with mother" changes with changing conditions, as when younger siblings arrive with resulting changes in the availability of the mother and her investment in children's contributions to maturational achievements.

These illustrations of factors in change cannot possibly do justice to the sensitive, thorough studies of prediction in relation to changes in the children that Escalona and Heider presented in their important book, *Prediction and Outcome* (1959). Further analysis of continuity and change was carried out by Heider (1966), focusing on the problem of the relation of vulnerability to change. Moriarty (1966) analyzed factors related to change in I.Q., and I made still other studies of continuity and change between infancy and the preschool and also prepuberty stage (Murphy and Moriarty, 1976).

Heider (1966) focussed on vulnerability and found that almost half of the group she studied became more vulnerable in the preschool years than they were in the first six months of life. Vulnerable babies had disturbances in feeding, digestion, bowel functioning, or breathing, and generally had a fragile physique and low energy. In addition, they often had developmental imbalances, with some functions ahead and others lagging behind the typical group level. In contrast, babies of low vulnerability were robust, energetic, resistant to infection. They were functionally stable, that is, free from marked autonomic lability reflected in tendencies toward blushing or paling, or variability in respiration, heart rate, pulse, and blood pressure. Vegetative functioning, including digestion and elimination was smooth.

Of special interest is the fact that all of Heider's babies judged to be vulnerable on the basis of a group of functions were disturbed in vegetative functioning and were relatively low in energy. Conceivably, low energy could be a result of digestive difficulties, which, in turn, could result from stress in the mother-baby relationship.

With all the vulnerable babies there was some inadequacy in attunement between mother and baby. Cynthia's mother was flighty and undependable at that time. Several years later, when she became more disturbed, she was hospitalized. But we cannot account for Cynthia's vulnerability solely by reference to her disturbed mother since her younger brother was not a vulnerable baby. We have to recognize differences in babies' vulnerability to maternal inadequacies.

Among the most outstandingly competent adolescents who graduated from college were some who had been vulnerable babies and had experienced some inadequacy in relationship with their mothers for different reasons. Terry's mother was a teaser, and Helen's mother was overly busy with three other little children. The competence and achievement of these two college students seemed to evolve from the children's own efforts to reach out to the environment and to use available resources outside of the family to supplement what was inadequate at home. This pattern of reaching out was seen in other children as well.

CHILDREN'S CONTRIBUTIONS TO MATURATIONAL ACHIEVEMENTS

When child development studies consisted of laboratory records of the average age of emergence of various functions, the emphasis was on the typical sequence, such as sitting up before walking and the like. The genetic factor was considered as all determining. Not until close, extended observation of infants in the home or in hospital settings did it become apparent to psychologists that infants themselves had something to do with their progress. This was just as true of their older brothers and sisters, who progressed with the support of their own efforts, trial and error experiments, insights, and imitation, along with their identification with older children or adults.

The genes provide the potentiality and the environment may provide opportunity, stimulation, and challenge. But it is the baby's effort which turns the potentiality into actuality. One has been moved to exclaim *bravo!* when an active four-month-old baby succeeds after repeated struggles in rolling over from a supine position to a position on his tummy where he can hold up his head and look around; again, when he successfully struggles to pull up to standing at the railing of his playpen.

Not all babies are equally determined. Some of them take it easy until coordinations are more nearly mature. But still it is the babies who have to actualize their developmental potentiality by their own efforts. And they have to continue to grow themselves up all through childhood.

PROCESSES OF PERSONALITY DEVELOPMENT

In going over records through successive years, I have been struck with the fact that when you follow through a particular theme like Molly's successive ways of dealing with fear of thunder, or Patty's ways of dealing with fear of bugs or any of these themes that extend over a period of years, you don't see anything that fits neatly into a learning theory type of explanation of what children do. Each response is a new, spontaneous integration that utilizes maturation, motivation, and insight and all the child's coping resources at that moment. It is new and different from what the child did a few months before.

Now, at what point do static structures come into being, and in what areas? Certainly, up to the preschool stage and into latency, there is so much new development that the balance is more on the side of spontaneous integration. The role of differentiation is very important in this. In reaction to thunder, Molly's being able to say to herself that thunder is really just a big loud noise, and it doesn't hurt you, permits an advance over getting into bed with her sister.

In what ways does the family, anybody in the family, promote *differentiation of self* which we see the child working at? We see it in some little girls who have an intense identification with their mother, or are resisting it—like Joanne saying, "My mother's afraid of mousies, but I'm not," or Darlene's saying, "My mommy says Jesus doesn't like bracelets, but I do." The differentiation that has been most conspicuous has been differentiation in the context of somewhat hostile separation of self from mother. But that was not true with Barbie, who was also a very differentiated child.

Are children whom we see as passive or withdrawing just "being good"? Are the children active enough at home so that the mothers don't know that the children are passive away from home? We need to explore the mother's attitude toward withdrawal or quietness. Rachel's mother was very much surprised when she saw how quiet Rachel was in a medical examination. I wonder whether some of the children in being quiet were sustained by feeling that this is being "good," and whether the parents think it's "goodness."

In addition to withdrawal and activity, there is the matter of how much limit the child puts on his or her own behavior. We saw children who pushed themselves to the brink, as well as children who gave themselves plenty of margin. Is this a family pattern, or is it just the mother's pattern to use everything that she's got? It would be important to find out whether the children who push themselves to the brink also have mothers who do.

One of our staff reported that when she called Mrs. Stevens one day, she said she was really just dead, that she was staying home to sleep. She had pushed herself too far. What happened was that she pushed herself too far in the sense of trying to meet Susan's needs at the hospital and Bee's needs at home at the same time. She would go over to the hospital at night, but be at home during the day with Bee. She let Bee stay home with a cold on Monday because she thought Bee needed some babying. She couldn't let herself say, "Well, this is an emergency for Susan, and we'll just have to make it up to Bee another time," or even *tell* Bee "We'll make it up to you another time." It was hard while Susan was away trying to balance everything for Bee. Bee would put up a fight and demand attention for herself, and her mother recognized it and felt that it was fair; she was determined not to let Bee feel gypped. Even in a crisis like this she had to try to meet the needs of both little girls.

COGNITIVE ASPECTS OF PERSONALITY

There are other qualitative aspects of cognitive orientation and coping that come from a family atmosphere or way of behaving. Most of them are included in questions about family aspiration, family stimulation to know and to understand, or support for curiosity. What are the mother's feelings about the child's curiosity? Does she welcome it or tend to curb it, and how? And how does this differ for boys and girls? We saw some girls who had it, but there were more boys who were curious. The children knew that the mothers carry the babies and they go to the doctor and to the hospital, and the doctor helps them or something like that. The mothers in our study did not think their children had curiosity about "how the baby gets in there and how it really gets out." Perhaps some children who show no curiosity about babies show their curiosity in connection with other things, which could be displacement.

INDIVIDUAL DIFFERENCES IN IDENTIFICATION PATTERNS

The quality of an infant's identification with his mother and with other people in the environment will be affected by the resources that he has developed before the time when deliberate imitation and identification emerge. Think of the baby of eight months who is able to crawl around, stand, even walk a little by herself, or hold onto furniture without special assistance from an adult; she has thereby been able to reach furniture that she has seen handled by grownups, pull out drawers and investigate the contents, get at pans and other objects in the kitchen, reach for musical instruments if there are any around the house. In these and other ways, she attempts to explore many of the areas in which she has observed adults being active.

Compare her with the baby who, though perhaps ultimately equally intelligent and equally observant, at about the age of eight months has not yet developed locomotion as did the first baby. The baby who is still sitting and perhaps even lying down much of the time has a relation with the adults dominated in the first place by vision; he watches their activities from his crib, playpen, and buggy. Second, he experiences more skin and kinesthetic contacts as he is held, walked, rocked, and in other ways handled by the adults upon whom he is still completely dependent for change from place to place. We might hypothesize that the second baby would have more fantasy and a richer emotional range. Perhaps there is even greater depth in his identification experience than that of the first baby, who is so busy doing what she has seen the grownups do that her experience is largely dominated by her actions and the consequences of them.

However, these factors cannot be considered in isolation. Other factors, such as thresholds to the quality of the environment, including voices of adults, sensitivity to facial expressions and capacities to achieve the integrations which are involved in imitations of facial expression, would be among the many also involved.

Briton and Susan were both extremely active and very much interested in getting into things and conquering the small world of their own home. During the peak of this exploratory activity, neither Briton nor Susan showed evidence of playing out fantasies as did Amy, who was much less active and did not venture about in the same way. Amy would move around from one piece of furniture to another at this age, but whenever other people were present or when she was out of her own home, she insisted on being carried by her mother. However, along with this greater closeness to her mother, she carried on much more fantasy play than did the other two at this age. Before eighteen months she even formed her own fantasy play object, folding a piece of cloth into a bundle as if it were a baby which she cradled and nursed, doing the things to her baby that her mother did with hers.

Gross differences in activity, sensory contact, and social interests are also involved in the differences between the active identification of the child who adopts the roles, attitudes, activities, and problem-solving interests of the parents as contrasted with the passive identification of children who adapt to mother's demands. Here we can note Sally's preschool active take-apart and put-together activities which came from watching her carpenter daddy; in contrast were the polite and ladylike behaviors of the little Howe girls, whose identification was with the mother's idea of what they *should* be, rather than with the activities and roles of the mother.

The pattern of identification also will be influenced by whether the child needs to identify to be safe, or to be free, strong, big, and masterful. What aspects of the adults available to him are chosen for identification will be selected by drive patterns that have matured before the identification process escalates.

SITUATIONAL VARIATIONS IN PERSONALITY EXPRESSION

Within the general personality pattern of a child we often find variations, sometimes dramatic, when we see the child in different situations. This was documented in some of the early studies of variability, such as those by McKinnon at Teachers' College, Columbia, some thirty-odd years ago (McKinnon, 1942). Also, my own records (Murphy, 1937) include a child whose ratings on cooperation, sympathy, and aggression shifted from a low level in the group to a top level when she was moved from a group where she was the youngest and the smallest, to a group in which she was at a top maturity level. Situational changes are greater or smaller depending on the range of variability available to the child. Different levels of functioning are seen as the child perceives him- or herself differently in different groups. Shifts within a range were also seen in a child whose level of sympathy or cooperation varied with the level of security or threat she experienced at different times in the same group. In other words, the kinds of behavior which occurred were functions of both objective and subjective variations in the child's relation to the group at a given time.

The same can be said of Tryon's (1939) records of changing peer appraisals of children in the older latency years. Lewin, Lippitt, and

White's (1939) records of changing levels of cooperation and aggression as children experienced different levels of autocratic or democratic leadership belong within the same category. All of these children undoubtedly had certain tendencies that remained relatively continous within these changing social situations, tendencies such as those which I reviewed related to constitutional factors, which tend to persist through different situations. When we consider the Barker, Dembo, and Lewin (1943) study, however, we see that we are not dealing with a finding of exceptionless validity. When two-thirds of the children regressed under frustration, one-third of them maintained their level and style of active, effortful functioning, oriented toward solving the problem.

PERSISTENCE AND VARIABILITY AS VARIABLES IN PERSONALITY GROWTH STYLE

The observations from this other work, as well as the work in Topeka, lead us to the *tendency toward persistence* or *variability* in the child's reactivity to changes in his relation with the environment as a possibly continous variable in child personality. In saying this we imply no value judgments at all, since certain strengths are implied on each side of this dichotomy.

Where the growth style of a child is gradual and smooth, and where both the child and his or her environment can count on a dependable pattern of response, we can see the way smoothed for consistent interactions with the environment; the mother knows what to expect, and a steady relationship can be developed. The mutually reinforced expectancies continually support integration at the level at which this dyadic stability has been achieved. (I put it this way because this level of consistency does not necessarily promote creativity even in an intelligent child, so the integration may remain at a rather simple, if deep level.)

When the growth style brings more surprises—for which the expectancies developed out of previous interaction with the environment are not prepared—there is a greater demand on both the child and the environment, especially parents, to integrate the new development into the previous relationship. If the new development is culturally appreciated, increased ease and integration may result (as with Raymond in our group). If the new development (such as prepubertal fatness, or restlessness and hyperactivity) is culturally disapproved, both the environment and the child, and their resulting interaction, are strained, so that secondary change is added to the primary, if temporary, change due to growth.

Constitutional tendencies, such as low energy or drive, or fatigability, may be accepted comfortably by the child and by his environment at certain stages. This was true of Sam during infancy and early childhood. At later stages, when the greater insistence of environmental demands in the schoolroom and the peer group bring unmanageable pressures, discouragement or even depression sets in. Sam's low drive was consistent from the age of four weeks. His twelve-year-old depression was, however, something new. That is, major shifts in the child's orientation to, and relation with, the environment may develop out of changed experience at the point where the environmental demands, formerly congruent enough with his capacities, can no longer be met. The child is not dynamically inconsistent; changed feelings have arisen in reaction to the environment's inconsistency.

The growth drive referred to by Bender (1953) and others as present even in very sick children includes some capacity for effort which we can see even in the youngest infants. A newborn baby may struggle in the process of nursing to maintain his grip on the nipple and to improve the sucking process, or he may struggle to get rid of, or shove off, the tight covers which are a nuisance to him. More obvious to the observer unaccustomed to watching babies, is the enormous effort that many slightly older babies will put into the struggle to turn over, to raise their heads or shoulders when lying prone on the floor, to reach for and try to grasp objects while the grasping capacity is still incomplete. In other words, energies intrinsic in the development of the baby's muscles find their way out through expression of such efforts to utilize the environment. This is reinforced by the interest, excitement, approval, and stimulus from the environment. But the growth drive itself is not dependent upon such stimulation.

The growth drive is as spontaneous, then, in a child as it is in a pine tree, a fern, a puppy, or any other living organism; to be alive is to have the energy to grow. At the same time, growing does not go on in a vacuum but in exchanges with and use of the environment, uses which involve struggle and coping efforts on the part of the growing organism. When we are talking about children rather than pine trees, the coping efforts include increasing potentialities of creativity which vary from one child to another, but which are just as intrinsic in normal human equipment as are the design-forming tendencies in the pine tree.

THE CONCEPT OF COPING

We have tended to carry over from biology the concept of adaptation, with its implications of fitting in, of accepting the limits imposed by the environment. Plants, and to certain extent animals, which are the object of study by the biologists, are limited in mobility and in capacity to restructure the environment. The greater the organismic mobility and the greater the cognitive resources, the greater the possibilities for restructuring and for creativity. The greater the potentiality of creativity, the less satisfactory the term adaptation seems as a description of the relation of the organism to the environment. The more active term "coping," which can include the creative restructuring possibilities of human beings as well as the more passive adaptive processes used where the environment is regarded as setting intransigent limits, would seem to be fairer to the wide range of potentialities of a growing child.

As J. E. Anderson commented at the 1957 Brussels Congress of Psychology, the longitudinal study offers an opportunity to look not only at the behavior that goes on at a given phase or stage, but also as the *transformation* that occurs between one phase and the next in the course of development. Such transformations involve the sometimes sudden reorientations of behavior after a series of steps, which can subsequently be seen as leading up to them, although they could not always be predicted.

It may be as Anderson stated that simple laws break down when confronting complex behavior; coping is one example of this complexity, which cannot be adequately explained in terms of learning. This, however, seems to us to be a further problem to be dealt with after we have adequately delineated the behavior. This is enough of a task at present. Here we are studying complex behavior in and for itself, in a way which could make it possible to look at the structures or organizations that occur within limited periods of time in the development of one sample of children.

In the presentation of the development of coping, through the records of Molly and Trudy, we often see what appear to be *sudden reorientations* in behavior; sometimes the steps leading up to these reorientations are clear, sometimes they are not. This is inevitable when our methods fall short of a complete record of a child's behavior over an extended period of time. If we wish to get sequences over a matter of months or even a few years, we have to rely upon arbitrarily chosen time intervals or upon salient episodes recorded at the time they occur, which may involve wide differences in the intervals between specific examples. In some instances, there will have been time for a considerable physiological maturation, acquisition of vocabulary, concepts, other related adjustments, values, motor resources, and new complexity of thinking and levels of integration. In such a simple change as the one we saw when Molly moved from a panicky, disorganized reaction, expressive of her terror of thunder at the age of two, to the capacity to maintain her equilibrium within some limits with the assistance of comfort from her older sister or an adult, we are dealing with an increase in capacity. This manifests itself in understanding, an increase in capacity for control, and an increase in capacity to hold onto the stimulus value of a positive, reassuring, comforting person and to use this as a supporting defense against fear of the threatening stimulus. When Molly moved, subsequently, from the stage of dependence upon comfort and support from someone else to a stage of giving herself comfort, she had become able to maintain her cognitive orientation, her complex integration of the effort to understand and the effort to keep the positive stimulation going as a support for mastery of her fear. Such a capacity, the ability to hold onto the positive-supporting-comfort-stimulus and to utilize it as a defense against the fear, is a type of maturity.

COPING AND SELF-IMAGE

From these sequences of Molly's development we see evidences of the emergence of a positive self-image as a brave, self-controlling girl who "does not cry" and who is not afraid, and who is able to *remember* that "thunder doesn't hurt you, it's only noise." The capacity to utilize the positive self-image in a stabilizing way is another product of development.

We have recognized the role of the self-image, in clinical terms, as a motivating force in social behavior, but our scientific spotlight has not been focused on the early emergence of this or the processes which contribute to its development. We do not know, for instance, whether a clear, firm, self-image which serves a controlling function in the child's effort to master disintegrative feelings, is itself a reflection of the forcefulness, energy, autonomy, and decisiveness characteristic of a child with strong drives as Molly had. Some believe it is a function of the way in which the child has been handled, the degree of self-consciousness that has been induced, and the clarity and positiveness of the self-image that has resulted from things that adults have said to the child. Or it may be a product of conflict between different concepts of the self to which the child has been exposed, and which are resolved with effort in a way that contributes more vividness and force and influencing power to the self-image itself.

SEQUENCES IN THE ACHIEVEMENT OF COMPETENCIES

When we look at the development of children during the first ten years of life, we find individual differences in the sequence of areas with which the child can cope both easily and with satisfaction to those in the world around him. We recognize that the development and coping problems of every child are greatly influenced by certain *universal* sequences: the dominance of feeding and oral needs during the period of most rapid growth in infancy, especially in the first six to eight months; followed by the dominance of motor drives, conflicts created by activity needs of the child, by new sensitivities and differentiations of people and by new possibilities of sphincter control; and problems dominated by sexual awareness and sexual impulses along with increasing interaction with peers, siblings, and changing relation with parents. But each child has his or her own early pattern of sequences in changing of these interests as his or her maturational pattern brings new possibilities of activity, interest, mastery, and problems connected with these. At the simplest level, we see Trudy changing from an early predominant interest in things, to a later interest in, and sensitivity to people; Kim changed from predominantly passive, sensory interests before the period of active motor development, to vigorous, active, masculine interest from the second year of life on.

I think of stages as follows: *At any time that structures have matured to a point which makes the behavior possible, the appearance of the behavior will depend upon the inner state—that is, the motivation, together with the experienced demand or opportunity of the environment.* A child might develop motor coordination, which would make it possible for him to get to the stage of preoccupation with a bicycle; but whether or not he actually showed this type of stage-connected behavior would depend upon whether or not he was in an area where children had bicycles and whether he had one himself. The relation between the degree of *mastery potential* available to the child, in terms of maturation and the timing of the environmental opportunity, would have much to do with the tempo of moving through a stage. This includes beginning an activity, then mastering it, and then becoming less interested in it in favor of interest in new activities which still remain to be mastered.

THE CONCEPT OF STAGES IN RELATION TO THE DEVELOPMENT OF COPING ASPECTS OF PERSONALITY

Since we have longitudinal data, we are committed to studying sequences in development; to many minds this implies stages. But we need to look at the concept of stages in relation to this type of material rather critically. It seems much easier to see clear-cut stages of skeletal, motor, and cognitive development than it is within a social and coping framework. Skeletal, motor, and cognitive development lend themselves to the analysis of sequences from global, to differentiating, to integrative stages on the one hand; or to initial confusion, the development of partial clarities, and achievement of insight on the other hand. Early social responsiveness and coping initiative can be documented in the infants; changes are the outcome of experience, not just genetically controlled growth stages.

In our material, we are constantly being impressed by certain continuities; some of them are apparently structurally or constitutionally determined and express themselves in different ways as the child gets older. Others are heavily influenced by continuities in parent-child ineraction from infancy on. These continuities are in contrast to changes that result from shifts in the transactions of the child with his or her surroundings, as the relationships between the parents change, or the relationship between parents and the child change, and so on. They affect the patterning of the child's behavior within the "stages" brought about by development.

Stages can also be seen where we are dealing with relatively clear cultural demands. The child may be unaware of these and ignore them at first. In one case, he or she begins to accept partially or in piecemeal fashion; in another, he or she fights before finally coming to terms with the patterns in the way in which he or she can use them and integrate them into his or her approach to problems. In such cases, the stages will be different for different children, depending upon their ways of struggling and coming to terms with the demands from the external world.

Other stages may be apparent but are actually secondary to stages in motor, cognitive, or drive development and their interaction. Because of the specific patterns of interaction in these aspects of development, the specific manifestation will, therefore, be different for different children, as these interactions are shaped by differing capacities, cathexes, and experiences.

Thus, we would expect to find limits in the extent to which we could talk about stages of realism, or of affective development, or use of fantasy. The contribution of the culture, the family life and the temperament of the child each would be large in modifying the characteristics of the stage.

Similarly, the degree to which the child's coping style fitted the demands of the culture would have an influence on the tendency of the child to progress toward increasing coping capacity. For instance, Taddy didn't fit the nursery school culture pattern at age four, when her puzzle interests were at odds with the social demands of the teacher. Later, she began to expand socially as her intellectual capacities were appreciated in school, along with other qualities.

CHANGES IN COPING ORIENTATION

When we analyse the changes in coping orientation, we can see the following basic contributing factors:

First, a major change in the hierarchy of systems which can appear in some children who relinquish old interests as new resources become available. For instance, with certain children strong motor drive emerges most clearly as the child develops a capacity for locomotion and the motor interest displaces oral preoccupations. A similar result can occur when blocks in functioning are removed.

Second, changes may be caused by shifts or distortions, which are most likely to arise during a critical phase in the development of a new function. For example, when Arthur was frightened by a loud fog-horn on an ocean-liner just at the age of two, when language was increasing rapidly, he developed a stammer.

Third, changes may be the result of extreme affect pressure, such as anxiety or conflict in a disturbing, dynamic, interpersonal context, or major frustrations that restructure the need system of the child and the ways of dealing with his needs.

Another type of change may occur when the child is confronted with the experience of overwhelming social pressure in starting school, when coping approaches that have been useful up to this time become forbidden. A talented child who has used verbal communication to an unusual degree and finds himself in a schoolroom, where she is forbidden to talk or whisper to other children or even to speak to the teacher without going through the ritual of raising her hand and getting permission—which is not always granted—would be in such a predicament. When there is an unresolvable conflict between a deeply rooted coping approach of this sort and the rigid limits of the social situation, symptoms may appear which were not apparent in the previous situations in which the child has been seen.

INDIVIDUAL DIFFERENCES IN CHANGE

Our discussion up to this point suggests that we ought to try to find out why some children change more than others. This calls for a study of the *range of variability* when the child is seen in infancy, as compared with the range of change over a longer period of time, for instance from two or three to seven or eight. One question would be whether the child who shows a wide range of variability when observed in a fairly limited situation is also more apt to show wide changes over a long period of time. Does he have an intrinsic elasticity which shows itself at both points?

The question of why some children change more than others must also take into account differences in the depth, intensity, number of important, disturbing, or otherwise stimulating experiences to the child, and differences in gross changes in the environmental situation of the child. We offer the interactive hypothesis that the child with a relatively low degree of elasticity whose first six years were relatively free from major disturbing experiences or trauma and also whose life situation was free from major changes in his most important relationships is less likely to change than are children who were more elastic initially, and/or were exposed to more external changes. In this connection, certain children seemed to us to be almost unrecognizably different at the prepuberty stage from what they were when we first saw them. The children for whom Escalona made the best predictions (p. 170–171) could be assumed to have less tendency to change in basic ways or were subjected to less dramatic environmental influences.

Irrespective of individual differences, the culture too plays a role; children will change in certain ways typical of personality development in this culture; the child who clings to a personality pattern at the expense of not being able to make the expected changes runs into difficulties. In other words, we have to think of a certain optimal amount of change in this culture in terms of the kinds of demands it makes on the children as they develop.

STAGES AS COMPARED WITH LIFE-STYLE

New stages may be initiated by way of a number of different pathways: by the maturation of structure and the possibilities made available for practice in, and mastery of, new functions; or, sometimes after this, by new opportunities not previously available or offered by the environment; or by systematic and consistent presentation of new demands by the environment, as when a child goes to school, provided he or she is structurally ready for the demands which are being made.

New stages following or concomitant with maturation of structures may be characterized either by predominant concern with one functional area, such as mastery of locomotion, or by a combination of functional areas, as when mastery of locomotion goes hand in hand with mastery of speech (in some children, one comes first and the other later; in other children the two seem to go in parallel). Or, in a different way still, it can be seen when a group of new functions have been mastered and the child is now free for a stage made possible by the integrations emerging from this mastery. For instance, after locomotion is mastered and after speech is mastered at the age of four years, the child is free for a level of fantasy and emotional play that was not possible when his or her energies were being focused on the process of mastering locomotion and speech. This freeing of cathexis or emotional energy around the age of four, when the exciting problems of motility and speech have been pretty well met, may be a major factor in the development of the "first adolescence" or "oedipal phase," when the child is emotionally involved in relationships with like-sexed and opposite-sexed parents. In fact, this emotional involvement may be stimulated in part by the child's feeling of competence and bigness, following on the fact that he or she can now talk like a big person and do so many of the things that big people can do. He may be stimulated by a kind of pseudo-grownupness, that phase which is familiar to us with adolescents who have suddenly become as tall as their parents, and who are intensely stimulated toward feelings of independence and the desire for grownup experience and freedom by their new equality in stature.

PERSISTENCE OF COPING ORIENTATION IN RELATION TO CHANGE IN STAGES OF DEVELOPMENT

We saw earlier (Tables 1–3) that some areas of functioning were better predicted by Escalona than others, implying that there is more continuity in certain areas while others are more likely to change as an outcome of interaction with a changing environment. This leads us to consider continuity in relation to change accompanying developmental stage sequences.

Baby Vernon showed a strong striving to cognitive mastery that was congruent with a later I.Q. of 140. This striving was but a part of a stable hierarchy of systems in which motor skill emerged later as a positive resource, without displacing the drive toward cognitive mastery. The latter included a tendency toward delay in the service of clarification. The total pattern of cognitive and motor precision was supported by the father's precision as a carpenter. In Vernon's case, as with Taddy, a drive toward cognitive and motor mastery with the accompanying delay went along with a slower development of social ease and social techniques. Vernon had a sensitive expressiveness and directness at the rare times when he confided his feelings. This total pattern was characteristic throughout the entire period we knew him. His coping, in the sense of meeting social expectations for participation and spontaneity, was not good in group settings. However, there was no evidence that Vernon was overwhelmed or affectively flooded; when he was able to choose his own terms and select that part of the situation in which he felt completely at home, he could be spontaneous.

With Susan there was a strong continuity of affective responsiveness and social interest. At the age of seven months when she was seen in infancy, her mother handled upsets or expressions of discomfort first by comforting her daughter and then if this failed, by laughing with her and trying to substitute laughter for crying. There was an invitation to imitate and identify or introject this pattern, which was seen at a phase already known to be a sensitive one for identification. We may infer then that maximization of identification at a critical phase would tend to promote internalization of coping patterns offered by the mother at this time. In this case, the pattern was one of substitution of a positive affect for the negative affect; it involved denial and repression, also, in the process of substitution. This was a major coping approach which carried Susan through a severe (later) experience of polio.

So far we have given illustrations of, first, constitutional tendencies maximized by support from the parents, and, second, further maximization by special stimulation during the developmentally "sensitive" or "critical" phase. Another process may be illustrated by Patsy, who had a strong need for tactual experience and contact. Her otherwise "good mother" tended to give reassurance from a distance rather than through physical contact and comfort. Thus distance receptors were maximized as substitutes for tactual contact and came to be used intensively by Patsy. This did not compensate for nor meet her need for physical contact, which continued. The end result was an overdevelopment of visual and auditory perceptiveness—that is, sensitivity in these areas, along with the persistence of oral and contact needs. In addition we saw a strong development of fantasy, which may be assumed to have resulted from the deprivation combined with inadequate gratification from the substitutes. Here, then, we see constitutional tendencies which were deprived and led to persistent or exaggerated needs. These were accompanied by compensatory solutions which were strong, but did not completely relieve the need and thus left the child sensitive and vulnerable.

In other instances we find that critical phase experiences are the predominant factor in determining direction of the coping orientation. In the case of Rachel, whose activity was average during early infancy, we saw the impact of a particular set of experiences at the period when motility and language were at a peak of development—that is, between the age of ten and twenty months. During this time she was exposed to an almost total blocking of motility due to the wrappings and immobilization in a crib necessary to protect her from infections during a severe infantile eczema. This was combined, of course, with much physical care, including skin contact, use of ointments, and so forth, which offered positive gratification. It is not surprising to find a relative failure of development of autonomous motor initiative under these circumstances. The expectation was that things would be done to her and the implication was that her role was to wait and to delay in the service of being guided or taken care of. We can assume that a child with more vigorous motor drive might have reacted differently to this experience; the physical care offered during the immobilization might then be experienced as a less adequate substitute for motor freedom. The essential point here is the importance of the developmental critical phase in determining outcome and direction of coping orientation, even when the system under consideration is not at the top of the hierarchy for the individual child.

Finally, we can use the case of Brennie to illustrate the persistence of the coping orientation for a long time when it is strongly rooted in a dynamic configuration. In this case, the arrival of a premature baby brother when Brennie was thirteen months old placed severe restrictions on Brennie's activity. This occurred at a critical period of expanding motility, when this activity involved expression of impulses and feelings toward the delicate little brother who needed special care and attention and preoccupied the family for a considerable period of time. Brennie's vigorous approaches to his baby brother were firmly stopped. The compromises, the high tension level and the repression which developed in this context led to patterns of conflict which continued through Brennie's childhood.

At the same time Brennie was one of the most imaginative and creative children in our Topeka study when observed with projective tests. When we consider this along with the fact that at least three of our high achievers in adolescence and college years had been vulnerable babies, we are led to reflect on the positive contributions to personality development of the combination of challenge, even frustration, with high drive and basic family support. Early on we spoke of the contribution to maturation of even the young baby's own efforts. With the positive response to frustration, along with challenge, we see a further dimension in the range of forces contributing to personality.

THE INTERACTION OF STRUCTURE AND PROCESS

Our understanding of stages of development is likely to be confused when we focus upon continuity of individual style and, similarly, our understanding of the role and extent of influence of individual style is likely to be threatened by a preoccupation with successive stages of development.

The influence of a certain stage is apt to dominate our thinking when we are dealing with *groups* of children seen at a given stage, especially when we ourselves are preoccupied with a certain learning problem typical of the stage in question (for instance, when we are dealing with a group of children learning to read or beginning to understand arithmetic or learning to ride a bicycle). For all new learnings and developments, as Piaget and Inhelder (1969) point out, there is a stage of confusion and incomplete mastery which yields to increasing clarification and integration. This process occurs at differing rates and even with different sequences for different children. However, when we put children into experimental situations where certain behavior is explicitly demanded, the differences between the children may be minimized. Only when the situation itself permits spontaneity of attack on the problem is it possible to do justice to the individual style of each child. Thus in school situations where we have an opportunity to observe small classes we see individual differences in motive and approach to even the most standard and familiar activities. Each child's style is expressed in his mode of coping with the new problem or new demand.

It is certainly true, in line with Barker and Wright's (1954) studies of the influence of settings on behavior, that each setting provides a certain range or set of limits to the behavior which is possible for a child, and certain directions in which behavior is most likely to go. At the same time, whether the child is at Sunday school or in a drugstore, at a party or taking intelligence tests, sitting in a class of fifty children in a schoolroom or going out for recess, he or she is still him- or herself, and his or her behavior occurs within a characteristic and available range of tempo, integration, use of observation, motor restlessness, or initiative.

Part of the child's individuality includes the degree of *elasticity* which determines the extent to which his behavior will be influenced by the setting or the demands of the individual situation, as compared to the extent to which he or she must behave in certain ways regardless of where he or she is. At one extreme, sick children are considered sick or maladjusted partly because of lack of the elasticity which permits sufficient modification of their behavior in response to the varying demands of different situations. A flexible child with strong motor drive may confine her motor activity in church or Sunday school to relatively small dimensions which will not be too disturbing to others, where a sick child, who has difficulties in impulse control, may not be able to control his scope of activity at all and becomes a disturbance in Sunday school or other large group situations where motility is severely restricted. Coping capacity thus implies some degree of elasticity. However, elasticity to the point of fluidity, implying lack of firm character structure and stable guidelines, is more likely to be found in a very dependent child or a psychopathic personality with no consistent inner direction.

THE NATURE OF PROCESS OF PERSONALITY DEVELOPMENT

Process may thus be seen as continuation through time of behavior which has aspects both of continuity and of change. When we are doing a chemical experiment and watch the gradually changing color of the liquid that emerges as we put one liquid into another, we speak of watching the process of change; or we watch cell division through a microscope and can see at first the gradual enlargement of the single cell, then the gradual bulging of two parts and the gradual pulling apart of the two halves. Thus marked off, we speak of watching the process of division. The process goes on without interruption. It is only in our observations that we verbalize recognizably different gestalts, as they emerge in the course of the process.

These recognizably different gestalts, if described separately, represent then, steps or points during the process. When we are watching the development of the behavior of a child, the steps have to be sufficiently close together structurally and functionally for continuity to be apparent, and for the changes to be seen in relation to the continuity. Otherwise, the changes appear as differences which may not be recognized as part of a continuity and therefore are not appreciated as steps in a process.

Continuity may be provided by the setting or the stimulus, or it may be provided by the behavior of the child him- or herself. Thus when we study Molly's reactions to thunder, we talk about the process of change in her reactions to thunder because the thunder stimulus itself remains more or less the same. This provides the continuity in the light of which we can look at the successively different ways in which she copes with her fear of the thunder, and also the successive changes and diminutions in the fear itself with the help of her coping methods. Similarly, when we observe children exposed to intelligence tests or miniature life toys or other comparable stimulus situations, we speak of the process of development of change of ways of coping, because the stimulus situation provides continuity of a frame of reference.

Even where situations are different, however, we may speak of process in terms of the recognizable continuity of the child in whom we are at the same time watching changes. For instance, Janice appeared in many different situations to be rather detached or lacking the kind of warm emotional responses that many other children showed at the age of four and five. Later in certain situations, she showed more warmth and contact with the experimenter. Thus without comparing the situations themselves too closely, we refer to a process of development of greater warmth in this child.

DIRECTION OF DEVELOPMENT

In connection with the study of the total sweep of longitudinal sequence in all our records of each child, we can arrive at groupings according to the *direction of development.*

One group would be the progressive[3] group: children who develop increasing scope and increasing capacity to overcome difficulties. This would include both children who are effective in handling difficulties from a very early time, such as Molly, and also children like Donald who were immobilized in certain situations at certain periods, then became very active later on. The important thing is that regardless of ups and downs or temporary limitations of the child, the "progressive" child continues to grow and make progress and to show increasing capacity to

---

[3]See Lester's (1945) unpublished analysis of college students.

cope with a wider range of situations, while maintaining his or her own inner integration.

A static group consists of those like Daryl whose methods are limited and stay more or less limited in comparison with those of her peers. This group includes children who are always playing safe or always sticking to patterns of a conventional and proper sort, and do not give themselves leeway to try out new ways, or extend the range of situations which they can utilize.

A defensive group would include children who handle certain kinds of problems very well, but whose reaction to stress includes a high degree of hiding (like Martin), or other devices and approaches which do not succeed in dealing with the problem or meeting the child's needs. In certain cases this could be forced by circumstances, as with Susan in the hospital; but in her case, the defensiveness is necessary in certain areas and actually has the effect of preserving the possibility of being progressive in other areas.

Another group would include those who, within our period of observation, progressed for a period, then lost ground—usually because of extreme external pressures and family stress—but who later recovered their earlier strengths.

An unresolved group includes children who seem unformed and have neither developed nor excluded the possibility of developing definite coping styles. It appears that children whose coping orientations exclude trial and error, exploration, and comfort, or satisfying refuge devices, tend to lack the possibility for progressive development or increasing the breadth of their coping resources. In other words, different combinations of coping orientations go along with different developmental directions.

CONCLUDING REMARKS

I have reviewed some of our observations of individual personality development and change in childhood without reference to recent theoretical formulations. An adequate discussion of these would need another chapter or a book. David Freedman's brilliant paper, "The sensory deprivations," (1979) includes a basic formulation of processes of development which I believe underlie the patterns I have described. He states that relatively independent, gene-determined maturational processes are going on simultaneously in disparate regions of the nervous system. He continues, "How they will be expressed in psychic structures and functions is dependent on the ambiance in which they emerge," following Spemann (1938). He adds that the whole organism's maturation when the individual is placed in a given environment also influences the expression of specific epigenetic processes. This is in effect a refinement of Gardner Murphy's (1947) field theory which in turn was influenced by Murray's concept of the interaction of needs and the press of the environment. Murphy emphasized that the environment offers opportunities and rewards, challenges and models, in addition to the demands and frustrations implied in press. Wide individual differences in both organisms and in environments are assumed here, and in fact Murphy illustrated them with examples from anthropology and different geographical settings.

What does not emerge in these formulations is the role of the infant and young child's autonomous efforts and initiative in these interactions. A two-month-old baby cannot grasp a visible object unless he tries to reach it; later he struggles to sit up so that he can see a wider range of the environment; a little later the baby experiments with throwing things—if the initiative is there. There are wide differences in autonomy and initiative in the first year of life and these are not purely a matter of issues or of opportunities offered by the environment, but rather of complex psychological development only vaguely understood in terms of precursors of the self and its psychological relation to the environment. The degree and quality of psychic activity is not merely an expression of physical energy. Without a sufficiently directed use of available energy, nothing much will happen. Much more work needs to be done to clarify the contribution of the child's own effort—its relation to the child's perception of self and the world—to the pattern of continuity and change in personality development.

A child who was extremely shy in her early years said to me later, "When I was ten years old I decided not to be shy any more." Molly could not seek and gain protection from the threat she felt from thunder without a psychically active approach. She might have cried and screamed or froze in terror. Instead, she just sought comfort, and later was able to cognitively master it. This is an active ego effort.

REFERENCES

Anderson, J. E. Unpublished comments, International Congress of Psychology. Brussels, Belgium, 1957.

Barker, R. G., T. Dembo, and K. Lewin. Frustration and regression: an experiment with children. *University of Iowa Studies: Studies in Child Welfare*, 1943, **18**, No. 1.

Barker, R. G. and H. F. Wright. *Midwest and its Children: The Psychological American Town*. Evanston, IL: Row Peterson, 1954.

Bayley, N. Consistency and variability in the growth of intelligence from birth to eighteen years. *Journal of Genetic Psychology,* 1949, **75,** 165–196.

Bender, L. Childhood schizophrenia. *Psychiatric Quarterly,* 1953, **27,** 663–681.

Bernfeld, S. *The Psychology of the Infant.* New York: Brentano's, 1929.

Bowlby, J. The nature of the child's tie to his mother. *International Journal of Psychoanalysis,* 1958, **34** (5), 1–23.

Brody, S. *Patterns of Mothering.* New York: International University Press, 1956.

Escalona, S. Emotional development in the first year of life. In *Problems of Infancy and Childhood.* Transactions of the Sixth Conference. New York: Josiah Macy, Jr. Foundation, 1952.

Escalona, S. *Roots of Individuality: Normal Patterns of Development in Infancy.* Chicago: Aldine, 1968.

Escalona, S. and G. M. Heider. *Prediction and Outcome: A Study in Child Development.* New York: Basic Books, 1959.

Escalona, S. K., M. Leitch, et al. Early phases of personality development: A non-normative study of infant behavior. *Monograph, Society for Research in Child Development,* 1952, **17** (1), Serial Number 54.

Freedman, D. A. The sensory deprivations. *Bulletin of the Menninger Clinic,* 1979, **43** (1), 29–68.

Freud, S. *Group Psychology and the Analysis of the Ego,* standard ed., Vol. 18. London: Hogarth, 1921.

Freud, S. *Ego and the Id,* standard ed., Vol. 19. London: Hogarth, 1923.

Fries, M. and P. J. Woolf. Some hypotheses on the role of the congenital activity type in personality development. *Psychoanalytic Study of the Child,* 1953, **8,** 48–62.

Gesell, A. and L. B. Ames. Early evidences of individuality in the human infant. *Scientific Monthly,* 1937, **45,** 217–225.

Gesell, A., B. M. Castner, H. Thompson, and C. S. Amatruda. *Biographies of child development: The mental growth careers of eighty-four infants and children.* New York: Hoeber, 1919.

Gordon, I. *Baby learnings through baby play.* New York: St. Martin's Press, 1970.

Gordon, I. Letter in *Human Nature,* 1978, **1** (10), 96.

Heider, G. M. Vulnerability in infants and young children: A pilot study. *Genetic Psychology Monographs,* 1966, **73** (1), 1–216.

Horowitz, R. and L. B. Murphy. Projective methods in the psychological study of children. *Journal of Experimental Education,* 1938, **7,** 133–140.

Isaacs, S. *Social Development in Young Children.* New York: Harcourt, 1933.

Klein, M. *The Psychoanalysis of Children.* New York: Norton, 1932.

Lerner, E. and L. B. Murphy (Eds.) Methods for the study of personality in young children. *Monograph, Society for Research in Child Development,* 1941, **6** (4).

Lester, M. Unpublished manuscript, 1945.

Levy, D. M. *Maternal Overprotection*, New York: Norton, 1943; 2nd ed., 1966.

Lewin, K., R. Lippitt, and R. K. White. Patterns of aggressive behavior in experimentally created "social climates." *Journal of Social Psychology*, 1939, **10**, 271–299.

Macfarlane, J. W. From infancy to adulthood. *Childhood Education*, 1963, **39**, 336–342.

McKinnon, K. M. Consistency and change in behavior manifestations as observed in a group of sixteen children over a five-year period. New York: Bureau of Publications, Teachers College, 1942.

Moriarty, A. E. *Constancy and I.Q. Change: A Clinical View of Relationships between Tested Intelligence and Personality*. Springfield, IL: Thomas, 1966.

Murphy, G. *Personality: A Biosocial Approach to Origins and Structure*. New York: Basic Books, 1947.

Murphy, G., L. B. Murphy, and T. M. Newcomb. *Experimental Social Psychology*, 2nd ed. New York: Harper, 1937.

Murphy, L. B. *Social Behavior and Child Personality*. New York: Columbia University Press, 1937.

Murphy, L. B. *Methods for the Study of Personality in Young Children*. Volume 1. New York: Basic Books, 1962.

Murphy, L. B. (Ed.). *The Widening World of Childhood: Paths Toward Mastery*. New York: Basic Books, 1962.

Murphy, L. B. Some aspects of the first relationship. *International Journal of Psychoanalysis*, 1964, **45**, 31–94.

Murphy, L. B. and A. E. Moriarty. *Vulnerability, Coping and Growth*. New Haven, CT: Yale University Press, 1976.

Murray, H. A. *Explorations in Personality*. New York: Oxford University Press, 1938.

Piaget, J. *Origins of intelligence*. New York: International University Press, 1952.

Piaget, J. & B. Inhelder. *The psychology of the child*. New York: Basic Books, 1969.

Rheingold, H. L. and C. O. Eckerman. The infant's free entry into a new environment. *Journal of Experimental Child Psychology*, 1969, **8**, 271–283.

Rorschach, H. *Psychodiagnostik*. Bern, Switzerland: H. Huber, 1921.

Shirley, M. *The First Two Years of Life*. New York: John Day, 1930.

Sontag, L. W. and R. F. Wallace. The movement response of the human fetus to sound stimuli. *Child Development*, 1935, **6**, 235–258.

Spemann, H. *Embryonic Development and Induction*. New Haven, CT: Yale University Press, 1938.

Spitz, R. Anaclitic depression. *Psychoanalytic Study of the Child*, 1946, **2**.

Sroufe, L. A. Attachment and the roots of competence. *Human Nature,* 1978, **1** (10), 50–51.

Stone, L. J., H. Smith, and L. B. Murphy. *The Competent Infant.* New York: Basic Books, 1973.

Tryon, C. M. Evaluation of adolescent personality by adolescents. *Monographs of Social Research on Child Development,* 1939, **4** (4).

Washburn, R. W. A study of the smiling and laughing of infants in the first year of life. *Genetic Psychology Monographs,* 1929, **6** (5), 397–535.

White, R. W. Motivation reconsidered: The concept of competence. *Psychological Review,* 1959, **66,** 297–333.

Woolf, P. The causes, controls, and organization of behavior in the behavior of the neonate. *Psychological Issues,* 1966, **5** (1), 1–105 (Monograph No. 17).

CHAPTER 7

Children under Stress: Perspectives on Antecedents and Correlates of Vulnerability and Resistance to Psychopathology

Norman Garmezy

INTRODUCTION

This volume which honors one of psychology's truly major figures, Professor Henry Murray, takes as its theme a series of new *Explorations In Personality*—forty years after the appearance of Murray's seminal volume (1938). In this portion of the volume, as in the symposium that preceded its publication, a creative developmental psychologist who has pioneered the study of stress and coping in young children and an experimental psychopathologist who had originally been assigned the task of discussing maladaptation of personality have been paired. But to emphasize *failures* of coping seemed a most downbeat way of reflecting on the great contributions of Professor Murray.

And so this chapter was reshaped to present two areas of research—one focused on children at risk for psychopathology and the second on children seemingly resistant to the negative consequences of stress. The first area—the study of vulnerable children—has occupied our research group at Minnesota over the past decade. In these investigations the emphasis has been on children at risk for subsequent psychopathology. These studies reflect a natural continuation of prior years of research on deficient functioning of schizophrenic adults—studies in which conditions of laboratory stress were presumed to reflect analogues of possible antecedent events in the lives of patients (Garmezy, 1973). From this nondevelopmental approach (with its weak inferences about developmental continuities) there evolved in natural progression an effort to study, at an earlier period of life, children who appeared to have a greater proneness for psychological disability in later life—a proneness which could, perhaps, anticipate a range of severity of maladaptation extending from overt schizophrenia at one end of the spectrum of psychopathology to more benign forms of maladjustment at the other. At least that appeared initially to be the potential spectrum of risk. It was only after twelve years of research by our Minnesota group and the happy circumstance of having been invited to chronicle the development of studies of risk-for-schizophrenia in laboratories in this country and abroad (Garmezy and Streitman, 1974) that it became apparent that there was not only a range of maladaptation, but that there existed a substantial number of adaptive children for whom more positive outcomes in later life could be anticipated. This finding has led our group to a new set of studies of these intriguing groups of "invulnerable" or stress-resistant children. It is this more positive note that I will introduce in the latter part of the chapter, thus disposing of the implication that failure-proneness is an inevitable accompaniment of children who are at risk.

To those familiar with the range of Dr. Murray's contributions to psychological science, it should be evident that the impetus for much of the research on stress, coping, and stress-resistance has been derived from the work of that extraordinary pool of professional talent that was assembled during World War II in Washington DC and Fairfax, Virginia (with branch offices in Ceylon, China, and India) to undertake the enormous task of selecting agents for the wartime Office of Strategic Services. Their task was to select persons capable of gathering "strategic information concerning the activities and vulnerabilities of the nation's enemies, to analyze and evaluate this information, and to report it to those concerned." On a different plane of activity was the selection of others who were "to conduct a multiplicity of destructure operations behind enemy lines, to aid and train resistance groups, and, by radio, pamphlets, and other means, to disintegrate the morale of enemy troops and encourage the forces of the underground" (OSS, 1948, p. 10).

The psychologists of World War I vintage had sparked the growth and development of intellectual assessment. In World War II psychologists brought new dimensions to the study of personality attributes; behavioral manifestations under situational trauma were measured by new types of situational tests, systematic observations of molar behavior, and intensive interviews. The goal of these distinguished clinical and experimental investigators was to relate such measures to critically important outcome variables. The predictive validity of these new methods of stress arousal, with their attendant clinical judgements of performance under unique task demands, involved the lives of thousands, perhaps millions of soldiers and innocent civilians. Here indeed was a test for psychological science; that it was well met is the ultimate tribute to Dr. Murray and his wartime colleagues.

VULNERABLE ADULTS AND CHILDREN

The nature of vulnerability and risk has its own vital history to commend it. Since we have been restrospecting about World War II let me cite for a moment the many studies of combat fatigue and exhaustion, those traumatic neuroses of battle, that were conducted during World War II in an effort to trace possible developmental or life-span antecedents to these large scale psychiatric losses. When Eliot Slater, Britain's famed psychiatric geneticist, studied the backgrounds of British military personnel who underwent the stress of combat he reported a "monotonous uniformity" to the basic personalities of these men. The psychiatric casualties tended to be "worriers"—pessimistic, moody, sexually inhibited and inadequate men. (Slater, 1943). In more than half of a group of 2,037 soldiers admitted to psychiatric wards over a 20-month span, he found a family history of psychiatric disturbance in first-degree relatives, one-fourth of the patients had had a previous history of breakdown, and more than 40% revealed abnormalities in earlier personality development. Poor home environments (poverty, alcoholism, fighting) appeared in 21% of the cases, and poor relationships with the father existed in 15.6% of the cases. Slater divided his group into those whose levels of stress exposure prior to breakdown were severe, moderate, or minor. Those who broke under a relatively minor degree of stress showed the strongest degree of predisposing elements and poor outcomes subsequently. Those who broke under severe combat stress gave less indications of strong predispositional qualities and had more positive outcomes.

Slater could have been describing a large part of the literature of prognosis in schizophrenia for here too one can correlate manifest personal competence prior to breakdown, reduced prevalence of mental disorder in family members, and acute onset under the press of an identifiable stressor with relatively brief periods of psychosis usually followed by recovery from disorder. This is the group of the so-called "reactive" cases. Contrasted with this group are those cases of true or process schizophrenia which are marked by premorbid patterns of incompetence, heightened incidence of the disorder in family members, insidious onset often without an evident stressor and subsequent chronicity of disorder with attendant rehospitalizations. (Garmezy, 1970; Kantor and Herron, 1966; Stephens, 1978; Strauss et al. 1977; Vaillant, 1978). The atypicality of the first group is such that one finds these types of "schizophreniform" disorders now excluded from the classification of schizophrenia in the draft version of the DSM III. (American Psychiatric Association, 1979).

What Slater and others attempted for the traumatic neuroses of war, students of schizophrenia had done for decades, namely to gather data retrospectively in order to derive correlations of factors linked to developmental attributes of those individuals marked by behavior pathology. If we consider the two great orientations to research into mental disorder—the structural as exemplified by Kraepelin and the developmental with Freud as its great progenitor—we note that both men used the contemporary status of the adult patient to render their clinical judgements. But where Kraepelin studied the patient's attributes in the present, which led him to create a descriptive psychiatric nosology, Freud looked at life history factors (more than personality attributes) in the past and was led to his creation of a dynamic psychiatry. Only as we have added to our literature multiple studies of the process and limitations of retrospection have we become aware of the error variance such a method tends to generate. One need only contemplate Freud's experience in which a succession of reports of incest experiences by his young Viennese patients led him initially to a belief in their reliability until the apparent base rate forced his retreat into a theoretical reconstruction of the motivating power of fantasy in such clinical accounts.

The undoing of retrospective error lies in developmental research. A masterful clinical-developmental psychologist such as Lois Murphy observes children at work and play, studies their coping efforts and uses her observations to create volumes whose titles depict the subject matter: *The Widening World of Childhood* (1962) and *Vulnerability, Coping and Growth* (Murphy and Moriarity, 1976). By contrast, one can survey the more dismal picture provided by tradition-bound clinicians whose adherence to retrospective inquiry has provided us with erroneous one-sided views of the early lives of schizophrenic patients which could well earn the sobriquet, *The Narrowing World of Childhood*.

Sometime ago in presenting the Frieda Fromm Reichmann lecture (Garmezy, 1977a) to the Washington School of Psychiatry I looked back to the era of the so-called "schizophrenogenic" mother. That harpy was so predatory in behavior instigated with less than innocent intent that she fulfilled the image of classical mythology (a woman's head with the body and claws of a vulture, acting as the instrument of a divine vengeance). Here was an era marked by the view of the mother as a potent instigator of psychosis, of a belief that the family can will one of its members to be ill and woe betide the victim who refuses victimization lest a sibling be chosen to take his or her place.

This era, which has been replaced by a more rational accounting of schizophrenic disorder based upon genetic and biochemical factors that are joined in (as yet) unspecified ways to complex, interactive environmental forces, was marked by a powerful belief in the mother's etiological role. Yet those most closely touched by the disorder, the parents, were presumed capable of serving as the most reliable observers of the early years of the disordered family member. Alternatively, reports of early family interactions were accepted as veridical that were obtained through the recitals of the hospitalized offspring or his or her siblings. The curious twin element in this formulation was that first, a distinguished core of psychoanalysts, no strangers to the distortions produced by defense, could accept such a limited proposition so readily, and second, that an equally distinguished core of developmentally minded psychologists could allow it to happen. The answer lacks a malignant component. The simple fact is that neither developmental psychology nor clinical psychiatry were yet ready to set forth an equally, if not more tenable hypothesis of the potential reactivity of parents to their offspring. (Leff, 1976; Lewis and Rosenblum, 1974; Vaughn and Leff, 1976; Brown, Birley, and Wing, 1972). That awareness of the possibility that parental behavior can be conditioned by the early prodromal signs of disorder in a child came surprisingly late (Bell, 1968). And so the decision suggested in certain quarters was that the effects of socialization in the etiology of schizophrenia were unidirectional: parents were the influencing agents; children the tabula rasa.

On this basis countless innocent parents were themselves labeled and stigmatized by an errant psychiatry that, trapped within its own historical methodology, lacked an orientation to true rather than reflected childhood and lacked as well the necessary developmental data on samples of children considered to be predisposed to schizophrenia. This can be viewed as scientific error, but one that warrants some ethical weighting. In the 1930s and 1940s—at the same time that the "schizophrenogenic mother" was getting her start in the scientific life, there were many false hopes that filled a biological literature devoted to the pathogenesis and pathology of schizophrenia. These descriptive statements were also scientifically inaccurate but they had the redemptive quality of not assigning blame for mental disorder of unknown etiology to other family members who had to live their lives under the mistaken assumption that they might be guilty of inducing schizophrenia in their offspring.

Realities such as these brought the study of risk factors in schizophrenia to the forefront and it is this change in orientation that owes so much to early investigators such as Barbara Fish, Sarnoff Mednick and Fini Schulsinger, and others (Garmezy, 1974; Wynne, Cromwell, and Matthysse, 1978). Fish (1957) provided (and still provides) a longitudinal study of a highly selected but small sample of infants born to schizophrenic mothers. Out of this ongoing project the first systematic data suggestive of a possible neurointegrative defect was actually observed in some infants at risk. This pattern marked by erratic and disorganized motivational patterns in activity, alertness, vestibular function, autonomic stability, and proprioception has been confirmed by several other investigators although it is evident in only a very restricted subset of children born to mothers who have received a diagnosis of schizophrenia. The subsequent studies of Mednick and Schulsinger (1973) enlarged the research enterprise: more substantial *N*s with more substantial controls in terms of the samples used; sophisticated research designs; a nomothetic orientation that moved beyond the intensive idiography of case reports; and a multivariate approach to data aimed at searching out precursor signs that might anticipate later disorder.

From these studies have come a proliferation of other projects, many in this country (e.g., UCLA, Stony Brook, New York State Psychiatric Institute, Washington University, Universities of Denver, Chicago, Minnesota, Rochester) and abroad (Sweden, Denmark, Israel).

The basic assumption underlying subject selection in most, but not all, of these studies is that the offspring of schizophrenic parents are more likely than control cases to be at risk for the later *development* and subsequent *maintenance* of schizophrenic pathology. That assumption is strongly supported by empirical data derived from genetic studies of schizophrenia in which the anticipated incidence rate of approximately 1% in the general population rises to 10–12% in offspring born to a union in which one of the biological parents has had a history of schizophrenia, and to 35–40% in those who are unfortunate enough to have had parents both of whom have experienced schizophrenia (Erlenmeyer-Kimling, 1975; Gottesman, 1978; Kety et al., 1978; Gottesman and Shields, 1972; Rosenthal, 1970).

With the identification of such cohorts has come the more difficult problem of the variables to be studied in evaluating these children. I will take the liberty of quoting from an earlier paper (Garmezy, 1974) in which I catalogued some of the variables under study. These read like a "who's who" (or a 'what's what') of generic psychology's own offspring.

First there are those tasks and procedures that have been shown to differentiate, with consistency, *adult* schizophrenic patients from others, such as measures of reaction time; attention, set, and vigilance; information processing tasks including sensory integration measures; psychophysiological measures of arousal, habituation, and recovery rate following onset of a stressful stimulus; electrophysiological studies of average evoked potentials during the course of fluctuations in attention; vestibular functioning; conditioning and generalization;

cognitive disturbances as revealed by word association tests; variants in individual cognitive styles; measures of social competence; intellectual competence as adjudged from school records and teacher's ratings; parent-child interaction; deviant patterns of communication manifest in the course of family interaction tasks; referential communication between parent and child; potential genetic markers such as eye-tracking dysfunction reported to be present (among others) in adult schizophrenic patients and their relatives (Holzman et al., 1974) and the reduction of monoamine oxidase (MAO) activity in the blood platelets of schizophrenics (Murphy and Wyatt, 1972).

Second, there are those assessment procedures that are designed to measure either fundamental trait dispositions, manifest state disturbances, or developmental lags of a neurological, motoric or behavioral sort. Included under this rubric would be structured interview procedures to assay current psychiatric status in parents and offspring, tests and interviews to measure personality traits of children, and assessments of neurological and visual-motor functions.

Third, there are variables borrowed by risk researchers from other colleagues whose preliminary investigations suggest they have chanced upon potentially fruitful differentiators. Among these I would include the use of pregnancy, birth, and obstetrical records, and the assessment of significant life events in parents and children.

Finally, there are those variables derived from current research in developmental psychology that reflect lags in social or cognitive development. These would include systematic observation and categorization of mother-child play interaction, the teaching styles of mothers in relation to their children, the use of Piagetian-type tasks to measure egocentrism-perspectivism behaviors, evaluations of infant temperament singly and in relation to maternal competence variables, assessments of attachment behavior, stranger anxiety, and socialization patterns, children's performance on attention and memory tasks, language development, assessment procedures to measure physical anomalies and psychophysiological responsivity, and sleep states in the neonate (Garmezy, 1974, pp. 192–193).

Many of these wide-ranging sets of variables are bound to prove nonproductive as present differentiators or future predictors of children at risk and controls, or for ultimate outcomes that are pathological or normal. It is however, possible to tag those currently most popular and seemingly more productive. These include arousal states, indicators of social and academic competence, pregnancy and birth complications in the maternal cohort, neurological evaluations, and measures of cognitive and attentional functioning.

These factors are indicative of two aspects involved in selecting for risk: (1) there are those variables that measure attributes associated with adult schizophrenia (attentional, cognitive, social and psychophysiological deficits); and (2) there are other variables that are associated with developmental lags.

It seems appropriate for now to suggest the following: (1) variables with the greatest predictive power may well be those that tap deficits or retardations in maturation as evidenced in the earliest years of children of schizophrenic parents; (2) later in childhood and adolescence, other factors, reflecting a failure to meet anticipated stages of cognitive, emotional and social development, or the absence of those that reflect the growth of competencies, may prove to be the most effective variables to study.

At the present time a great amount of data are still being collected. A future issue of the *Schizophrenia Bulletin* is expected to update the risk research scene. But one thing can be said at this point. This area of study, like all emergent areas in science, began on a high tide of enthusiasm. Without such powerful expectations it is unlikely that the study of children at risk for later psychopathology would have emerged with the rapidity with which it did. In such a climate of positive regard, disappointments are inevitable and risk researchers are no strangers either to depressive affects or to a "burned-out" phenomenon.

When various risk research groups first got underway there appeared to be relatively little awareness of the experimental realities that would have to be overcome. Those realities are now increasingly evident, and so when invited to write an editorial for *Psychological Medicine* by Professor Michael Shepherd of the Institute of Psychiatry, I titled it "On Some Risks in Risk Research" (Garmezy, 1977a). Here are some observations of the methodological problems that are now apparent to researchers. While these observations have been applied to schizophrenia I believe that many of them are also applicable to other areas of risk research involving children.

1. In the case of risk for schizophrenia, there is in many instances a long waiting period between the time at which observational and laboratory studies were made in childhood and the emergence of disorder in adulthood. The risk period for schizophrenia extends to age 45 and more recently some have suggested that an extension to age 55 would be appropriate. Consider the dedication demanded of researchers who have to await the final determination of risk over a period that extends through decades. It is true, however, that a peak incidence for schizophrenic occurs in the late teens and early 20s and this ameliorates the problem somewhat. However, prognostically more favorable cases (which may reflect quite different antecedents) do occur in later adult life.

2. Hovering in the background is the ubiquitous problem of reliability of the parental diagnosis which often must be adjudged from in-

adequate case records marked by brief histories that are replete either with contradictory or with limited information. For diagnostic interviews conducted with released patients the problem is one of inferring the prior disordered status of an adult currently in remission.

3.   The ascertainment of offspring poses a problem too. Immigration, and mobility downward (or upward) can result in irretrievable sample losses. Losses are also affected by the placement of offspring of disturbed parents in foster homes or by their adoption by relatives or strangers.

4.   The absence of any signs of disorder in many of the children at risk generates a pressing ethical question. Given the realities of informed consent, are the potential results to be obtained commensurate with the arousal of anxiety, guilt, and shame that may be generated in parents and in children since identification and explanation of the purpose of one's project is required by committees on the use of human subjects in research?

5.   An additional problem is generated by the small samples available to investigative teams, and this limitation inhibits broad generalizations. The identification of disturbed parents in selecting a cohort of their biological offspring implies that one may be dealing with a fertile, more intact, certainly more cooperative parental group and this too provides constraints in seeking to generalize to the more fragmented world of many preschizophrenics who have been exposed to less competent parental backgrounds.

6.   Data analysis based upon small N's constrains multivariate analyses and makes necessary a combining of multiple subgroups that may vary in ways that transcend their similarities in phenotypic behavior. Examples of such differences may include the adaptive qualities of the nondisordered spouse, or the acuteness-chronicity qualities of the disordered spouse. Such dissimilarities pose problems when interpreting group differences.

7.   The absence of national registries—psychiatric, adoption, and geographic—and marked restrictions in the contents and usage of those few that are available, block the longitudinal pursuit of outcome data in a markedly mobile United States.

In a recent paper Reider (1979) has added observations on five other substantive and methodological problems that face risk researchers:

1.   The heterogeneity of the transmitted genotypes may preclude any likelihood that all cases of breakdown will reveal common precursors.

There is a major problem (already touched upon) as to which variables to include in the search for causative environmental factors or predisposing biological components. Reider points out that "most of the high-risk studies have not focused on deviant family interaction, nor on biochemical abornormalties, and these hold leading places in environmental and genetic theories of the etiology of schizophrenia." (While the neglect of biochemistry appears to be evident, attention to family interaction continues to be investigated by several risk research teams.)

2.   Studies differ widely both in the measures employed and in the ages of the children evaluated. This makes replication across samples difficult and restricts efforts to combine the data secured by different research teams.

3.   Variance in parental samples contributed to by differences in both type and severity of parental schizophrenia as well as lack of information about disabilities in the presumably "well" spouse limit generalization of findings about offspring who are quite likely to vary in their risk for psychopathology.

4.   There has been an increasing number of reports of offspring of schizophrenic parents whose diagnoses would seem to warrant assignment of a "schizophrenia spectrum" category. Such cases are markedly different from "consensus schizophrenia" cases and comprise a diagnostic concept that lacks universal acceptance.

5.   The unsuccessful search thus far for the elusive genetic marker poses the greatest problem of all for its absence prevents identification and control of these relevant genetic-biological factor(s) with which the child is presumably endowed and which could reflect risk potential. Without such indicators the search for environmental factors that interact with biological components to lower or to raise the predispositional factor cannot be ascertained.

Given these marked limitations, one would expect a falling off of efforts to assay children at risk. But this is not the case. Why? As the discussant of a risk research symposium that constituted a portion of the recently held Second Rochester International Conference on Schizophrenia (Wynne, Cromwell, and Matthysse, 1978) I attempted to deal with this question (Garmezy, 1978a). What would be the consequences, I asked a panel of leading risk researchers, if twenty years from now the effort to map the lives of these vulnerable children revealed that we hadn't been able to predict the course of their disordered or nondisordered development at all? Would there have been any value gained from support of the multiple programs of risk research now underway?

Two other questions framed the reply: First, did the research groups do a scholarly job of tracking the development of children born of schizophrenic parentage (or selected on the basis of any alternative etiological model) through infancy, childhood, adolescence, and early maturity? Second, had it proved possible to predict who in time became schizophrenic?

Clearly if the answer to the first question was negative, the second question would likely be in the negative too. But if the answer to the first question proved to be an affirmative one, then even a negative response to question two would have made the venture into risk research worthwhile for four reasons. It would have provided for clinical psychiatry and developmental psychopathology the descriptive knowledge essential for understanding (1) the nature of predisposition to schizophrenia, and perhaps (2) the conditions required for its actualization, (3) the diversity of likely outcomes in such children, and (4) the probable factors that influenced the diversity of the behavioral expression of risk.

But to track that development brings us back to the critical question of the attributes to be measured in the growing child. Risk research has contributed to a radical modification in the method whereby one seeks to understand the relevant past of the individual who develops schizophrenia. But the longitudinal-developmental-prospective method is only as powerful as the variables it houses and herein lies a problem.

The range of variables that are now being studied is a substantial one—a conservative observation given the wide spectrum of biological, psychological, psychosocial, and familial factors now being tested.

THE MINNESOTA STUDIES OF RISK FOR PSYCHOPATHOLOGY

Faced with this problem and with very limited funding we at Minnesota made a set of experimental decisions:

1. We fixed on multiple risk groups against which to compare children of schizophrenic mothers. One such group was the selection of mothers with similar aged offspring whose "consensus diagnosis" pointed either to nonpsychotic depression or to a personality disorder. Other groups included different forms of behavior or symptom expression shown by children, many of whom had been referred by school personnel to a community child guidance clinic. In various studies we have included antisocial children, overinhibited children, and hyperactive children.

2. We forswore a longitudinal study in favor of a cross-sectional design reasoning that a first step in the process of searching for pay-off

variables was to evaluate rapidly the differentiating power, via cross-sectional comparisons, of those risk groups that had been initially selected for study.

3. We sought to differentiate children within risk and control groups by measures of social competence as indexed by peers. Reasoning that since empirical studies of peer rejection have proved to be a reliable predictor of a variety of later psychiatric problems while peer acceptance is a powerful correlate of healthy adult adaptation (Cowen et al., 1973; Roff, Sells, and Golden, 1972), we included a sociometric measure of social competence (Bower, 1969) in our studies to specify subsets of children within risk groups who might be at even higher levels of predicted risk for later psychopathology.

4. We decided to focus primarily on a single construct that admittedly always has had a great deal of surplus meaning both in experimental psychology and psychopathology but which we hypothesized would likely be related to competence. This is the study of *attention,* whose history and multiplicity of meanings both in the biology and experimental psychology of psychopathology has recently been described (Garmezy, 1977b; Matthysse, 1977).

5. At Minnesota, Marcus (1972) had observed that children of schizophrenic parents as well as acting-out clinic children showed deficits in a reaction time study. The latter group, however, under conditions of heightened motivation were able to overcome this deficit whereas the children who were at risk for schizophrenia were not able to do so, although their cooperativeness in the task remained at a high level.

Other supporting data of an attentional deficit in similar types of children have been reported by Erlenmeyer-Kimling and her colleagues (1975, 1978; Rutschmann, Cornblatt, and Erlenmeyer-Kimling, 1977 and by Gallant, 1972; Cohler et al., 1977; Asarnow et al., 1977). Reviews of these studies in the context of attentional functioning in children at risk for schizophrenia and related disorders have appeared elsewhere (Garmezy, 1978b; Nuechterlein, 1978; Phipps-Yonas, 1978).

In the final three studies of our research program on risk, which now conclude the Minnesota project on vulnerable children, we decided to focus simultaneously on three different forms of attention—*sustained, shift,* and *selective attention*—in a major effort to evaluate possible attentional dysfunction in four groups of children who may be at risk for adult psychopathology. These four groups were (1) children of schizophrenic mothers, (2) children of nonpsychotic depressive and personality-disordered mothers, (3) hyperactive, but essentially nonantisocial school children who had been seen in a community child guidance clinic, and (4) an antisocial (externalizing) group of children drawn from the same clinic or from special schools within the school system to which such acting-out children are assigned. Control groups of children consisted of classroom peers who were matched for demographic factors (age, sex, social class, etc.) and social competence as indexed by peer judgments obtained through a sociometric technique, an adaptation of Bower's Class Play (1969). Other classroom controls drawn from grades 3–6 were stratified by level of social competence and served as an adjunct to the control group aspect of the current investigations.

Primary investigators of this collaborative study were Dr. Keith Nuechterlein (1978) who measured *sustained attention* using a variant of the Continuous Performance Test (CPT), Dr. Susan Phipps-Yonas (1978) who used a mixed modality reaction time test to measure *shift attention,* and Dr. Regina Driscoll (1979) who created two unique studies of incidental versus central learning as a means of evaluating *selective attention.*

The subjects (*N*'s varied very slightly in the different experiments) totaled approximately 230 children (Group 1 [schizophrenic mother and controls] = 23-24 pairs; Group 2 [depressed mother and controls] = 20 pairs; Group 3 [hyperactive children and controls] = 14-15 pairs; Group 4 [externalizing children] = 16 [4 controls]; stratified control subjects = 100).

Different measures of attention were used with the same subjects in these three independent but interrelated studies. A characteristic of all three investigations was the use of differing experimental conditions designed to enhance or to interfere with attentional functioning in an effort to provide indications of the modifiability of attention in the risk and normal control children.

As an example of the complexity of these experiments, Nuechterlein devised several conditions for administering the CPT. These included a basic number version with the number "5" as the target stimulus (to which the child was to respond with a button press) with exposure time reduced for the older as opposed to the younger children to equalize difficulty level and raise the ceiling of the task. A more difficult version that met the assumptions required for data analyses based upon signal detection theory utilized distraction, decreasing exposure, illumination, and cycling time and degraded stimuli.

Nuechterlein's "feedback" condition for correct and incorrect responses provided the opportunity to study reinforcement effects, while a response reversal condition in which the subject was to respond to each number *except* the previously used target number, tested the child's ability to shift set and to inhibit his or her previously acquired responses.

The experimental conditions in Phipps-Yonas cross-modality reaction time study were a partial replication of earlier work (Marcus, 1972) and were marked by conditions in which trials utilizing a visual imperative stimulus were presented, followed by trials with auditory stimuli alone, followed in turn by a mixed group of trials. After these three initial conditions there was another mixed set of trials but with prior correct information provided the child as to the stimulus modality that was to mark the trial to follow. This condition, in turn, led to the presentation of partially incorrect information and a final condition that involved the child in guessing the stimulus modality for the trial that was to follow. In this condition half of the child's guesses were arbitrarily delineated as "correct" and half as "incorrect."

The incidental learning study was similarly of a complex nature, making use of incidental stimulus features that were in one study extrinsic to the central stimulus and in another experiment intrinsic to a comparable set of stimuli, thus placing increased demands for scanning by the child in coping with the latter task.

A disproportionate subgroup of children born to schizophrenic mothers showed deficits in sustained attention relative to the matched and stratified controls. Nuechterlein (1979) affirmed this by his signal detection analysis indicating lowered scores on the index of sensitivity, d'. In a unique factor analysis in which he integrated the signal detection indices from the CPT conditions as well as the experimenter's ratings of the subject's behavior in the course of performing the task, Nuechterlein was able to demonstrate that there was a tendency for a number of children born to schizophrenic mothers to fall into a group marked by high emotionality. Following a growing pattern of analyzing the results of high-risk groups to search for a smaller subset that may be particularly predisposed to later disorder (e.g., Asarnow et al., 1977; Hanson, Gottesman, and Heston, 1976) Nuechterlein successfully isolated a small subset of attentionally deficient high-risk children in his sample that approximated the proportion of anticipated "breakdowns" one would expect based upon extrapolation from schizophrenia genetic research.

The complexity of the issue of "attentional deficit," however, is revealed by Phipps-Yonas' failure to find differences between these same children of schizophrenic mothers and their matched controls in terms of speed of their reaction times, the individual variability of their performance, or other behaviors on her irregular reaction time task. Furthermore the effort to identify a special subset of these high-risk children on this task has also proved unsuccessful at this point. Phipps-Yonas (1979) writes:

Regardless of the variables and scoring criteria used, it was not possible to select a subset within the sample which was larger, more abnormal, or different in anyway from comparable low status subsets within other groups of subjects.

In the final analyses 4 of the 22 children of schizophrenic mothers were identified as especially deviant across the measures studied. That proportion is identical to that found for their matched controls and comparable to that overall for the other 209 individuals in the study.

The data of the incidental learning study (Driscoll, 1979) is now undergoing extensive analysis and will be reported at a later date. But preliminary analyses reveal commonalities across the attentional studies. First, the hyperactive children show consistently defective performance. With the data of a third study still to be analyzed, earlier appraisals of the marked attentional deficits of antisocial children have been strongly confirmed in these most recent investigations. However, the data across studies for the cohort of children born to schizophrenic mothers are variable. Extended analyses are now underway to collate and integrate all three studies in a further search for the elusive subsets of particularly vulnerable high-risk children in these various groups who are marked by deficient performance in the three attentional studies. A subsequent step will be the search for the correlates (e.g., peer and teacher ratings, cumulative school record data, family data) of such deficient performance if the attentional data were to yield such subsets.

If a relationship were to be found between children showing a markedly consistent attentional dysfunction and maternal and child life history variables suggestive of maladaptation, it would not necessarily indicate that an attentional deficit is a precursor attribute of the preschizophrenic child. However, it would suggest the importance of following such a subset of children (and their controls) into adolescence and early adulthood with a view to determining their patterns of later adaptation. The task is a difficult one.

Risk researchers are now essentially engaged in a long-term "bootstrapping" operation. What could make their task infinitely easier would be the discovery of genetic and (possibly) psychological markers that could assist in determining the risk status of children. Thus far the search has been a disappointing one. But whatever the outcome of these studies of vulnerable children, the methods of risk research will likely come to be recognized as a contribution of value to a true developmental orientation for elucidating some of the precursors to later forms of psychopathology. Even in the absence of any imminent breakthrough researchers have demonstrated a methodological approach that is necessary if we are to study effectively the development of psychopathology, with its social, psychological and biological correlates, in a more sophisticated fashion. It is hoped that both method and emergent content will, in time, contribute to our understanding of the complex nature of etiology in schizophrenia.

STRESS-RESISTANT ("INVULNERABLE") CHILDREN

Despite these many difficulties, the study of populations of children at risk constitutes an advance not only for psychopathology but for generic psychology as well. For in this research, in which we observe not the already disordered but those who seemingly have the potential for later disorder, we are studying individuals—typically children—who are victimized by severe stress. Yet, despite this overarching stress component in their everyday lives, risk researchers can observe many whose patterns of ongoing behavior clearly indicate manifest competence in comparison with peers and others who, similarly stressed, reveal behavior patterns that reflect a growing move toward incompetence. Such findings warrant the attention of clinical and personality psychologists but not necessarily for purposes of intervention to stay the course of psychopathology. Rather, exposure of psychologists to children and adults who survive the most distressing life experiences invites a humility about the knowledge we lack regarding the sources of security and competence in stressed but adaptable mentally healthy people and of incompetence in their stressed, maladaptive, mentally disordered counterparts. *Risk status* in psychopathology implies a diversity of outcomes in which the minority—the *minority* mind you—who become the victims of mental disorder in later life is exceeded by others drawn from similar backgrounds who seem destined to lead happier, more productive lives.

Support for this viewpoint comes from the results of a lifetime of research pursued by Dr. Manfred Bleuler, former Director of Burghölzli Hospital in Zurich, and famed son of a famous father, Eugen Bleuler. For twenty years Professor Bleuler (1974, 1979) served as family physician, resident psychiatrist, friend, and confidante to 208 schizophrenic patients who constituted his research sample. Over that twenty-year span, 104 of his patients married and generated 169 offspring. Fifteen other children were born out of wedlock. Of these 184 children, only ten in time were diagnosed as definitely schizophrenic and five of these ten had recovered by the time the research was concluded. Three-quarters of the children were mentally sound in adulthood; 120 of the 143 children who were over 20 years of age at the completion of the study worked at jobs that exceeded expectations based on their level of training and education with all but ten exceeding the paternal occupational level. Eighty-four percent of the offspring who had married had happy and successful marriages.

Bleuler concluded that "the accomplishments of these children are remarkable when one considers their handicaps—the emotional suffering, social ostracism, and economic disadvantages to which their parents' psychoses subjected them." My favorite passage from Bleuler's recent writings is this:

But despite their miserable childhoods . . . , and despite their presumably tainted genes, most offspring of schizophrenics manage to lead normal productive lives. Indeed, after studying a number of family histories, one is left with the impression that pain and suffering can have a steeling—a hardening—effect on some children, rendering them capable of mastering life with all its obstacles, just to spite their inherent disadvantages. Perhaps it would be instructive for future investigators to keep as careful watch on the favorable development of the majority of these children as they do on the progressive deterioration of the sick minority (Bleuler, 1974, p. 106).

Bleuler is not implying that these children are free of the trauma they have witnessed. "Even normal offspring," he writes, "who are successful in life can never fully free themselves from the pressures imposed by memories of their schizophrenic parents and their childhood." He records the words he has often heard in one form or another. "When you've gone through that . . . you can never really be happy, you can never laugh as others do. You always have to be ashamed of yourself and take care not to break down yourself" (p. 106).

Bleuler, clinician-physician had a distinct advantage over the experimental psychopathologist. The setting for his observations were naturalistic, the time span lengthy, the orientation a longitudinal-developmental one. The psychopathologist's observations of competence, if laboratory bound and short term do not permit a search for the price that some pay for their stress-resistant qualities. Contacts are too brief, too superficial, and the expression of competency too bounded and too distant from the world of work, social exchange, and marital and sexual adequacy. Risk research with its emphasis on resistance or capitulation to psychopathology provides the most appropriate setting for the collaborative efforts of researcher and clinician. Under the best of circumstances these are joined in a singular figure of talent. So I pause in this recital to bring forth our "guest" of honor and add my homage to that proferred by other contributors to this volume.

Thirty years ago, research on concepts such as stress, coping, and defending was not in its infancy so much as it was *in utero.* Yet here in that milestone volume, *Assessment of Men,* is a passage that resonates with the sound of the voice of Henry A. Murray, for it projects a future aspect of psychological science that to this day is one of the foundation stones of personality study. In referring to a need for future assessment institutes, an exemplar of which was the famed Harvard Psychological Clinic, the volume takes this position:

There are scores of strategic questions about the determinants of effective behavior which might eventually be answered by an assessment institute that employed the system outlined in this book. For example, there is the great problem of the consequences of various traumatic occurrences in childhood. According to the psychoanalytic formula, neurotic symptoms are resultants of repressed dynamic complexes engendered by traumatic situations in early life. Many different types of traumatic situations have been described, as well as the dynamisms of ego-defense and of complex formation, and also the different conditions in later life under which a complex is likely to erupt as a manifest symptom. Although certain links in the chain of causation are still obscure, many now believe that the chief determining processes leading from the series of traumata to the final psychological disorder have been convincingly formulated.

One of the striking findings of the OSS assessment staff, however, was the frequency of such traumata and such complexes in the past histories of very effective personalities. In not a few instances, indeed, the staff concluded that the complex was more influentially related to the proficiencies than to the deficiencies of the personality. There is nothing very novel about this observation: it conforms to Adler's notion of ambition overcompensating for an initial narcissistic wound. But in many of our cases there was no evidence of an exorbitant craving for superiority: the underlying complex had apparently been integrated into a personality structure that was both balanced and competent. *And so, to supplement our present knowledge of pathogenic tendencies it seems that we require a much clearer understanding of the positive, creative, and health-building forces which so often succeed in checking, counteracting, or transforming the complexes of early life in such a way as to produce characters which in certain respects are stronger than they would otherwise have been. The question is, what determinants must be taken into account in predicting whether this or that hurtful occurrence will impede or encourage the development of an effective personality?* We have learned a great deal about the defense mechanisms of the ego, but a personality cannot flourish by defense alone. Surely it is the forward-reading and constructive forces which are chiefly responsible for integrated growth. And so, since these long-overlooked positive forces can be best investigated in normal personalities, an assessment institute would be in a favorable position to make a significant contribution to our knowledge of human development (OSS Assessment Staff, 1948, p. 168, italics ours).

Having witnessed the range in adaptation of many "vulnerable" children during a decade of experimental study, our research group at Minnesota decided to devote the next decade of our research to the other side of the coin of risk, namely to study "invulnerable" children—a term so replete with drama, expectancy, and buoyancy that our own fear of overstatement and overpromise has led us now to adopt the more prosaic, less media-oriented term, "stress-resistant."

It is a curious paradox indeed that a phenomenon so ubiquitous in the real world can be so neglected by the scientific community. I have tried to consider why this should be so and can only suggest that those of us who are clinical psychologists have been victims of Abraham Kaplan's "law of the hammer." Stated in its simplest form this pervasive behavioral law is summarized by the following postulate: "Give a kid a hammer and everything he (she?) runs into will need pounding." Our hammer is psychopathology and everywhere we turn we see disorder or dynamic substitutes for disorder. We seem to forget that psychology is that branch of science that deals with the study of behavior. Within clinical psychology the scientific thrust is directed more specifically to the study of deviant behavior and its amelioration. But unlike psychiatry with its ubiquitous preoccupation with abnormality, the roots of our discipline (and its specialty areas) lie in the study of basic normative behavioral processes. It is this quality that serves as our hallmark of distinction among the mental health disciplines—that and our appreciation of the critical importance of research for understanding the normal and the abnormal in the realm of personality, cognition, and affective and social-emotional development.

Without a base of observation focused on normality, the exploration of deviance, whether for purposes of assessment, therapy, or research, presents enormous pitfalls for the unwary. The relationship has been set forth by Nobel Laureate Tinbergen (1972) in the importance he accords to ethological studies of children. He writes:

> It is surprising, how much is being discovered which so far has simply been ignored by professional psychologists; on the one hand, it is clear that this simple, careful observation of normal children is going to be a very demanding task indeed. But, it will give a wider scope and more purpose to human studies. And, no less important: by gradually building up an ethogram of our species, (such) work will provide the yardstick by which behavior pathology can be measured (p. ix).

And to these wise words I add those provided by another Nobel Laureate, Sir Peter Medawar: "It is not informative to study variations of behaviour unless we know beforehand the norm from which such variants depart."

Knowledge of such "norms" of behavior can fill us with unparalleled regard for the human psyche and the human spirit.

When Robert Coles (1964) wrote *Children of Crisis* in the turbulent mid-1960s and described for the country the initiative, courage, and talents of black children who ran the gauntlet of white adults' hostility during the desegregation of the public schools of the South, he added an observation that deserves repetition a decade later:

For some time students of literature and psychology have tried in bewilderment to understand the paradoxes like Dostoevski's early traumas and Kafka's terribly twisted childhood. Lives such as theirs illustrate more than the triumph of genius over illness. They are exceptional examples of how very hard it is—or should be for us in our present state of knowledge to define the sources of "health," "creativity" or "maturity" in many people. We see the wide behavioral variations of children from relatively similar neighborhoods. We are struck by the common cause and ethical commitment of children from widely divergent ones. Growth in children seemingly challenges as well as responds to a wide and complicated assortment of influences; social, economic, psychological—spiritual (Coles, 1964, p. 234).

There is only one element in that paragraph with which I disagree. In general psychologists, with or without bewilderment, have made few efforts to understand the development of competence amidst stress. It is to this critical topic that I would like to direct my comments in the closing section of this chapter.

THE STUDY OF STRESS-RESISTANCE IN CHILDREN

It is difficult to present a format for research in an area in which there exists neither a substantial body of empirical data nor a formal conceptualization. Unfortunately this is the present status of the study of *stress-resistant children*. The term "invulnerability" has been used to designate such children (Anthony, 1974; Garmezy, 1974, 1976). This overly dramatic word implies the presence of two components in the lives and makeup of these children: (1) the presence of sustained and intense life stresses and (2) the maintenance of mastery and competence despite such stress exposure.

There has been a curious neglect of such children and their adult counterparts by the mental health disciplines. Lois Murphy (1962) one of American's foremost observers of coping behavior in children was moved to comment in the opening pages of *The Widening World of Childhood* on the paradoxical nature of the involvements of most of the nation's mental health researchers:

It is something of a paradox that a nation which has exalted in its rapid expansion and its scientific technological achievements, should have developed so vast a 'problem' literature: a literature often expressing adjustment difficulties, social failures, blocked potentialities, and defeat. . . . In applying clinical ways of thinking formulated out of experience with broken adults, we were slow to see how the language of adequacy to meet life's challenges could become the subject matter of psychological science. Thus there are thousands of studies of maladjustment for each one that deals directly with the ways of managing life's problems with personal strength and adequacy. The language of problems, difficulties, inadequacies, or antisocial or delinquent conduct, or of ambivalence and anxiety is familiar. We know that there are devices for correcting, bypassing, or overcoming threats, but for the most part these have not been directly studied (p. 3).

These "devices" can be inferred from the many case studies that dominate the literature of stress-resistance. One such source are the observations of children who overcame adversity and achieved fame through their attainments. Examples of such volumes include *Cradles of Eminence* (Goertzel and Goertzel, 1962), *Three Hundred Eminent Personalities* (Goertzel, Goertzel, and Goertzel, 1978), and *Lessons from Childhood* (Illingworth and Illingworth, 1969). Worthy as these volumes may be, they do not provide an optimal framework within which to study the components of stress-resistance, for developmental biography is often influenced by later achievement. Of even greater importance, such accounts of the lives of famous people removes the study of "invulnerability" from what is typically the more commonplace and provides a low base-rate context of the extraordinary. The traumatic familial, physical, or social experiences that beset such greats as Beethoven, Edison, Kepler, Keller, the Roosevelts (Theodore, Eleanor, and Franklin), Einstein, Louis Armstrong, G.B. Shaw, Dylan Thomas, Kafka, T. E. Lawrence, and numerous other personages scarcely seem to be the foundation stones on which to build a research program on "stress-resistance" as observed in "ordinary" children who show mastery over their stressful environments. Many of the individuals cited came to greatness with rather extraordinary predispositional qualities and potential talents. A focus on eminence, whether from the viewpoint of the cradle or the rocking chair, can cause us to lose sight of the many children and adults who lead ordinary lives and who are not destined for greatness, but whose very "ordinariness" can be heroic when placed against the highly traumatizing backgrounds out of which they have come.

As noted, our Minnesota group first became interested in the study of stress-resistant children as an outgrowth of a research program in which we compared the attendant performance characteristics of different subsets of children who were considered to be at increased risk for the future development of psychopathology (Garmezy, 1976). The lives of these children have, in some cases, been marked either by maternal disorder (e.g., schizophrenia, depression, personality disorder) or poverty; others have exhibited patterns characterized by antisocial or withdrawn, asocial behavior. Yet observations of these children in laboratory or school settings made evident their range of individual differences in social and work competence, motivation level, task orientation, and performance efficiency. Greatness may not be the future lot of many of the children we have studied over the past decade, but if their present levels of adaptation are sustained, one can anticipate lives characterized not merely by survival but by self-sufficiency.

Such observations led us to comment on the prolonged neglect of the "invulnerable" child, the healthy child in an unhealthy setting—a neglect that has provided us with a false sense of security in erecting prevention models that are founded more on values than on facts. If we can study the forces and attributes that seemingly move such children to survival and adaptation, then society may derive benefits far more significant than our current efforts to construct primary prevention models designed to curtail the rising tide of vulnerable high-risk children.

The experimental and clinical literature with respect to such potential forces and attributes is sparse. The literature that does exist emphasizes case reports of individuals who have been exposed to different types of stress: poverty, the holocaust, uprooting and migration, economic and social deprivation, psychotic parentage, natural disasters, bereavement and loss, parental separation and divorce, and so forth. There are in this literature reports of individuals who have remained demonstrably resistant to breakdown and who, under the most dire circumstances, continued to exhibit positive, adaptive strivings (e.g., Engel, 1967; Krystal, 1968; Sobel, 1973); other case histories describe those who have overcome manifest psychopathology and have gone on to marked achievements following recovery from severe mental disorders (Freeman, 1972).

Observations by researchers provide some highly generalized insights into stress-resistance. A report (Shepherd and Barraclough, 1976) on the aftermath of parental suicide for children, five to seven years following the traumatic event, notes that despite the fact that the suicide contributed to a radical and forced change of living circumstance for the children, marked behavioral disturbances occurred in only a *minority* of them. The account is suggestive in identifying that this minority embraced those whose parents' lives had been previously marked by mental difficulties, separation, and abnormal personality manifestations. A similar theme runs through a volume reviewing research on *Psychological Deprivation in Childhood* (Langmeier and Matejcek, 1975). Commenting on "extraordinary life situations" such as the evacuation of children from urban centers in England exposed to air bombings during World War II, the authors write:

Although undoubtedly evacuation, with all its demands and consequences, produced a considerable amount of stress and certain behavior problems in the majority of children, the incidence of disorder and maladaptation, relatively speaking, was considerably lower than we might expect (p. 153).

A clue to one source of resistance to stress is suggested by this observation:

Generally, children who had healthy positive relationships with their parents tolerated evacuation with relative ease. It is clear that this relationship with their parents provided the basis for security which helped them to adapt to the new situation (p. 152).

In this same volume reports of children exposed to the barbarities of Nazi concentration camps describe comparable patterns in that psychological damage was less severe in those children who retained contact with their families. Commenting on the critical factor of individual differences, the authors observe a recurrent emphasis in the literature on the critical importance of "stable families," "happy early lives," a prior history of having been "mentally very healthy," and possessing "character traits developed in early childhood." Elsewhere, the authors also refer to children who are *"constitutionally* [italics ours] more resistant to adverse life conditions."

Although those factors are suggestive, the imprecision of the formulations and the personal attributes cited are disconcertingly vague. What is evident as one pursues an admittedly sparse literature is the lack of *systematic* research on such individual variations both under naturalistic conditions and under the more rigorously controlled conditions that can be imposed in the laboratory.

Stressful Life Experiences: The Negative Concept of "Disadvantaged Children"

A major stressor in the lives of many children, for which a research literature does exist, is one imposed by poverty, discrimination, poor housing, overcrowding in the ghetto, and restricted educational and cultural opportunities. A decade ago, the first effort of our group to track competence amidst stress, took form in a *summa cum laude* thesis written by Nuechterlein (1970) which was, at that time, a definitive review of the attributes of competent black children of the ghetto. Two years later the review was updated (Garmezy and Nuechterlein, 1972) and a further updating of the more recent literature is now underway.

It is of some interest to place side by side the heavy focus on "disadvantage" that dominates the literature of children in poverty when compared with our review of the attributes of competence despite severe economic discrimination. A quotation from Warden (1968) is revealing:

The left out is disadvantaged in his potential for school adjustment in that he often has a lower *social-class* background, which is less likely to have socialized him adequately to the social and academic demands of the heterogenous social situation . . .

Parents in the lower socioeconomic strata (in relation to middle-class parents): (1) more often employ object-oriented rewards and punishments; (2) are more apt to punish the child physically; (3) are more rejecting of dependency behavior; (4) are apt to be less able to provide the bases of achievement motivation; (5) are less apt to have the educational or experiential background to offer specific help in attaining school success; (6) are less likely to provide a verbally oriented environment; (7) are less likely to place value on intellectual accomplishment per se as opposed to valuing occupational training; and (8) are more likely to be separated or to be inadequate sex-role models (pp. 146–147).

In commenting on the consequent lacks in the children, deficits are specified in the areas of "achievement motivation," "functional anxiety," and "a future time orientation."

In an introduction to one of the earlier volumes on the *Disadvantaged Child,* Marans and Lowrie (1967) write in a similarly discouraging vein:

When we speak of the disadvantaged child, we refer to a child deprived of the same opportunity for healthy growth and development as is available to the vast majority of other members of the large society in which he lives. . . . We will further limit this definition to children born into the poor families which produce a disproportionate incidence of academic failures and of lower socioeconomic group memberships among their full-grown offspring. These are the families that perpetuate their own conditions in their children through their child-rearing patterns rather than genetic inheritances, although . . . the issue of the effects of malnutrition, inadequate prenatal care and the like, on the physical constitution of the children is an extremely important one.

There is no intention to minimize the impact of the economic, social and physical environments which also serve to perpetuate the culture and status of poverty. That these factors are major contributors to the disadvantaged stature of the child and his family is accepted, but we would contend that were the child less handicapped early in his life as a result of certain child-rearing patterns, his chances for success in overcoming the other environmental factors might be significantly advanced (p. 21).

And the authors then proceed to catalogue the defects in poor families: "excessive dependency," "magical thinking," "inadequate perceptual stimulation," "perceptual overstimulation," "inconsistency of handling," "multiple mothering," "punitive maternal discipline," excessive demands by mother despite the child's precocious development, "paucity of verbal communication," "emotional overstimulation"—all these leading to "survival techniques" which the child learns as would the "soldier in combat."

Disadvantaged Children: A Positive View

Reading this catalogue of negatives one would find it difficult to believe that there is another literature, admittedly scant but not because there are too few poor children who provide clear evidence of competence (a nation's history attests to their presence both in the past and in the present), but because too few investigators have been oriented to a view of adaptive as opposed to maladaptive behaviors under stress, economic or otherwise.

Compare the dire predictions that have been cited with some of the realities that have been observed by researchers who have studied achieving poor children. In highly abbreviated form (and sparing specific references for the summary statements), here are some of the tentative conclusions derived from our literature review (Nuechterlein 1970; Garmezy and Nuechterlein, 1972).

1.   Teachers and clinicians rate these children as possessing social skills. They are friendly and well-liked by peers and adults. They are more socially responsive, interpersonally sensitive, less sullen and restless. Teachers see them as lower in "defensiveness" and "aggressiveness" and higher on "cooperation," "participation," and "emotional stability."

2.   They tend to have a positive sense of self, manifesting self-regard rather than self-derogation, and a sense of personal power rather than powerlessness.

3.   Theirs is an internal locus of control and a belief that they are capable of exercising a degree of control over their environment. (The literature of internality suggests its correlates include a warm, praising, protective, and supportive family environment.)

4.   Intellectually these children reveal their cognitive skills, but a dominant cognitive style appears to be one of reflectiveness and "impulse" control.

5.   An intact family is *not* an identifiable consistent correlate. One is struck immediately by the lack of any consistent evidence in the studies reviewed that father-absence has an adverse effect on academic achievement. Mother's style of coping with and compensating for an absent father is a powerful redemptive variable.

6.   The physical and psychological environment of the home is important. One investigative team describes the households of these achieving lower-class children as less cluttered, less crowded, neater, cleaner, and marked by the presence of more books.

7. Parents are more concerned about their child's education, they assist willingly with homework, and participate in school-related activities.

8. Parents carefully define their own role in the family as well as the child's. Mothers of underachieving youngsters use their children to meet their own needs and stand more in the role of a pseudosibling than that of parent. The role relationships for the competent children were more structured and orderly.

9. Parents accord their children greater self-direction in everyday tasks and take cognizance of their children's interests and goals.

10. The children, several studies suggest, seem to have at least one adequate identification figure among the significant adults who touch their lives. In turn the achieving youngsters hold a more positive attitude toward adults and authority in general.

The intriguing point to be made about the findings of these studies is that despite the harshness of life that the families encounter, some parents appear to be able to foster or enhance in their children the confidence, self-control, determination, flexibility, and cognitive and social skills that accompany the development of competence and positive adaptation. These appear to be important precursors to the establishment of stress-resistance in children.

The positive findings of these studies of children from the nation's high-stress, inner-city areas are tempered by some common methodological limitations of many of the studies. All utilize a cross-sectional design and compare, at certain ages, a group of competent "disadvantaged" children and a group of their less competent peers as adjudged from psychometric tests, rating scales, and interview data. Such studies supply valuable descriptive data but make difficult the ascription of cause and effect. Moreover, many of these studies have failed to establish rigorous criteria for the socioeconomic level of their samples, have provided limited statistical analyses of their findings, and have imposed a marked restriction on potential criteria of competence by an excessive reliance on academic success as the measure of work competence.

These divergences in views of the child at risk have been brought together by Escalona (1974) in a summary statement that comes closest to matching the author's viewpoint. In urging that preventive and remedial efforts be directed at young children who although at risk are not yet impaired or damaged in their functioning Escalona writes:

Retroactive study, whether in the form of individual case studies or in more systematic clinical research has shown beyond a doubt that particular life stresses, deprivations, frustrations, and trauma during the preschool years are significantly related to later psychiatric illness or deviant impaired development. Among psychiatric patients, as well as among persons showing learning failure, psychosocial pathology, and other overt malfunctioning, the incidence of maternal psychopathology, of family disruption, of separation and loss at crucial times, of neglect, conflict, isolation, of harsh, punitive, or inappropriate child-rearing practices and many other malignant features is greater than in so-called normal, that is, unselected populations. . . .

However, prospective studies—the effort to predict on the bases of identified risk factors a greater frequency of developmental deviations and psychopathology—have not fared as well. The fact is that none of the specific high-risk factors, such as child-rearing practices, family disruption, psychopathology of the parents and the like, predict later psychopathology. The very same traumatic events or deficits that do produce maladaptation and illness in those who become patients are also found among a large number of normal individuals who, *for reasons we have yet to learn,* sustain these risks without significant impairment of personality development. In other words, knowing the child-rearing practices of parents, and knowing that events potentially disruptive or traumatizing have occurred, does not predict the developmental outcome for the child. . . .

In all respects normal development is threatened by being born and reared under poverty conditions. However, even this unquestionable fact leaves unresolved two issues of great importance. First, while the incidence of cognitive deficit, maladaptation, and psychiatric illness is higher among the poor, the prediction is statistical and not case-specific. No one has yet succeeded in predicting which individuals among the high-risk population defined by low socioeconomic status will show deviant developmental outcome, and which individuals will survive intact. Much less can we predict the kind or the severity of later pathology for individuals in such a population. Second, we do not know at what ages or developmental time spans poverty conditions critically interact with the child's functioning. Recent research suggests that, except for the greater incidence of neurological and other physical disabilities, socioeconomic status does not significantly contribute to either cognitive or social and emotional maldevelopment during the first two years of life. (Escalona, 1974, pp. 35–37, italics ours.)

This lengthy quotation provides still another affirmation of that curious aspect of the limited citations in our literature on stress-resistance in children—the observation of the phenomenon in many individual case studies, and the paucity of systematic studies on normal development of adaptive children under stress. To learn about stress-resistance one must turn to research in relevant, if tangential, areas.

THE HEALTHY PERSONALITY AS A SOURCE OF HYPOTHESES ABOUT STRESS-RESISTANCE

One source of hypotheses about stress-resistance is to be found in the literature of the "mentally healthy" personality. This concept appears recurrently in articles and books citing the nature of normality, the attributes of psychological health, the patterns and manifestations of competence, and so forth. Such studies of psychologically healthy people, largely adult samples, have taken a variety of forms (Lazarus, 1975):

1. There have been a number of studies that report psychiatric and psychological assessments of individuals who are seemingly free of any signs or symptoms of neurotic problems or of the anxieties and conflicts that beset even the garden-variety type of normal persons. Illustrative of such research are Grinker's (1962) studies of so-called "homoclites"— normal, healthy college people training for YMCA work who show few if any signs of distress. Brewster Smith's (1966) studies of competent Peace Corps candidates are of the same genre.

2. There are studies of adapting individuals observed at significant transition points in their lives. An example of such a focus is Coelho, Hamburg, and Murphy's study (1963) of graduating high school students and their modes of preparing for college entry. Kelly's (1971, 1979; Kelly et al. 1971) research on adaptive behavior in contrasting high school environments is of a similar nature.

3. There is a small core of studies of individuals selected for dangerous tasks because of their presumed high resistance to stress, such as the early studies of personality and stress responsivity of the Mercury astronauts (Korchin and Ruff, 1964). Rachman's (1978) recent volume on *Fear and Courage* constitutes a preparation for his forthcoming studies of the attributes of volunteer bomb disposal crew members in Britain's armed forces (personal communication).

4. Then there are the studies of creative persons (Barron, 1963). These are based on the assumption that psychological health is not the primary attribute of healthy adaptation, but rather that true health is best conceived as self-expression in the context of high achievements.

The Literature of Competence as a Source of Hypotheses about Stress-Resistance

Efforts to describe the attributes of competence represent still another source of hypotheses about stress-resistance, without regard to whether such attributes are cast within a trait or a developmental framework. Unfortunately, the concept of competence, too, presents a number of difficult problems, several of which have been described by Anderson and Messick (1974) in their review of the indicators of social competency in young children. One can look to a problem posed earlier in the twentieth century when lists of instincts were being conceived in an ever-expanding fashion (McDougall, 1908). Reflecting on this era Boring (1950) wrote: "There is never an end to such a list, . . . anyone can make up his own list of instincts and . . . there is no way to prove that one list is more certainly correct than another." (pp. 717–718.) The concept of competence may be similarly endangered. The Anderson-Messick list is the best example of a search for inclusiveness but it is obvious that even this extended catalogue lends itself to a further expansion of the subset of cognitive skills in keeping with the growing body of research in cognitive psychology. Similarly, social competence can be adumbrated to include behaviors drawn from both the ethological and ecological perspectives, (e.g., adaptive behavior in relation to specific environments in which it occurs), or from a structure-of-personality viewpoint (e.g., positive traits associated with different competent behaviors), or from a social interaction viewpoint, (e.g., competence as the ability to establish and maintain "productive and mutually satisfying interactions between a child and peers or adults," see O'Malley, 1977, p. 29).

The extensiveness of such listings is of great importance to a researcher heading out into an unchartered domain. Where does one begin a program of research on competence? Should the focus be on an analysis of adaptive behaviors that are trans-situational? Should there be an evaluation of likely trait structures including cognitive skills? Or should the emphasis be placed on positive social interactions with others? The initial Minnesota choice has been to use test and interview procedures, systematic observation, and experimental tasks to provide data relevant to all three issues.

Definitional Problems: The Concept of Competence

Before cataloguing the many indicators of competence there are definitional problems to be resolved (Anderson and Messick, 1974).

1. There is the problem of "distinguishing between behaviors that are prized by many segments of society across a large number of situations, and behaviors that are not necessarily universally admired or

are differentially appropriate to different situations." (Anderson and Messick, 1974, p. 287.)

In our preliminary work at Minnesota we interviewed principals, social workers, and teachers to see if they could go beyond a focus on formal academic achievements by helping us identify children who were "street smart." It is more difficult to secure information about a child's adaptation that goes beyond the confines of the school. We have, as yet, not enjoyed great success in doing so.

2. The second problem of definition is to be able to distinguish "between proficiency and performance and between maximal and typical performance." (Anderson and Messick, 1974, p. 287.)

These important distinctions have their counterpart in research on psychopathology. In studying performance deficits in schizophrenia, Shakow (1963, 1971) invariably sought to differentiate between *capacity* or optimal performance and *ability* or typical performance.

In making this differentiation with children important components of task and of personality must be assessed including motivational factors, sensitivity to specific types of reinforcement and their contingencies, age-specific appropriateness of various assessment procedures, and so forth. The differentiation is also important when considering interventions designed to foster competence and to enhance effective performance in children.

3. A third problem is the recognition "that variables may have different meanings—and thus different implications for social/educational action—at different levels of intensity or in their positive and negative ranges." (Anderson and Messick, 1974, pp. 287–288.)

Extreme behaviors at either end of several unipolar or bipolar dimensions of personality (e.g., impulsiveness/reflectiveness, externalizing/internalizing behavior) may reveal incompetence. What constitutes an optimal range of behavior is a question that can only be answered by gathering adequate normative data on tasks that reflect different forms of competence functioning.

4. Finally, there is the problem of "identifying different classes of variables in terms of their developmental trends." (Anderson and Messick, 1974, p. 288.)

This problem demands awareness, accompanied by data, of the nature of changes in competence-related variables over time. Relevant variables may have different developmental courses; some may remain constant over fairly long periods of time, some may show an incremental trend with age, others a decrement, while still others may show marked variations at specific transitional points in development. Again, age developmental norms are needed and can only be secured by research on competence attributes across age groups. Such data collection is best served initially by cross-sectional studies and subsequently by longitudinal-developmental methods (Baldwin, 1960; Garmezy and Devine, 1977).

THE LITERATURE OF COMPETENCE: MANIFESTATIONS IN HEALTHY INDIVIDUALS

Coping, adaptation, competence—these are relatively new areas of psychological research, in contradistinction to an older and more extensive literature built around *maladaptation, incompetence, defense* and *defeat* as adduced from the studies of the behavior pathology of adults and children.

Illustrative of the newer trend in volumes over the past five years are those of Antonovsky (1979), Coelho, Hamburg, and Adams (1974), Connolly and Bruner (1974), Gilmore (1974), Haan (1977), Kohn (1977), Lowenthal, Thurnher, and Chiriboga (1976), Moos (1976), Murphy and Moriarity (1976), Offer and Sabshin (1974), Vaillant (1977), and White and Watts (1973). An earlier bibliography on coping and adaptation is already clearly outdated (Coelho et al., 1970).

If one turns to the dictionary for a lay definition of competence it becomes immediately apparent that the word is strongly linked to achievement. "Competence," according to *Webster's Third New International Dictionary,* "is the quality or state of being functionally adequate or of having sufficient knowledge, judgment, skill or strength as for a particular duty or in a particular respect."

The dictionary definition is akin to Connolly and Bruner's (1974) distinction between a broadened concept of "operative" intelligence of "knowing how" rather than the simpler state of "knowing what." Competence for these investigators implies action, the ability to change or to act upon the environment as opposed simply to adapting to it. The three features implied in such an action orientation are:

1.   Selectivity in which the features of the environment which would facilitate solution are recognized and utilized.

2.   Planning a course of action and initiating activities necessary for achieving one's objective.

3. Utilizing the successes or failures encountered in the past to formulate new plans in the present or for the future.

It is particularly interesting to find Connolly and Bruner referring not only to nonspecific intellectual skills but to the importance of nonspecific emotional skills as well, of which confidence in oneself or self-esteem is based upon learning what we can do successfully and learning how to overcome failure when we encounter it.

Definitions such as these link the abstract notion of competence to specific competencies and require a determination of which areas of "functional adequacy," both in the spheres of concrete performance and affective and attitudinal patterns, are most significantly reflected in those individuals society looks upon as its competent members.

Here is where the problem grows more difficult. Although many speak and write about "competence," there exists no agreed-upon definition for it. In a recent volume devoted to *Normality* (Offer and Sabshin, 1974) there is no substantive definition offered, that responsibility being relegated by the authors to individual investigators:

> Do we see a profile emerging which reliably and validly describes "the normal man or woman"? Definitely not. The more we study normal populations the more we become aware that healthy functioning is at least as complex and varied as our psychopathological entities . . . It is our belief that continued empirical investigations will lead us to a better understanding of the complexity of healthy development. We are presently shifting from deduction and theorizing about normal development to empirical investigations of the relationship among the multiplicity of variables which contribute to the healthy, or normal development of individuals. Greater efforts in studies of coping and adaptation will prove to be useful in elucidating the theoretical perspectives of normality and mental health (Offer and Sabshin, 1974, pp. 197–198).

Offer and Sabshin are atypical in not volunteering a definition such as those that have been derived in armchairs and subsequently published under such rubrics as criteria for "positive mental health" or the "productive personality."

Twenty years ago under the prestigious institutional sponsorship of the early Joint Commission on Mental Illness and Health, Jahoda (1958) set forth her criteria in the volume *Current Concepts of Positive Mental Health*. With the passage of two decades it is somewhat surprising that her six criteria seem to have stood the test of time when placed against new listings of the attributes of competent functioning.

Basing her list on a survey of relevant literature Jahoda provided six major categories of concepts for defining positive mental health:

1. "The adequacy of an individual toward his own self." Jahoda's reference here is to a positive self-concept and a sense of identity.

2. "Growth, development or self-actualization" as expressions of mental health.

3. An "integrated" coherent personality accompanied by the ability to withstand adverse events and other forms of stress.

4. "Autonomy and independence" from social influence and effective regulation of behavior from within.

5. Adequacy of an individual's "perception of reality"; empathy, social sensitivity, and a concern for and attention to others.

6. *"Environmental mastery"*; the ability to love, work and play; adequacy in interpersonal relations; efficiency in meeting situational requirements; capacity for adaptation and adjustment; efficiency in problem-solving.

In her concluding statement Jahoda posed the still unresolved problem of translating these criteria into a systematic framework for research using the tools and strategies for observation that were then available. We would add to observation, the tools and strategies of laboratory investigation, survey methodology, and case study as well. The obvious problem of the reliability, validity, and representativeness of situations in which behavior is to be observed remains every bit as realistic (and difficult) an issue as it was two decades ago.

Other category sets seek to be more staunchly operational and down-to-earth, while still others are imprecise statements of positive virtues. Some spell out a developmental orientation ranging from the patternings of *The Competent Infant* (Stone, Smith, and Murphy, 1973), to the prosocial behaviors exhibited with adults and peers by preschoolers (White and Watts, 1973), to the strong patternings of *set* in the aged as described by Simone de Beauvoir (1972) in the *Coming of Age*. ("Habit . . . provides the old person with a kind of ontological security. Because of habit, he knows who he is. It protects him from his generalized anxieties by assuring him that tomorrow will be a repetition of today." p. 469.)

Gilmore (1974) writing of the "productive personality" has provided a set of criteria drawn from the work of others (e.g., Kohlberg, 1964; Murphy, 1962) that strikingly parallels Jahoda's earlier formulation. Using "ego strength" as the global concept, Gilmore has assigned to it the following behaviors: intelligent action, a reflective cognitive style, the ability to delay gratification, a perspective toward the future, a desire for autonomous achievement, a pattern of stable focused attention, internal locus of control, a lowered level of anxiety, and positive self-esteem (National Institute of Child Health and Development, 1968).

Gilmore also refers to integration of personality organization, a strong sense of personal identity including gender identity and adds an interesting congeries of personal attributes: altruism, sympathy, moral development marked by a sense of conscience, guilt, and shame for wrongdoing, and social responsibility.

A parallel is to be found in the aphorism provided by John Whitehorn (cited by Grinker, 1968), that the mentally healthy person is one who "works well, plays well, loves well and expects well"—a simple statement but one well rooted in the empirical literature of factors correlated with good and poor prognosis for recovery from psychopathology.

Whitehorn's "expects well" speaks to the concept of self-esteem which is derived through the achievements marked by his first three criteria of efficacy in work, play, and love.

The correlation of self-esteem to achievement, which is certainly one aspect of the "functional adequacy" alluded to earlier, is seen both at the elementary school level (Campbell, 1966; Coopersmith, 1967) as well as at the college and graduate school levels (Silverman, 1964).

A study by Blair (1968) of black students in the ninth grade demonstrated that I.Q. test scores and academic attainment were found to be related to self-esteem, independence behavior, and degree of inner control—all factors cited by Jahoda among the attributes she assigns to the concept of positive mental health.

Several other efforts to delineate the criteria of competence deserve review.

Smith (1974) gathered data from selected interview transcripts with Peace Corps volunteers to generate a set of descriptive personality items that were then Q-sorted to characterize each volunteer. A factor analysis of the data provided a first evaluative factor which was labeled *self-confident maturity*. The components of this factor included "self-confidence, high self-esteem, energy, responsibility, autonomy, trust in others, persistence with flexibility, and hopeful realism." In terms of their Peace Corps efforts these volunteers were rated very favorably, as highly competent, and committed to their work.

By contrast those low on this factor were marked by low self-esteem, dependency, high anxiety, pessimistic in terms of life's expectations, low energy level, gives up easily when faced with setbacks, unable to accept help from others, unrealistically minimizes or denies difficulties that are to be faced, lets things drift, irritable.

Finally, there are the set of attributes established by a panel under the auspices of the Office of Child Development to define the meaning of "social competency" in young children. The committee (Anderson and Messick, 1974) managed to generate twenty-nine statements to match their task (see Table 1).

This inclusive list embraces a goodly portion of work (i.e., school) effectiveness, social mastery, motivational skills, prosocial behaviors, impulse control, empathy, attentional focusing, and high self-esteem. Incorporative as it is, the list does parallel those of other list-makers. It is longer as befits a committee of twenty-one distinguished members.

Table 1.   Aspects of Social Competency in Young Children

1. Differentiated self-concept and consolidation of identity
2. Concept of self as an initiating and controlling agent
3. Habits of personal maintenance and care
4. Realistic appraisal of self, accompanied by feelings of personal worth
5. Differentiation of feelings and appreciation of their manifestations and implications
6. Sensitivity and understanding in social relationships
7. Positive and affectionate personal relationships
8. Role perception and appreciation
9. Appropriate regulation of antisocial behavior
10. Morality and prosocial tendencies
11. Curiosity and exploratory behavior
12. Control of attention
13. Perceptual skills
14. Fine motor dexterity
15. Gross motor skills
16. Perceptual-motor skills
17. Language skills
18. Categorizing skills
19. Memory skills
20. Critical thinking skills
21. Creative thinking skills
22. Problem-solving skills
23. Flexibility in the application of information-processing strategies
24. Quantitative and relational concepts, understanding, and skills
25. General knowledge
26. Competence motivation
27. Facility in the use of resources for learning and problem-solving
28. Some positive attitudes toward learning and school experiences
29. Enjoyment of humor, play, and fantasy

Source: Based on Anderson and Messick (1974).

COMPETENCE FROM THE VIEWPOINT OF DEVELOPMENTAL PSYCHOLOGY VERSUS DEVELOPMENTAL PSYCHOPATHOLOGY

There is an empirical area of research seemingly far removed from the study of competence, namely research in psychopathology. The behavior of the disordered person appears to be the obverse of the coin of competence, for the very act of breakdown under stress implies a more fragile personality structure. This is not inevitably the case, but its qualification would take us into a lengthy discussion of predispositional factors in relation to acute and chronic stress, and biogenetic and psychological factors in the mentally disordered and in normal individuals in situational crises.

The current scene in the study of competence is energized by research in both developmental psychology and psychopathology. In both cases older and newer perspectives on competence are evident. In developmental psychology the earlier orientation centered on intellectual competence, on the assessment of intelligence and the elaborate network of behavioral correlates that characterizes effective versus ineffective cognition. More recently, research contributing greatly to the study of children's competence has focused on social adaptation and competence in relation to attachment, socialization, parenting, and the development of prosocial behaviors.

By contrast, if one looks toward research in psychopathology for insights into the nature of competence, the gaze is distracted by two facts: (1) the narrowness of the behavioral criteria that are used; and yet (2) the power of such criteria to predict highly significant events such as resistance to stress or recovery from the stigmatizing status of mental patienthood. Educational achievement, friendships, sexual attachments, and employment history record the statistics of one's adaptation. They share the uncommon virtues of being readily measurable and of bearing some degree of predictive validity. But are there other manifestations of competence that may have equivalent or perhaps even greater power to provide a firm perspective for considering the adult futures of children? Baumrind and Black (1967) among others (e.g., Becker and Krug, 1964; Schaefer, 1961) have written of the multidimensional nature of competence, two-dimensional in the preschool years (socialized/responsible versus disobedient/unfriendly; independence/autonomy versus dependence/suggestibility), three-dimensional in middle childhood (responsible-altruistic/social independence and dominance/cognitive agency). Baumrind's general factors embrace positive mood stages, self-esteem, and physical fitness, while her specific competencies include social responsibility, (compliant facilitative behavior with adults, prosocial behavior with peers, moral maturity) agency (social cognition, achievement orientation, internal locus of control and creativity), and social confidence (egalitarian attitudes toward adults, leadership behavior with peers, and purposive, persistent, goal-oriented behavior).

Empirical Findings on the Early Sources of Security and Competence

Michael Rutter (1978), in his Wolfson Lecture delivered at Oxford University, turned to the intriguing paradox of children who fail to fit our prediction formulations. There are children, he notes, who emerge out of desperate circumstances, relatively unscathed, and yet appear to have developed healthy personalities. What do we know about the roots of their emotional security and social competence?

In his review of research relevant to this question, Rutter has considered several aspects of the problem including the thesis of a vulnerable age phenomenon in relation to specific stresses, such as separation and loss. These can have particularly powerful effects if they occur at an age at which a child is particularly susceptible to that stressor. Thus age itself can serve as a powerful determinant as to whether a child will show a greater likelihood of behaving in a manner that reflects security or insecurity.

Other factors can also operate to produce adaptive as opposed to maladaptive behavior (Rutter, 1979). One is the multiplicity of stresses to which a child may be subjected. In looking at the antecedents of child psychiatric disorder as observed in epidemiological studies conducted on the Isle of Wight and in the inner city of London, Rutter and his colleagues successfully isolated six family variables that were found to be associated with such disorders: "(1) severe marital discord; (2) low social status; (3) overcrowding or large family size; (4) paternal criminality; (5) maternal psychiatric disorder; (6) admission into the care of local authority" (Rutter, 1979, p. 52). Rates of psychiatric disorder proved to be a function of the *number* of familial risk factors to which the children had been exposed. A *single stress,* even if chronic, did not increase significantly a child's risk for psychiatric disorder over those children who had not been exposed to *any* of the risk factors. Two or three stresses, however, operating concurrently resulted in a fourfold increase in psychiatric disorder. The presence of four or more simultaneous family risk factors produced a tenfold increase in the rate of disorder.

On the side of reducing risk were found positive temperament factors in the child, such as regularity, flexibility of response to impinging stimuli, and positive mood—attributes of the "easy" child (Thomas and Chess, 1977) that can attenuate the likelihood of the child becoming an irritant to parents and the target of their censure. On the other hand, Rutter reports that children with adverse temperament attributes were twice as likely to be the victims of parental criticism than were those children with the aforementioned positive temperament characteristics. It thus appears that genetically determined constitutional variables can help to shape the reward or punishment aspects of a child's environment. Similarly, Rutter reports sex of the child seems to play a role in adaptation: male children tend to be more vulnerable to physical and psychosocial stress than are females, provided there is an absence of identifiable brain pathology.

The role of parents too is an obviously critical one. A warm, empathic relationship between parent and child that provides for a secure emotional bonding is an important source of security. Even in highly discordant and unhappy homes, Rutter has found that if a child has had a relationship with one of the parents marked by "high warmth and the absence of severe criticism" it appears to provide substantial protection for the child. Rutter reports that in such homes only 25% of the offspring manifested a conduct disorder, compared with 75% of children from similar but quarrelsome families in which such a supportive relationship did not exist. Placement in a harmonious home setting, even when such placement was dictated by the presence of mentally disordered biological parents, also seemed to reduce significantly the probability of psychiatric risk in the offspring.

Influences beyond the home may also exercise a major impact on the adaptive behaviors of children. Of the many possible social influencing agents, the school, in which the child spends such a large portion of the working day, is undoubtedly one of the most significant. Rutter and his colleagues (1979) have investigated the stable and relatively long-term (four to five years) contribution different inner-London schools make to a wide variety of behaviors: absenteeism, delinquency rates, teachers' ratings of misbehavior, school retention, success in later public examinations, and so forth. These different behavioral outcomes between schools proved not to be related to physical factors such as school size, age of building, or availability of space, nor were they a function of differences in administrative organization. The important correlates of adaptive behavior were rooted in the attributes of the schools as social institutions.

Factors as varied as the degree of academic emphasis, teacher actions in lessons, the availability of incentives and rewards, good conditions for pupils and the extent to which children were able to take responsibility were all significantly associated with outcome differences between schools (Rutter et al., 1979, p. 178).

These factors are not fixed by unmodifiable external limitations, but are open to change by faculty and administrators, and thus suggest a more hopeful augury for the futures of children in settings where the requisite leadership is present. The authors' overarching conclusion is this: ". . . to an appreciable extent children's behaviour and attitudes are shaped and influenced by their experiences at school and, in particular, by the qualities of the schools as a social institution." (Rutter et al., 1979, p. 179.)

The causal inference is based upon the longitudinal data available to the investigators that affirm differences in student outcomes following specific placements in schools with specific characteristics *after* controlling for relevant features of the children when initially admitted to these different secondary schools.

What are these specific school characteristics that appear to conduce to good outcomes? The investigators point to these as the major influencing factors: (1) Fundamental to the school's effectiveness is its *ethos,* the culture or climate of the school as an institution, (2) the efficacy of the school's management as exemplified by the teacher's effectiveness in organizing the classroom, and in providing a quiet, positive, firm, nonobtrusive style of discipline in which punishment and reprimand are not primary modes of control, (3) high expectations by staff and their confidence in the student's academic competence and behavior; (4) assignment of responsibility to students for maintaining the physical resources of the school, and a pleasant working environment; (5) the teacher as a model of concern for and responsiveness to pupils, including the use of positive reinforcement and rapid feedback in response to pupil achievements; (6) widespread acceptance of school values and norms by staff and students; (7) an active sharing in activities between staff and students; (8) a well-balanced mix of students in terms of intellectual abilities, whereas a mix of other behaviors as well as of socioeconomic and sociocultural background seems to be of secondary importance; and (9) stability of class assignments throughout schooling to foster the students' identification with the school and its goals.

By providing a much-needed empirical investigation of multiple school settings, their characteristics, and their effects on students, Rutter and his co-workers have begun to fill in gaps in our knowledge of the role of major societal institutions for influencing the nature and development of children's competencies. Furthermore, the message has a ring of optimism as reflected in Rutter's (1978) concluding commentary in his Wolfson Lecture:

Development is fluid and it is never too late for changes to take place. Even with the worst circumstance that human beings can devise only a proportion of the children succumb, and ameliorating factors can do much to aid normal development. There is a widening—although still limited—knowledge of how children and parents can overcome stresses and disadvantages. If we can increase our understanding of these influences and harness the knowledge already available to our policies and to our patterns of treatment, perhaps something useful can be achieved. Of course, we will not eliminate suffering. Nevertheless some children who would otherwise have succumbed may be helped to survive stressful circumstances and to develop emotional security and social competence (p. 57).

ON THE NATURE OF STRESS

Volumes have been written about stress and its correlates. Although the emphasis in the literature has been largely on adult reactivity, a growing literature has begun to be focused on the adaptations of children under threat (e.g., Clegg and Megson, 1968; Fraser, 1973; Lash and Sigal, 1976; Lewis, 1954; Stewart, 1976; Tonge, James, and Hillam, 1975; Varma, 1973; Wedge and Prosser, 1973; Wolff, 1973; and Young, 1964).

The breadth of volumes in the more general literature of stress include the effects of specific stressors: natural and man-made disasters; war and its aftermath; surgery; death, dying, and bereavement; economic deprivation; social stresses; and so forth. Added to this literature, of course, are the even more voluminous writings on stress-related behaviors: emotion, anxiety and conflict, frustration and aggression, psychophysiological disorders and other forms of psychopathology. Perhaps the breadth of the field can be summed up in this observation. When Selye first introduced the concept in 1936, there was a paucity of research on stress. By the time his major formulation appeared in 1950, later to be popularized in *The Stress of Life* (1956, 1976), the volume of articles on the physiology of stress alone had reached a level approximating 6,000 annually.

Selye restricted the definition of the concept of stress to a pattern of physiological responses which he termed the general adaptation syndrome (GAS) with its specified stages (alarm, resistance, and exhaustion) that reflected the changes in such responsivity when stress was prolonged. The stressors in Selye's formulation were such events as infections, marked temperature changes, injury, sugical trauma, other physical trauma, and so on. In such circumstances it is less difficult to retain Selye's clear though perhaps oversimplified view of stress with its consequences in disease and physical debility.

Psychological research on stress evolved from the physiological research and rapidly came to be perceived as a legitimate area for study. But the elaboration of Selye's formulation to include psychological stressors provided new difficulties. Eysenck, Arnold, and Meili (1972) noted:

> The range of psychological stressors is so wide as to be virtually endless . . . when examined in a psychological context, the stress reaction must . . . take account of complex cognitive processes as well as physiological reactions and feedback from the effects of these reactions (pp. 282–283).

Commenting on the incorporative nature of stress Appley and Trumbull (1967) noted that:

> Since the term gained some attention, and apparently some status, as a research topic, it has been used as a substitute for what might otherwise have been called anxiety, conflict, emotional distress, extreme environmental conditions, ego-threat, frustration, threat to security, tension, arousal, or by some other previously respectable terms (p. 1).

It is the implicit linkage evident in these overlapping terms that has broadened the appeal of research on stress. It holds forth a promise of the potential power offered by combining the modes of clinical and experimental research. But the definitional problem has remained. In a broad sense stress is both stimulus and response. On the stimulus side it relates to those actions and events that require individuals to put forth special levels of physical or psychological response in order to regain an equilibrium that has been disrupted by situations marked by newness, rapid change, danger, threat, boredom, fatigue, and so on.

On the response side stress is indexed by marked shifts in performance, increased propensity to error or to fatigue, and perhaps most marked of all by a tendency to disruption or disorganization of behavior.

The problem of definition is clouded however by the reality of individual differences. An imposed stimulus does not necessarily generate an intended effect. Stress, thus, can also be challenge, just as a two character Chinese notation for the word "crisis" is used to denote both danger and opportunity.

It is only with regard to life-threatening stresses or to the severance of deep-seated attachments (via traumatic severe injury, or disability, natural catastrophies, combat, death, and bereavement) that one is enabled to refer to universal stressors which appear to have consequences for almost all individuals. The threshold for arousal is markedly lowered in these special cases, whereas in most other instances responses suggestive of a stress state require a period of delay while the organism appraises or interprets the event as threatening. Only then does the stress response become manifest.

Referring to the relationship between stress and individual vulnerability, Appley and Trumbull (1967) write:

> It is consistently found that these reactions vary in intensity from person to person under exposure to the same environmental event . . . It has also been noted that, with few exceptions, the *kind* of situation which arouses a stress response in a particular individual must be related to significant events in that person's life. Many people have used the terms "ego-strength," "stress-tolerance," and "frustration-tolerance." It is perhaps doubtful that there is such a thing as a general stress-tolerance in people. There is more likely to be a greater or lesser insulation from the effects of certain kinds of stress-producers rather than others . . . It seems more likely that there are differing thresholds, depending upon the kinds of threats that are encountered and that individuals must be differentially vulnerable to different kinds of stressors . . . To know what conditions of the environment are likely to be effective for the particular person, the motivational structure and prior history of the individual would have to be taken into account. Where the particular motives are known—where it is known what a person holds important and not important, what kinds of goals he will work for and why, what kinds of situations have for him been likely to increase anxiety or lead to aversive or defensive behavior—a reasonable prediction of stress proneness might be made (pp. 10–11).

This passage sets forth in part the programmatic research effort *(Project Competence)* of the Minnesota group. Is stress-responsivity a highly generalized or a more specific attribute to the individual? Is stress-responsivity situation-specific for most individuals, or is there a strong element of trans-situational consistency for those persons who despite placement at the higher end of the stress-exposure dimension show consistently either very high or very low levels of mastery of their environment?

Stress-reactivity, however, is not wholly an intraindividual phenomenon. Other persons, the social and culture matrix of an individual's environment, the family in terms of its integrative or disintegrative state, all contribute to exacerbating or reducing stress and to inhibiting or facilitating mastery.

These factors suggest the necessity for an investigator not only to pursue the trait and state attributes of stress-resistance but also to take into account the social matrix in which an individual functions.

Defining Stress

Stress in its most neutral and extended definition is defined as "any action or situation that places special physical or psychological demands upon a person—anything that serves to unbalance an individual's equilibrium or homeostasis." Losing a job, by this definition is stressful; so is going to a new job that represents a promotion. The sound of footsteps behind one on a darkened city street produces a state of heightened arousal, so does the appearance of a loved one. Excess stress can be hurtful; the absence of it may also do harm to an individual's moves to maturity. *Stress* is not equivalent to *distress,* although it has come to be viewed in that way.

If one considers any event that is destabilizing, momentary or otherwise, the way is clear to perceive both positive and negative events as stressful. It is such a definition that has brought research on life events schedules to rapid prominence, for it provides in simple form a catalogue of destabilizing events that can be positive and negative, of short duration or long duration, of serious or of more moderate consequence. But there are marked limitations and constraints that such a simple schedule places on both respondent and investigator (Dohrenwend and Dohrenwend, 1974).

Lazarus' (1971) view of stress by contrast requires the presence of a "damaging transaction" between an organism and a condition in the environment. Thus the stimulus in stress and the reaction to it are both integral elements of any effort at definition:

> From this point of view, it would be well to allow the term "stress" to extend to the whole area of problems, sociological, psychological and physiological in which organizations and individuals are taxed by stimulus demands up to the limits of their potential ability to adapt. The concept thus includes stimulus causes, mechanisms, and response effects, more specific terms being required to differentiate each variable and process, at each level of analysis. Stress refers, then, to a very broad class of problems differentiated from other problem areas because it deals with *any demands which tax the system,* whatever it is, a physiological system, a social system, or a psychological system, and *the response of that system* (Lazarus, 1971, p. 54).

In Lazarus' analysis the key components in appraisal are determined by the balance of forces evident in the person's interactions with the environment. When environmental demands exceed the availability of the individual's resources to meet them, the appraisal generates an awareness of *threat* posed by the heightened probability of *harm* or *loss* that is to follow. If the individual's available resources exceed such demands, the appraisal is more likely to evoke a positive sense of *challenge*.

A "damaging transaction" involves, then, an individual interpretation of event, press, and personal resources. Such interpretations are heavily influenced by prior success or failure experiences, one's concept of the self, motivational structures, demographic and cultural factors, and so on. It is these individualized factors that pose the difficult problem of defining most stress experiences. "What is meat to one, is poison to the other" is an oft-heard statement (Mechanic, 1970). Persons who differ in age, sex, social, and cultural background can also differ in their appraisals of stress, threat, distress, and challenge.

Lazarus' "challenge" is Bernard's "eustress"—those pleasant stresses which must be separated out from "dys-stress" of the unpleasant variety. The distinction here too is a psychological one. Bernard (1968) writes:

Voluntary dys-stress is the kind associated with the assumption of activities and responsibilities beyond the call of duty . . . Such dys-stress is difficult, sometimes depressing. It is associated with the Protestant Ethic, with Puritanism, with blue noses. Eustress, contrariwise, is associated with excitement, adventure, thrilling experiences. It is fun, it enhances vital sensations, it 'turns people on,' it releases energy. Indeed one of the reasons for studying stress-seeking . . . lies in the key it may supply for unlocking the 'motivational reservoir for social actions' (pp. 8–9).

Taken in this context Bernard's eustress comes closer to the literature on "sensation-seeking" (Zuckerman et al., 1972), a pattern of behavior with which the Minnesota research project is not concerned. But the positive type of stressor described by Bernard has a less volatile parallel in Murphy's (1962) fourfold category of situations that require coping. Murphy describes coping as "some means-end element in the process of activity" that serves to secure mastery over a novel situation, obstacle, or conflict that is either new or has not yet been overcome. Such situations can be (1) gratifying (i.e. positively enhancing), (2) challenging (anticipated gratifications), (3) threatening (anticipated frustrations), or (4) frustrating. The continuum of situations so set forth establish a classification of situations ranging from the "eustress" to the "dys-stress" categories suggested by Bernard and others (e.g., Lipowski, 1969).

Such a category set is reflected in the different stressors that have been used as the basis for the selection of three different cohorts of children in the Minnesota research program. The category of "threatening" situations is reflected in the inclusion of children born with a life-threatening congenital heart defect. The search for a stress marked by a pronounced omnipresent "frustration" has led to our decision to study a separate cohort of physically handicapped children who are being "mainstreamed" in a school system. Positive and negative events that reflect variations in their degree of gratification and frustration and require efforts at mastery have led us to select a third cohort of families and children in the community who report exposure to a variety of life events that vary in their severity of stressfulness.

Stress-Resistance and the Trauma of Early Psychological Deprivation

One area of stress that has been given increasing attention in recent years is the problem of maternal and social-emotional deprivation in infancy and childhood: parental loss, bereavement, divorce, foster home placement of children, and adaptation to adoption. These studies supplement the observations of Rutter and his research group that have been described previously.

A striking aspect of studies in this area of separation and loss is the reversibility of the traumas many children sustain. Kadushin's (1967) follow-up study of ninety-one children who had been placed for adoption when they were 5 years of age or older and who had, prior to adoption, encountered considerable trauma is a case in point. These young boys (forty-nine) and girls (forty-two) had on the average been in foster homes for almost four years and had experienced an average of 2.3 foster home changes prior to permanent adoption. In all cases the children had been separated from their biological parents because of neglect or abuse, or both. Their childhoods had been spent in poverty marked by poor housing, conflictual family relationships, and family pathology (promiscuity, alcoholism, imprisonment of a parent, parental psychosis, etc.). Only one-third of the children had met with normal parental warmth and acceptance. In 70% of the cases the child was physically neglected, in 40% emotional neglect was evident.

Interviews were conducted with the adoptive father and mother by trained social workers and signs of parental satisfaction or dissatisfaction were rated independently by three qualified social workers. Of the group of ninety-one adoptive parents 87% expressed satisfaction with the adoption. Apparently, if these reports and observations are accurate, these traumatized children had been able to overcome satisfactorily their traumatic early years.

Other studies have provided comparable results. Theis (1924) who also evaluated foster children found a gratifyingly high level of adjustment that provided "a distinctive impression that there exists in individuals an immense power of growth and adaptation" (p. 163). Roe and Burks (1945) made similar observations of previously traumatized children who had been placed in foster care because of parental neglect. They found that their sample of thirty-six young adults were showing such healthy adult adaptations as to force the conclusion that these productive, contented persons generated in the investigators "a profound sense of awe at the biological toughness of the human species" (p. 391).

Finally Meier (1962, 1965) has provided follow-up data on sixty-one young adults who had been removed from their own homes and reared in foster homes, many prior to 5 years of age. By the time they were 18 years old the average number of foster home placements for the group was 5.6 different settings. And yet after interviewing these young people Meier found them indistinguishable from their neighbors; they were self-supporting, good parents, and contributors to community activities.

Out of this experience Meier observed:

> Child welfare workers are continuously baffled, as well as heartened, by the fact that over and over again they see children removed from impossibly depriving circumstances who, by all the "rules" ought to be irreparably harmed, who, nevertheless, thrive and grow and learn to accept love and affection and respond to it. (Meier, 1965, p. 12.)

Results such as these have been affirmed by Lewis (1954), Welter (1965), Renaud and Estess (1961), Brill and Liston (1966) and Bowlby and Ainsworth (1956). The phenomenon recurs too frequently in the follow-up studies cited above to be viewed simply as atypical outcomes of traumatizing early childhoods.

However, it also remains a fact that most studies of vulnerability to stress in adoptees and foster home-reared children suffer from sufficient methodological deficiencies and unevenness in the available data as to warrant caution in asserting sweeping global conclusions (Kirk, Jonassohn, and Fish, 1966).

Nevertheless, in commenting on these departures from clinical expectations, Kadushin points to the finding that in general a closer analysis of several of these studies suggests that the less pathological the background of the child, the higher the probability of a more successful adaptation in childhood. But it is also the case as affirmed by Thomas et al. (1963) that basic biological differences in resiliency and reactivity from infancy onward modify or temper environmental experience. These factors must also be considered in a search for those conditions and attributes that correlate with vulnerability or resistance to stress.

COPING BEHAVIOR

Coping as Concept and as Skill

Coping bears an intimate relationship to the concepts of stress and competence outlined in earlier sections of this chapter. In relation to a stress it is a pattern of response made to novel situations, obstacles, or conflicts (Murphy, 1962) present in the environment that carry "challenge" to one's self-esteem by virtue of posing threats of failure, danger, or loss of security (Gilmore, 1974). But it also defines a threefold form that such responses are likely to take: (1) a search for those expedients to action that will serve to overcome the problem, (2) the maintenance of continued motivation (effort) during that search for solutions, eventuating in a (3) solution that helps to attain mastery over the problem.

A distinction has been set out by some researchers to differentiate between the concept of *coping* versus that of *defending*. Coping mechanisms are looked upon as healthy, active, and adequate efforts to gain mastery over threat in the environment, whereas defenses are presumed to reflect inadequate or in some instances pathological methods of dealing with threat through protection-seeking from environmental challenge.

Perhaps the most explicit statement of such differences has been made by Haan (1963) who has elaborated upon her views in her recently published (1977) volume *Coping and Defending*. Haan's distinctions are set forth in Table 2. To her impressive set of distinctions, I have added several that Professor John Romano has suggested in a personal communication.

The Formulations of Lazarus and Colleagues

Lazarus (1966) more than two decades ago recognized some comparable distinctions with his category set for "defensive appraisals" or coping reaction patterns. For example, *direct actions* which are aimed at strengthening the individual's resources against threat can take the form of *attack patterns* (with or without anger) or *avoidance patterns* (with or without fear). This more nearly represents coping in contrast to *defensive appraisals* in which no direct form of coping is visible or *anxiety reaction patterns* denoted by threat reaction when no clear action tendency is generated.

More recently, Lazarus and his colleagues (see Lazarus and Launier, 1978) have described stress and coping in terms of a transactional model in which the *process* of stimulus and response incorporates a *sequence*

Table 2.   Analysis   of   Properties   of   Defense   Mechanisms   and   Coping Mechanisms

Haan's Differentiation

Properties of a Defense Mechanism	Properties of a Coping Mechanism
1. Behavior is rigid, automatized, and stimulus bound.	1. Behavior involves choice and is thus flexible and purposive.
2. Behavior is pushed from the past, and the past compels the needs of the present.	2. Behavior is pulled toward the future and takes account of the needs of the present.
3. Behavior is essentially distorting of the present situation.	3. Behavior is oriented to the reality requirement of the present situation.
4. Behavior involves a greater quantity of primary process thinking, partakes of unconscious elements, and is thus undifferentiated in response.	4. Behavior involves secondary process thinking, conscious and preconscious elements, and is highly differentiated in response.
5. Behavior operates with the assumption that it is possible to remove disturbing affects magically.	5. Behavior operates within the organism's necessity of "metering" the experiencing of disturbing affects.
6. Behavior allows impulse gratification by subterfuge.	6. Behavior allows forms of impulse satisfaction in an open, ordered, and tempered way.

Romano's Differentiation

Defense Mechanisms		Coping Mechanisms
Information-reducing	versus	Information-gathering
Intrapersonal	versus	Interpersonal in orientation
Self-devaluation/incompetence	versus	Mastery/self-esteem
Origins in guilt	versus	Origins in shame
Restrictive	versus	Innovative

Source: Based on Haan (1963) and Romano (1977).

of stimulus and response alterations. This sequence is triggered by a person's continued assessment and reassessment of ongoing experience and the consequent modification of response in an attempt to shape the course of future events.

Roskies and Lazarus (in press) write:

> The occurrence or anticipation of a given event is stressful and generates emotional reactions because the person construes it both as important to his or her well-being and as taxing his or her resources, and the type of coping response made is again based on *evaluation* of the best available way to achieve

the outcome which is *judged* as most desirable or least harmful. The static S-O-R linear model has been replaced by a dynamic cognitive one . . .

This new model radically alters the direction of the cause-effect relationship between stress and coping. Coping is no longer simply a response to an event that *has* happened, but instead becomes an active force in shaping what *is* happening and what *will* happen.

The role of appraisal in Lazarus' view is itself an active process that can meliorate or accentuate the perceived stressfulness of a situation since it entails as well the equally relevant evaluation of one's resources (intrapsychic, environmental, etc.) in deciding whether or not the stressful event can be met adequately or inadequately.

But the problem of the conceptualization of coping remains a challenge. Lazarus and Launier (1978) have generated a classification system for coping behavior in which two major categories are: (1) *altering the troubled transaction (instrumental)* and (2) *regulating the emotion (palliation)* (p. 313). This system considers both the *temporal orientation* (Is the appraisal one of a past/present or a future threat?) and the *instrumental focus* (Is the coping effort directed toward the environment or toward the self?) of the effort to cope as particularly relevant factors in deriving a classification system.

The coping modes they envision are fourfold: *information seeking, direct action, inhibition of action,* and *intrapsychic*. The last named is represented by the traditional defense mechanisms as well as more effective cognizing efforts.

The choice of the coping effort is seen as dependent upon the *degree of uncertainty* or *ambiguity* with regard to the posed threat, the *severity of the threat, conflict* (conceived in Millerian terms of approach-avoidance tendencies that constrain action and resolution), and the magnitude of the individual's perceived *helplessness* versus confidence in one's ability to control significant outcomes.

Recent papers by Lazarus and his colleagues (Lazarus, 1978; Lazarus and Launier, 1978; Roskies and Lazarus, in press; Lazarus, et al., in press; Lazarus, Kanner, and Folkman, in press; Folkman, Schaefer, and Lazarus, in press) have provided invigorating new analyses of the concepts of stress and coping that point the way toward research studies needed in this important area of adaptiveness or maladaptiveness under threat.

One effect of this large-scale effort may well be a broadened view of the problem of analyzing threat and its consequences. This has not always been the case in the past. In general, studies of coping have reflected discipline biases. Those that have been conducted by psychologists and psychiatrists have dealt in great detail with individual responsiveness and to a far less extent with environmental analysis. By contrast, sociological studies, often of natural disasters, have placed great emphasis on the collective environmental impact and have tended to evaluate individual behavior primarily in terms of group phenomena.

A recent volume on the destruction of an Appalachian community following the Buffalo Creek Flood by sociologist Kai T. Erikson (1976) recognizes a difference by reference to the concepts of *individual* versus *collective* trauma. But Erikson's catalogue of individual trauma remains essentially a collective pattern for individuals as a group with no attention paid to individual styles of coping. Mourning, loss of morale, depression, collapse of moral standards, disorientation, isolation, difficulty of problem-solving, loss of human trust, illness, and loss of identity are assigned to all victims of the disaster, but there is a failure to recognize, even in the superb descriptions provided by the observer, those individual variations in coping that are manifestly evident even in the presence of a universal stress.

This does not negate the critical importance of a societal context in evaluating individual coping efforts. Mechanic (1974), a distinguished sociologist, recognizes the validity of an individual's coping capabilities, his or her motivation to meet environmental demands, and the necessity for the maintenance of a state of psychological equilibrium by persons, but he also makes a telling case for the importance of society's contributions in solving the most pressing demands that are placed on individuals. Society, asserts Mechanic, does this in two ways. First by evolving preparatory institutions such as schools (see also Rutter et al., 1979) that help to provide the competence skills individuals need to cope successfully. Second by providing the social supports individuals need to meet the major stressors, such as natural disasters, that occur in their lives. To such unusual events must be added more common and extreme privations including transgenerational poverty, because the greater the stress and the more universal its presence, the less likely is its reduction to be amenable to individual intervention. The components of "major" in alluding to stressors are those that (1) are overpowering in that individuals can do little to modify them, (2) that are prolonged and intense, (3) that are cumulative in nature, and (4) may be of a form that persons have had little experience with previously. These aspects erode the individual's efforts at problem-solving. Poverty provides one example of such an eroding stress. The fight for survival by a family residing in the urban slums must have the support of a society committed to an eradication of disordered environments, the use of support systems for family members, and a commitment to the use of its "preparatory institutions" to train individuals in the skills necessary to escape the confinement of poverty.

The Implications for Research on Stress

These views of stress and coping point up some of the major methodological limitations that are evident in much of stress research. Mechanic's (1974) criticisms are cogent:

> Man attempts to take on tasks he feels he can handle, he actively seeks information and feedback, he plans and anticipates problems, he insulates himself against defeat in a variety of ways, he keeps his options open, he distributes his commitment, he sets the stage for new efforts by practice and rehearsal, he tries various solutions and so on. One cannot study such activities very effectively within an experimental mode that subjects man to specific stimuli and only measures limited reactions to these. But methodological models to successfully study such active processes of coping are very much undeveloped, and the lack of richness in the experimental stress literature reflects the lack of a successful experimental technology for studying adaptive attempts over time (pp. 38–39).

Mechanic decries the interview method as retrospective, and psychological assessment techniques as substituting labels for explanation. He strongly endorses the study of disasters and real-life stresses under natural conditions but recognizes the difficulty of anticipating such events and of isolating the most influential variables involved in coping in the presence of disaster.

In suggesting how best to study coping, Mechanic favors a "rich interaction between field studies and more precise laboratory experiments" designed to simulate real situations. Further, he urges an emphasis on prospective and process studies that are extended over time and thus allow study of the breadth of a person's adaptive repertoire rather than its artificial narrowing to the experimental demands of the researcher.

Mechanic calls for more than a descriptive array of behaviors that represent the individual's coping style. The need is for studies that permit differential predictions: Under what types of circumstances will one coping effort be attempted in opposition to another? Finally, he urges investigators to study successful people in the hope of learning how they go about organizing and preparing to deal with difficult tasks and to solve problems.

With these views there can be no quarrel. The issue of the ecological validity of laboratory studies of stress is a major problem as are the ethical issues of deliberately generating disruptive threats to people. But the call for a multimethod approach to stress responsivity is one consonant with the views of contempoary researchers of personality and one that is a requisite for studies of individuals under stress.

Coping Skills

What are the specific competencies that characterize good "copers" as opposed to poor ones? Here again one finds in the literature a catalogue not unlike those that serve as ascriptors used to designate competence (Gilmore, 1974).

1. Accuracy of perception including receptivity to environmental stimuli, the ability to select imperative stimulus aspects of the environment and then to focus attention on those components that are essential to problem solving.

2. The ability to exercise sound appraisal and good judgment in problem situations.

3. A sense of hopefulness and efficacy in that there is a positive anticipation of outcomes, and positive expectancies that problems can be solved by one's own resourcefulness and skills.

4. Cognitive skills implicating verbal ability, reading ability, math, and memory, and the use of such skills in the resolution of problems.

5. The control of affect and impulse; delay of gratification and a reasonably appropriate time perspective.

6. The regulation of affect to allow for effective cognitive processing of the problem and its solution.

7. The ability to order complex situations; to seek and to process information relevant to problem solving.

8. Persistence in problem solving.

9. A sense of autonomy, independence and responsibility for making one's own decisions.

10. A belief in one's control over one's fate.

What about poor "copers"? Are their attributes the mirror opposite of those described for good stress-responders? Haan (1977) takes a broader view of this group and her observations deserve attention, for she offers a number of alternatives to explain an individual's lack of efficacy in mastering environmental demands:

> Some people handle stress less ably than others. The most obvious reason
> . . . is that the nature of the particular situation has special ominous meanings to
> them, that is, it is similar in structure, content, or affective overtones to past

unsuccessfully resolved situations. A second reason may be that the particular situation requires ego capabilities that the person does not easily use or has not developed either because he is a child, he is retarded in some way, or he prefers processes that are inappropriate to the situation. A third reason may be that the person's chronically stressed and habitual defensive condition is only exacerbated by the onset of new stress. Finally, the alleviation of stress often requires the help of others, and some people are without such support systems because they are without intimates or because their cultural subsystem does not value and promote mutual aid (p. 172).

Is there not a more positive parallel to such situational factors in the lives of good copers? These individuals are likely to have the requisite skills necessary to meet stress more effectively. For them, a particular "stress" situation may not be as ominous because its "structure, content, and affective overtones" have been successfully challenged and met in the past. It is equally likely that even in the face of chronic stress the good coper has enjoyed the partial reinforcements of successes due in no small part to his or her own skills and perhaps to the inadvertencies of a more hospitable fate? And finally we can ask whether these people tend to have the support systems of a more beneficent family or of sets of friends, teachers and other adults who take pleasure in the presence of their maintained skills particularly when appraised against a background of marked stress.

This brings us to an interesting conjecture. The work of Michael Rutter and his Maudsley colleagues, joined with the studies of others, provide us with a starting point for understanding some of the types of experiences that may help to inoculate children against the deleterious effects of stress. We infer from such research that adaptive, stressed children seemed to have enjoyed compensatory positive experiences outside the family and a bond with some supportive surrogate figure(s). We infer too that they appear to possess cognitive skills that are critical for adaptation under stress—social problem-solving skills marked by greater variability, flexibility and resiliency (Spivack and Shure, 1974; Spivack, Platt, and Shure, 1976; Shure and Spivack, 1978; Pellegrini, 1980).

We may conclude, therefore, that modes of intervention are available to us for effecting change in less favored children. Surrogate figures are to be sought, models are to be observed, and more formal exposition invoked to teach those problem-solving skills so facilitative in crisis.

But a research question that requires resolution before we plunge into full-scale interventions of this sort is the need to know the attributes not only of surrogates but of the helped child. The interactions between helpers and those they assist is a two-way street. What attracts surrogates to children who subsequently prove by acts and thoughts that they are stress-resistant? Intellectual achievement, it has been said, favors the prepared mind. May not adaptational achievements favor equally well the prepared personality?

The initial search then must be for understanding the attributes and resources of children who maintain mastery in a stressful world.

To do so the researcher must leave the laboratory and search for answers in the "real" world that surrounds the child—the family setting, the school, the neighborhood, and the peer group.

Only through such varied approaches to the study of stress-resistance can the researcher hope to deal with an observation that Robert Louis Stevenson (who knew the stress of physical illness) was purported to have made: "Life is not a matter of holding good cards, but of playing a poor hand well."

And that brings a return to the question as to what are the factors that enable some individuals to play that very "poor hand well"?

In our search for such factors there is an added danger in the effort at analysis. The terms "good" and "poor" copers are heavily value-laden. All of the positive virtues and labels appear to fall to the competent and to the coper; all negatives to the incompetent and to the defender. Are the "good" ways to handle stress exclusively those of confrontation and grappling or are mechanisms of avoidance and retreat a better measure of reality-testing in some situations? Is the move to alleviate distress always a positive enterprise or is distress simply a necessary component of the human condition?

"In a way," writes Haan, "stress research seems to have unwittingly designed a scientific 'Catch 22' situation. If you do not admit you can be killed in a war, you are strong and courageous, but you are also a fool" (Haan, 1977, p. 157).

Further, there is the question not solely of studying the response to stress, but also the need to understand what price may be paid by the "coper" for long-term efforts to deal with the multiple and recurrent stresses life seems to deal out to some people?

Haan's (1977) observation of this problem is an important one and warrants quotation:

Just as we cannot, on rational grounds, avoid considering that some social arrangements are better for some people than others, or that some organizations of personality are better than others, we cannot avoid recognizing that some resolutions of stress are more socially and personally satisfactory for all concerned than are others. Strictly speaking, we are not permitted to say that the man who effectively turns his back on the interpersonal chaos surrounding him and thereby evidences little arousal is impervious to stress. Instead, he has made one kind of solution to stress that must inevitably have social and personal valuation and consequences. If his lack of arousal is based on his avoiding the recognition that his child has leukemia and a consequent need for medical attention, we may need to inhibit our Judeo-Christian propensity to "blame" him in the construction of our research designs and interpretations. Greater imagination and differentiation is needed to see that by his own necessity he chooses a resolution to stress that involves self-compartmentalization instead of disintegration . . .

. . . Large-scale naturalistic research on stress has been able, almost at will, to establish correlates between noxious social situations and various indices of breakdown in people, such as psychiatric and physical illness. However, correlates between inimical social conditions and personal damage do not form a basis for a psychology of stress. They only reinvent the wheel . . .

. . . Why do some people when they are faced with stress do far better or far worse than anyone had suspected they would, and why do they do better or far worse than they have done before? Why do some kinds of social conditions totally define the actors, and why are other conditions that seem equally monolithic susceptible to being revised by some people? (Haan, 1977, pp. 158–161).

Here again is a new phrasing to the central question of what is it that accounts for stress-resistance? The sought-for-answer frames the purpose and goals of the newly-initiated Minnesota program of research on stress-resistant children.

A Moderately Unsuccessful Pilot Study[1] of "Invulnerable" Children

Our initial attempt to identify and evaluate "invulnerable" children took the following form. Several years ago the author had offered a graduate course for elementary and secondary school principals in which the final class assignment was the preparation of a case description of an "invulnerable" child known to each principal. What rapidly became evident was that the principals not only could carry out the assignment, but seemingly relished the task as well. In particular, they seemed to resonate to the concept of the stress-resistant child as more positive in its orientation to the inner-city child. They reported having seen many children who seemed to fit our twin criteria of "invulnerability": manifest stress and maintained mastery. Most seemed as challenged as we were by the prospect of trying to understand these children better.

[1]The co-investigative team included Vernon Devine, Margaret O'Dougherty, David Pellegrini, Dana Fox, and Kathy Dwyer.

Subsequent to these case presentations which were discussed in the seminar, we expanded our case study approach by visiting many schools and tape-recording vignettes of anonymous children provided by principals, counselors, and social workers. We explicitly asked that the names of children not be mentioned, but that a recital of examples of the backgrounds and behaviors of different children be provided. These anonymous descriptions were transcribed and the investigators carefully reviewed the patterns of stressors and modes of coping that had been described to help us in choosing procedures and measuring instruments for a more systematic study.

During this phase of school visits, we came across a very interesting school and a very special principal and social worker. Our years of research in the city school system had reassured us that the descriptions of the crushing effects on children of public schools cited by numerous authors was neither applicable to the schools we worked in, nor to the teaching and administrative personnel we had encountered. The elementary school to which I refer, however, was unusual even within this concerned school system. The principal and social worker were active community participants. The principal knew all of his several hundred pupils by their first names, and in his relationship to the community, he seemed to serve as much in the role of a pastor as he did in the role of a principal. The school operated on a philosophy of an action-oriented, involved, concerned humanism. On the basis of further visits, it became apparent that this philosophy was shared by many of the teachers, and was translated into an exciting and effective school program that involved most of the faculty in the lives of the children beyond the doors of their classrooms. Teachers typically made home visits as did the principal and social worker, and not merely to the families of troubled children, but to those of adaptive children as well.

The support of the school and families was essential given the many difficulties that inevitably beset a pilot effort. The constructs of stress and adaptation were vague and encompassing and the problem of measuring and quantifying them difficult. How could severity of stress be measured? Much of the stress literature emphasized environmental change but some of the stressors we had in mind (poverty, illness, family disruption) were marked by relative stability rather than transiency. Adaptation posed a similar problem. Here too a heterogenous domain of academic performance, work habits, motivation, and social competence required measurement.

We presented our problems to school personnel, asking them to be our collaborators in the research enterprise, because their long-term knowledge of the children would be essential in our initial efforts to define stress and adaptation. The faculty accepted the challenge and the pilot study was readied.

And then our basic plans were turned around by the intervention of what life-span developmental psychologists term a secular variable. Significant and unanticipated changes took place in the school system as school integration began on a large scale with children being bussed all over the city. Specifically, one-half of the student body of the school we had selected was transferred out, and a new group of students took their place. Pupils whom teachers had known so well were gone, and other children who were unfamiliar to them and who came from distant neighborhoods, occupied their places. The changeover meant that one of the criteria we had considered important in research on stress-resistant children, namely knowledge of the child's background, had shifted in a most significant manner. That these changes were occurring simultaneously, of course, put additional strain on the faculty's time and energy, making it difficult for them to find the time to be involved in the structured interviewing and rating procedures that we were developing. Nevertheless, all teachers completed all measures that we requested, and showed a level of cooperation and commitment that exceeded our expectations. But the significant changeover of student personnel meant that almost half the pupils in the grades (3–6) we had selected for study could not be rated by their teachers.

Our first step was to define stress (we used the less negative word, "pressures," in our descriptions) in a way that was reasonably comprehensive for teachers and congruent with their orientation.

Descriptive vignettes about the children were recorded by hand substituting code numbers for all students' names. All descriptions provided by teacher, principal, counselor, and social worker for a given coded child were transferred verbatim onto a single card. Three members of the research team that read those descriptive background circumstances for each child. Raters did not have available to them the faculty's quantitative judgments of stress and, as with the faculty, they too retained the option of withholding a rating when faced with insufficient data.

The composite stress ratings between the teachers' scale ratings and the research team's ratings based on qualitative, descriptive content provided a reasonable but not overly high degree of agreement ($r = +.66$).

On the side of adaptation, teachers were asked to provide four judgments of adaptation based on different aspects of the students' functioning. To emphasize differentiation, an adaptation essay was written for the teachers to use as a reference base while rating the global adaptation of their children. The teacher rater was asked to weight these components in the way he or she considered to be most appropriate. Following this global rating of adaptation, each teacher rated each child successively on *academic competence, work habits* (without regard to achievement level), a measure of motivation or effectance competence, and *personal-social* competence (again without regard to the other two variables). These ratings also required assignment of a child to one of five categories of adaptation ranging from excellent to poor.

The co-occurrence of the ratings of stress and adaptation enabled us to define initially four specific statuses for the children as represented by a simple 2 × 2 matrix (see Table 3).

In this table, children in cell 1 were presumed to constitute an "invulnerable" or stress-resistant group. Cell 2 was composed of children doing well in a relatively low-stress environment—an outcome to be anticipated. Children in cell 3 lived under high stress and adapted poorly, and were by definition an identifiable "vulnerable" group, while children in cell 4 had an even lower threshold of vulnerability, as signalled by their adaptive failure despite relatively low levels of environmental stress.

Approximately three months later, the teachers repeated these three specific competence judgments for the same children. In addition, each teacher also rated a second group of children with whom they had some classroom contact as a result of the modular structure of the school curriculum. Having both a single teacher's ratings of his or her students on two occasions, spaced three months apart, as well as the availability of a rating by a second teacher on the same students, allowed us to calculate two types of reliability: the reliability of individual raters over time, and a measure of concurrent agreement between raters at the same temporal point.

Using a modification of the "Class Play" sociometric procedure developed by Bower (1969) we then had peers in each classroom complete sociometric ratings on their fellow students. Each respondent was asked to assume the role of a director and to cast other students in

Table 3.   Four Samples of Children Used in Pilot Study of Stress Resistance

| | | Stress | |
		High	Low
Adaptation	High	1	2
	Low	3	4

different roles in a hypothetical class play. These roles were written to reflect positive and negative academic and social behaviors (e.g., "a person who is a class leader," "a person who interrupts when others are speaking," "someone whose feelings get hurt easily.") We have had extensive experience with this procedure and have found it to be an excellent index of social competence in our studies of children vulnerable to psychopathology (Rolf, 1972; Marcus, 1972; Nuechterlein, 1978).

The class play made it possible to compare teacher's evaluations of students with peer evaluations, using different measuring instruments. This information was gathered on approximately 300 children in grades 3–6. The large number of students on whom data were collected allowed us to select subsets of children who differed in levels of stress-exposure and adaptation in addition to providing teacher-peer comparisons on several measures of competence.

The reliability results were reasonably satisfactory. Teachers tended to agree with their own ratings over a three-months span, providing reliability correlations of +.70 in the academic sphere and +.75 for work habits. In these areas when two different teachers judged the same pupils the correlations were +.65 and +.67 respectively. Agreement, however, was lower ($r = +.58$) in the area of personal-social competence. The correlations were also significant between teacher's and peer's perception of competence, with agreement on academic competence ($r = +.55$), somewhat higher than for the personal-social competence variable.

In filling the four cells, "high stress" assignments reflected ratings of 4 or 5 on the stress scale with preference given to the more extreme scores, while "low stress" was based on ratings of 1 and 2. Adaptation scores were summed across teachers, and students were selected as high and low adapting individuals if they fell in the highest and lowest 25% of the distribution. On the basis of these two scores children were assigned to one of the four cells. Although it was reassuring to locate students who fitted the four categories, it should be noted that the cell with the fewest number of subjects, as classified by the teachers, was the low stress/low adaptation group. Teachers apparently perceive very few poorly adapting children as being subjected to a low degree of external stress. There are a number of possible explanations for this covariation. First, it may simply reflect a bias or an assumption not uncommon in the mental health field ("if you are well-adapted, you are obviously not being subjected to stress"). Second, it may well be the case that these two factors do tend to covary in this fashion, particularly if category assignments are forced into dichotomies. This problem was more effectively resolved in our current research program.

With parental permission, further exploratory studies were then conducted with small numbers of students in each of the four cells, the total subject pool being 50. These measures included: formal academic achievement test (Peabody Individual Achievement Test), an abbreviated measure of intellectual functioning (Vocabulary and Block Design subtests of the WISC-R), the Porteus Maze as a measure of foresight and planning, and a test of role-taking ability in children that has been presumed to reflect social competence (Chandler, Greenspan, and Barenboem, 1974). The behavior of half the sample was also observed in the classroom.

The results of this pilot effort were at best suggestive. The low stress/high adaptation group obtained the highest scores on most of the measures; the high stress/high adaptation ("invulnerable") group was practically identical to its low stress counterpart on peer sociometric ratings and only slightly lower on achievement test scores. The peer ratings of the two high adaptive groups were markedly different from the ratings of the two low adaptive groups, the mean positive peer choice scores being almost three times greater for these groups. By contrast, the two low adaptation groups performed significantly more poorly across all competence measures, with the low adaptation/low stress group evidencing the poorest performance of all. This should not be surprising since the adaptation ratings tapped into several of the areas rated by the competence indicators. But it was encouraging to learn that peers viewed the high stress/high adaptation and the low stress/high adaptation groups in a comparably favorable manner, particularly so since the categorizations of the children were chosen, not on the basis of peer selection, but on the basis of teachers' judgments. In terms of future research, it was also encouraging to find that although there appeared to be differences in I.Q. and achievement scores among the four groups, there was sufficient overlap between the high stress/high adaptation and high stress/low adaptation groups in these areas to make evident that differences in adaptation was not a simple reflection of intellectual variation. As for the test of role-taking skills we found that a ceiling effect prevailed for the older children that precluded its possible differentiating power among the groups.

One further comment is of interest. We sent our letters to a number of parents informing them that we had obtained data from our studies that we would be willing to share with them and suggesting an evening meeting at their convenience to be held at the school. It is noteworthy that responsiveness to our invitation when forthcoming came primarily from the parents of our high adaptive children in the two stress groups, in contrast to the parents of the low adaptive children.

PROJECT COMPETENCE: THE CURRENT MINNESOTA
RESEARCH PROGRAM OF STRESS-RESISTANT CHILDREN

The pilot study served its purpose in modifying markedly the large-scale project now underway at the University of Minnesota with grant support from the National Institute of Mental Health and the William T. Grant Foundation.

Several of the characteristics of the new program are these: First we elected to include several different cohorts of children designed to reflect different forms of stress to which the children are being subjected. This decision we hope will enable us in time to evaluate the attributes and coping efforts of adaptive and nonadaptive children under different types of stress and to study the nature of commonalities and differences among the children. The base for one cohort is an inner-city school complex housed in a newly built architectural complex of contemporary design in which three different schools coexist, each run under a somewhat different educational philosophy. Our research program embraces two of the schools (the third, an "open" school has been used to test out, or pilot, various procedures intended for use with pupils in the other two schools). The demographic attributes of the two schools reveal a strong sampling of blue collar, working-class families, an increasing enrollment of minority children who are well represented (40%) but do not constitute a majority of the schools' enrollments, and a considerable number of single-parent families, many (50%) receiving aid for dependent children (AFDC) assistance.

Selection of children (grades 3–6) from this population comprise *all* families (approximately 150) that have indicated a desire to participate on the basis of letters and telephone follow-ups in which we have described quite openly our interest in learning about stress-resistance as revealed in how children fare in an increasingly technological society. Even with these families who elected not to participate the response to our goal has been largely a positive one.

A second cohort is comprised of virtually all members of the population of elementary school-age children who have survived (via surgery) a life-threatening congenital heart defect, transposition of the great arteries (TGA). This research program under the direction of Professor Francis Wright (ably assisted by Ms. M. O'Dougherty) of the Division of Pediatric Neurology in the Medical School of the University of Minnesota emphasizes the neurological and psychological sequelae as well as the patterns of parent and child adaptation following successful surgical intervention.

A third cohort, now underway, focuses on physically handicapped children. In this group the stress emphasis is on both the limitations posed by the handicap and the additional external stressor posed by the move toward mainstreaming of various cohort members in regular classrooms after a period of time spent in special classes.

In measuring adaptation of the children in the school/community cohort we have drawn a composite score based upon *work (academic) competence* as derived from a highly reliable schema for evaluating a child's school cumulative record, a measure of *motivational-attitudinal work patterns* (without regard to ability) provided by teachers using the Devereux Elementary School Behavior Rating Scale (Spivack and Swift, 1967) which is based on the teacher's observations of the child over many months in the classroom, and *social competence* as assessed by peers using the Class Play, but extended and modified from previous versions so as to increase the number of roles pertinent to social interaction.

Stress is measured by a modification of Coddington's (1972a,b) widely researched instrument, the *Social Readjustment Rating Scale for Children*, which includes different lists of experiences applicable to groups of preschoolers, elementary, junior high school, and senior high school students. Using scaling procedures similar to those first used by Coddington, we have modified the scale to incorporate additional events, some positive, some negative that we assume may be more relevant to the problems faced by some of our families (e.g., "family funds [food stamps, etc.] cut off by government agency").

We are not unmindful of the limitations of life events questionnaires and have provided, as part of our early preparation for the project, a literature review delineating the shortcomings of such procedures. In compensating for these limitations a unique aspect of the current project is afforded by our decision to engage mothers in three two-hour interviews, the last session being elevated to a carefully prepared and detailed contextual life events inquiry.[2] This final interview seeks to establish the context of each reported stressful life experience by inquiring into such factors as: (1) an extended description of the specific event; (2) immediate reactions to the event; (3) the adequacy of preparation for and anticipation of the event; (4) the degree and control the parent(s) believed she (they) had over the event; (5) the support services, re-

---

[2]This interview has been jointly developed by the author and Mr. Harvey Linder whose doctoral dissertation is focused on findings based on these lengthy interviews with the mothers of fifty families of the first cohort.

sources, or assistance that were available to the family in adapting to the event; (6) the impact, consequences, and alterations within the family that were probably outcomes of the event. In addition, the other four hours of interviews with mother include a lengthy inquiry into family and parental backgrounds, family relationships, caretaking, and child-rearing practices of the mother, mother's perceptions of the index child including the early developmental history as well as the current adaptation of the child.

In addition, there is a lengthy two-session interview[3] with the child that covers school, outside activities, chores and responsibilities at home, money and work, friends and peers, family and home, mood and emotions, fantasy and dreams, sex, self-concept, and perspectives on the future.

Accompanying this interview information are a series of experimental studies designed to help us delineate a variety of attributes in the children: social cognition (Pellegrini)[4], impulsivity-reflectiveness, impulse control, and delay of gratification (M. Ferrarese), creativity, cognitive flexibility, and the ability to generate and to appreciate humor (A. Masten), and adaptation to the transition stress of a move from elementary to junior high school plus a number of achievement and intelligence test measures. Studies now being planned include measures of both family and peer interaction, attributes of persistence, frustration tolerance, and level of aspiration, role taking and perspectivism, and self-esteem. These as well as systematic observations of the children at work and play are also being planned within a program that includes the author and faculty co-investigators V.T. Devine, A. Tellegen, F. Wright, and a research team composed of talented doctoral graduate students and undergraduate honors candidates. Seven doctoral dissertations are nearing completion or will have been completed by the time this volume appears. As published by these research associates the initial reports will elaborate upon the methodology of the study, the bases of cohort selection, the evidence favoring the reliability of many of the measures, procedures and tasks that constitute the central variables now under investigation.

[3]This interview format was developed by the author and Mr. David Finkelman whose doctoral dissertation is formed around the results of the interviews with 100 children of one of the two schools.

[4]The names in parentheses are doctoral students whose dissertations constitute the base of inquiry into a specific aspect of psychological functioning.

Over a span of the next five years we hope to be able to place before members of the mental health disciplines answers to four questions that reflect our goals:

1.   Can different cohorts of stress-resistant children be reliably identified?

2.   Assuming that success attends our efforts both to identify the cohorts and to elicit the needed family cooperation, what attributes characterize these children and their families in comparison with less adaptive control children subjected to similar types of stress?

3.   Are there antecedent events that appear to have played a relevant role in identifying stress-resistant and stress-capitulatory behaviors of these children.

4.   In terms of short-term longitudinal follow-up studies, what are the subsequent patterns of adaptation of children identified as stress-resistant and their attendant controls?

If our project can provide the first tentative steps toward answering some of these important questions they may serve as necessary building blocks in developing programs of primary prevention with less adaptive children. These in turn may help to meet the challenge of Sir Peter Medawar's admonition: "It is not informative to study variations of behavior unless we know beforehand the norm from which the variants depart."

ACKNOWLEDGMENT

Preparation of this chapter was facilitated by grants from the Schizophrenia Research Program of the Supreme Council, 33°.:A.: of the Scottish Rite, Northern Masonic Jurisdiction, the William T. Grant Foundation, the Graduate School of the University of Minnesota, and a Research Career Award 17H-K6-14,914. Appreciation is expressed to past and present members of Project Competence, a program of research that has been underway in the Department of Psychology at the University of Minnesota for a decade. The chapter was written while the author was a Fellow at the Center for Advanced Study in the Behavioral Sciences. The financial support provided by The Spencer Foundation during the author's stay at the Center and the assistance of the staff are gratefully acknowledged.

REFERENCES

American Psychiatric Association. *DSMIII-Draft*. Washington, DC: Task Force on Nomenclature and Statistics, January 1979.

Anderson, S. and S. Messick. Social competency in young children. *Developmental Psychology*, 1974, **10**, 282–293.

Anthony, E. J. The syndrome of the psychologically invulnerable child. In E. J. Anthony, and C. Koupernik (Eds.), *The Child in His Family: Children at Psychiatric Risk*. New York: Wiley, 1974, pp. 529–544.

Antonovsky, A. *Health, Stress, and Coping*. San Francisco: Jossey-Bass, 1979.

Appley, M. H. and R. Trumbull. *Psychological Stress*. New York: Appleton-Century-Crofts, 1967.

Asarnow, R. F., R. A. Steffy, D. J. MacCrimmon, and J. M. Cleghorn. An attentional assessment of foster children at risk for schizophrenia. *Journal of Abnormal Psychology*, 1977, **86**, 267–275.

Baldwin, A. L. The study of child behavior and development. In P. H. Mussen (Ed.), *Handbook of Research Methods in Child Development*. New York: Wiley, 1960.

Barron, F. *Creativity and psychological health*. Princeton, Van Nostrand, 1963.

Baumrind, D. and A. E. Black. Socialization practices associated with dimensions of competence in preschool boys and girls. *Child Development*, 1967, **38**, 291–327.

de Beauvoir, S. *The Coming of Age*. New York: Putnam, 1972.

Becker, W. C. and R. S. Krug. A circumplex model for social behavior in children. *Child Development*, 1964, **35**, 371–396.

Bell, R. Q. A reinterpretation of the direction of effects in studies of socialization. *Psychological Review*, 1968, **75**, 81–95.

Bernard, J. The eudaemonists. In S. Z. Klausner (Ed.), *Why Man Takes Chances*. Garden City, NY: Anchor Books, 1968.

Blair, G. E. The relationship of selected ego functions and the academic achievement of Negro students. *Dissertation Abstracts*, 1968, 1968a, **28**(8), 3013.

Bleuler, M. The offspring of schizophrenics. *Schizophrenia Bulletin*, 1974, No. 8, 93–107.

Bleuler, M. *The Schizophrenic Mental Disorders in the Light of Long-Term Patient and Family Histories*, translation by S.M. Clemens. New Haven, CT: Yale University Press, 1979.

Boring, E. G. *A History of Experimental Psychology*, 2nd ed. New York: Appleton-Century-Crofts, 1950.

Bower, E. M. *Early Identification of Emotionally Handicapped Children in School*, 2nd ed. Springfield, IL: Charles C. Thomas, 1969.

Bowlby, J. and M. Ainsworth. The effects of mother-child separation: A follow-up study. *British Journal of Medical Psychology,* 1956, **29** (Part 3), 211–244.

Brill, N. and E. Liston. Parental loss in adults with emotional disorders. *Archives of General Psychiatry,* 1966, **14,** 307–314.

Brown, G. W., J. L. T. Birley, and J. K. Wing. Influence of family life on the course of schizophrenic disorders: A replication. *British Journal of Psychiatry,* 1972, **121,** 241–258.

Campbell, P. B. Self-concept and academic achievement in middle-grade public school children. *Dissertation Abstracts,* 1966, 1966a, **27**(6), 1535–1536.

Chandler, M. J., S. Greenspan, and C. Barenboem. Assessment and training of role-taking and referential communication skills in institutionalized emotionally disturbed children. *Developmental Psychology,* 1974, **10,** 546–553.

Clegg, A., and B. Megson. *Children in Distress.* Middlesex, Great Britain: Penguin, 1968.

Coddington, R. D. The significance of life events as etiologic factors in the diseases of children. I. A survey of professional workers. *Journal of Psychosomatic Research,* 1972a, **16,** 7–18.

Coddington, R. D. The significance of life events as etiologic factors in the diseases of children. II. A study of a normal population. *Journal of Psychosomatic Research,* 1972b, **16,** 205–213.

Coelho, G. V., D. A. Hamburg, and J. E. Adams (Eds.) *Coping and Adaptation.* New York: Basic Books, 1974.

Coelho, G. V., D. A. Hamburg, and E. B. Murphy. Coping strategies in a new learning environment: A study of American college freshman. *Archives of General Psychiatry,* 1963, **9,** 433–443.

Coelho, G. V., D. A. Hamburg, R. Moos, and P. Randolph (Eds.) *Coping and Adaptation: A Behavioral Sciences Bibliography.* Public Health Service Publication No. 2087, National Institute of Mental Health, Washington, DC: U.S. Department of Health, Education and Welfare, 1970.

Cohler, B. J., H. V. Grunebaum, J. L. Weiss, E. Gamer, and H. D. Gallant. Disturbances of attention among schizophrenic, depressed, and well mothers and their young children. *Journal of Child Psychology and Psychiatry,* 1977, **18,** 115–135.

Coles, R. *Children of Crisis.* Boston: Little Brown, 1964.

Connolly, K. J. and J. S. Bruner (Eds.) *The Growth of Competence.* New York: Academic Press, 1974.

Coopersmith, S. *The Antecedents of Self-esteem.* San Francisco: W. H. Freeman, 1967.

Cowen, E. L., A. Pederson, H. Babigian, L. D. Izzo, and M. A. Frost. Long-term follow-up of early detected vulnerable children. *Journal of Consulting and Clinical Psychology,* 1973, **41,** 438–446.

Dohrenwend, B. S. and B. P. Dohrenwend (Eds.) *Stressful Life Events.* New York: Wiley, 1974.

Driscoll, R. Intentional and incidental learning as measures of selective attention in children vulnerable to psychopathology. Presented at the 87th Annual Convention of the American Psychological Association. New York, September 5, 1979.

Engel, M. Children who work. *Archives of General Psychiatry,* 1967, **17,** 291–297.

Erikson, K. T. *Everything in its Path.* New York: Simon and Schuster, 1976.

Erlenmeyer-Kimling, L. A prospective study of children at risk for schizophrenia: Methodological considerations and some preliminary findings. In R. D. Wirt, G. Winokur, and M. Roff (Eds.), *Life History Research in Psychopathology,* Vol. 4. Minneapolis: University of Minnesota Press, 1975, pp. 23–46.

Erlenmeyer-Kimling, L. and B. Cornblatt. Attentional measures in a study of children at high risk for schizophrenia. In L.C. Wynne, R.L. Cromwell, S. Matthysse (Eds.), *The Nature of Schizophrenia: New Approaches to Research and Treatment.* New York: Wiley, 1978, pp. 359–365.

Escalona, S. K. Intervention programs for children at psychiatric risk: The contribution of child psychiatry and developmental theory. In E. J. Anthony and C. Koupernik (Eds।), *The Child in His Family: Children at Psychiatric Risk,* Vol. 3. New York: Wiley, 1974, pp. 33–46.

Eysenck, H. J., W. Arnold, and R. Meili. In *Encyclopedia of Psychology,* Vol. 3. New York: Herder and Herder, 1972.

Fish, B. The detection of schizophrenia in infancy. *Journal of Nervous and Mental Disease,* 1957, **125,** 1–24.

Folkman, S., C. Schaefer, and R. S. Lazarus. Cognitive processes as mediators of stress and coping. In V. Hamilton and D. M. Warburton (Eds.), *Human Stress and Cognition: An Information Processing Approach.* London: Wiley, in press.

Fraser, M. *Children in Conflict.* London: Martin, Secker and Warburg, 1973.

Freeman, L. *The Story of Anna O.* New York: Walker, 1972.

Gallant, H. D. Selective and Sustained Attention in Young Children of Psychotic Mothers. Unpublished doctoral dissertation, Boston University, Boston, 1972.

Garmezy, N. Process and reactive schizophrenia: Some conceptions and issues. *Schizophrenia Bulletin,* 1970, No. 2, 30–74.

Garmezy, N. Competence and adaptation in adult schizophrenic patients and children at risk. In S. R. Dean (Ed.), *Schizophrenia: The First Ten Dean Award Lectures.* New York: MSS Information Corporation, 1973, pp. 135–137, 163–204.

Garmezy, N. Children at risk: The search for the antecedents of schizophrenia. Part II: Ongoing research programs, issues, and intervention. *Schizophrenia Bulletin,* 1974, No. 9, 55–125.

Garmezy, N. The experimental study of children vulnerable to psychopathology.

In A. Davids (Ed.), *Child Personality and Psychopathology: Current Topics,* Vol. 2. New York: Wiley, 1976, pp. 171–216.

Garmezy, N. On some risks in risk research. *Psychological Medicine,* 1977a, **7,** 7–10.

Garmezy, N. The psychology and psychopathology of attention. *Schizophrenia Bulletin,* 1977b, No. 3, 360–369.

Garmezy, N. Observations on high-risk research and premorbid development in schizophrenia. In L. C. Wynne, R. Cromwell, S. Matthysse (Eds.), *The Nature of Schizophrenia: New Approaches to Research and Treatment.* New York: Wiley, 1978a, pp. 460–472.

Garmezy, N. Attentional processes in adult schizophrenia and in children at risk. *Journal of Psychiatric Research,* 1978b, **14,** 3–34.

Garmezy, N. and V. T. Devine. Longitudinal versus cross-sectional research in the study of children at risk for psychopathology. In J. S. Strauss, H. M. Babigian, and M. Roff (Eds.), *The Origins and Course of Psychopathology.* New York: Plenum Press, 1977.

Garmezy, N., and K. H. Nuechterlein. Invulnerable children: The fact and fiction of competence and disadvantage. *American Journal of Orthopsychiatry,* 1972, **42,** 328–329 (abstract).

Garmezy, N. and S. Streitman. Children at risk: The search for the antecedents of schizophrenia. Part 1. Conceptual models and research methods. *Schizophrenia Bulletin,* 1974, No. 8, 14–90.

Garmezy, N., V. T. Devine, M. O'Dougherty, D. Pellegrini, D. Fox, and K. Dwyer. First Steps in the Study of Invulnerable Children. Unpublished paper presented to the Midwest Conference of School Social Workers, Minneapolis, MN, September 30, 1975.

Gilmore, J. V. *The Productive Personality.* San Francisco: Albion Publishing, 1974.

Goertzel, M. G., V. Goertzel, and T. G. Goertzel. *Three Hundred Eminent Personalities.* San Francisco: Jossey-Bass, 1978.

Goertzel, V., and M. G. Goertzel, *Cradles of Eminence.* Boston: Little, Brown, 1962.

Gottesman, I. I. Schizophrenia and genetics: Where are we? Are you sure? In L. C. Wynne, R. L. Cromwell, S. Matthysse (Eds.), *The Nature of Schizophrenia: New Approaches to Research and Treatment.* New York: Wiley, 1978, pp. 59–69.

Gottesman, I. I. and J. Shields. *Schizophrenia and Genetics.* New York: Academic Press, 1972.

Grinker, R. R. "Mentally healthy" young males (homoclites). *Archives of General Psychiatry,* 1962, **6,** 405–453.

Grinker, R. R. Psychiatry and our dangerous world. In *Psychiatric Research in Our Changing World.* Proceedings of an International Symposium, Montreal, Excerpta Medica International Congress Series, No. 187, 1968.

Haan, N. Proposed model of ego functioning: Coping and defense mechanisms in relation to I.Q. change. *Psychological Monographs,* 1963, **77**(8), Whole No. 571.

Haan, N. *Coping and Defending.* New York: Academic Press, 1977.

Hanson, D. R., I. I. Gottesman, and L. L. Heston. Some possible childhood indicators of adult schizophrenia inferred from children of schizophrenics. *British Journal of Psychiatry,* 1976, **129,** 142–154.

Holzman, P. S., L. R. Proctor, D. L. Levy, N. J. Yasellow, H. Y. Meltzer, and S. W. Hart. Eye-tracking dysfunctions in schizophrenic patients and their relatives. *Archives of General Psychiatry,* 1974, **31,** 143–154.

Illingworth, R. S. and C. M. Illingworth. *Lessons from Childhood.* Edinburgh: E. and S. Livingstone, 1969.

Jahoda, M. *Current Concepts of Positive Mental Health.* New York: Basic Books, 1958.

Kadushin, A. Reversibility of trauma: A follow-up study of children adopted when older. *Social Work,* 1967, **12,** 22–33.

Kantor, R. E. and W. G. Herron. *Reactive and Process Schizophrenia.* Palo Alto, CA: Science and Behavior Books, 1966.

Kelly, J. G. The Socialization of Competence as an Ecological Problem. Paper presented at the American Psychological Association Annual Convention, Washington, DC, 1971.

Kelly, J. G. (Ed.) *Adolescent Boys in High School: A Psychological Study of Coping and Adaptation.* Hillsdale, NJ: Lawrence Erlbaum Associates, 1979.

Kelly, J. G., D. W. Edwards, R. Fatke, T. A. Gordon, S. K. McClintock, D. P. McGee, B. M. Newman, R. R. Rice, and D. M. Todd. The coping process in varied high school environments. In M. S. Feldman (Ed.), *Studies in Psychotherapy and Behavior Change, No. 2, Theory and Research in Community Mental Health.* Buffalo: State University of New York at Buffalo, 1971.

Kety, S. S., D. Rosenthal, P. H. Wender, F. Schulsinger, and B. Jacobsen. The biologic and adoptive families of adopted individuals who became schizophrenic: Prevalence of mental illness and other characteristics. In L. C. Wynne, R. L. Cromwell, and S. Matthysse (Eds.), *The Nature of Schizophrenia: New Approaches to Research and Treatment.* New York: Wiley, 1978, pp. 25–37.

Kirk, H. D., K. Jonassohn, and A. D. Fish. Are adopted children especially vulnerable to stress. *Archives of General Psychiatry,* 1966, **14,** 291–298.

Kohlberg, L. Development of moral character and moral ideology. In M. L. Hoffman and L. W. Hoffman (Eds.), *Review of Child Development Research,* Vol. 1. New York: Russell Sage Foundation, 1964.

Kohn, M. *Social Competence, Symptoms and Underachievement in Childhood.* New York: Winston, 1977.

Korchin, S. J. and G. E. Ruff. Personality characteristics of the Mercury astronauts. In G. H. Grosser, H. Wechsler, and M. Greenblatt (Eds.), *The Threat of Impending Disaster*. Cambridge, MA: MIT Press, 1964.

Krystal, H. (Ed.) *Massive Psychic Trauma*. New York: International Universities Press, 1968.

Langmeier, J. and Z. Matejcek. *Psychological Deprivation in Childhood*. New York: Wiley, 1975.

Lash, T. W. and H. Sigal. *State of the Child*. New York: Foundation for Child Development, 1976.

Lazarus, R. S. *Psychological Stress and the Coping Process*. New York: McGraw-Hill, 1966.

Lazarus, R. S. The concepts of stress and disease. In L. Levi (Ed.), *Society, Stress and Disease: The Psychosomatic Environment and Psychosomatic Diseases*, Vol. 1. London: Oxford University Press, 1971.

Lazarus, R. S. The healthy personality: A review of conceptualizations and research. In L. Levi (Ed.), *Society, Stress, and Disease: Childhood and Adolescence*, Vol. 2. London: Oxford University Press, 1975.

Lazarus, R. S. The Stress and Coping Paradigm. Paper presented at a conference on "The Critical Evaluation of Behavioral Paradigms for Psychiatric Science," Oregon, November 1978.

Lazarus, R. S. and R. Launier. Stress-related transactions between person and environment. In L. A. Pervin and M. Lewis (Eds.), *Perspectives in Interactional Psychology*. New York: Plenum, 1978, pp. 287–327.

Lazarus, R. S., A. D. Kanner, and S. Folkman. Emotions: A cognitive-phenomenological analysis. In R. Plutchik and H. Kellerman (Eds.), *Theories of Emotion*. New York: Academic Press, in press.

Lazarus, R. S., J. B. Cohen, S. Folkman, A. Kanner, and C. Schaefer. Psychological stress and adaptation: Some unresolved issues. In H. Selye (Ed.), *Guide to Stress Research*. New York: Van Nostrand, Reinhold, in press.

Leff, J. P. Schizophrenia and sensitivity to the family environment. *Schizophrenia Bulletin*, 1976, No. 2, 566–574.

Lewis, H. *Deprived Children*. London: Oxford University Press, 1954.

Lewis, M. and L. A. Rosenblum. (Eds.) *The Effect of the Infant on Its Caregiver*. New York: Wiley, 1974.

Lipowski, Z. J. Psychosocial aspects of disease. *Annals of Internal Medicine*, 1969, **71**, 1197–1206.

Lowenthal, M. F., M. Thurnher, and D. Chiriboga. *Four Stages of Life*. San Francisco: Jossey-Bass, 1976.

Marans, A. E., and R. Lowrie. Hypotheses regarding the effects of child-rearing patterns on the disadvantaged child. In J. Hellmuth (Ed.), *Disadvantaged Child*, Vol. 1. New York: Brunner Mazel, 1967.

Marcus, L. M. Studies of Attention in Children Vulnerable to Psychopathology.

Unpublished doctoral dissertation, University of Minnesota, Minneapolis, 1972.

Matthysse, S. The biology of attention. *Schizophrenia Bulletin,* 1977, No. 3, 370–372.

McDougall, W. *An Introduction to Social Psychology.* London: Methuen, 1908.

Mechanic, D. Some problems in developing a social psychology of adaptation to stress. In J. E. McGrath (Ed.), *Social and Psychological Factors in Stress.* New York: Holt, Rinehart and Winston, 1970.

Mechanic, D. Social structure and personal adaptation: Some neglected dimensions. In G. V. Coelho, D. A. Hamburg, and J. E. Adams (Eds.), *Coping and Adaptation.* New York: Basic Books, 1974.

Mednick, S. A. and F. Schulsinger. Studies of children at high risk for schizophrenia. In S. R. Dean (Ed.), *Schizophrenia: The First Ten Dean Award Lectures.* New York: MSS Information Corporation, 1973, pp. 247–313.

Meier, E. G. Former Foster Children as Adult Citizens. Unpublished doctoral dissertation, School of Social Work, Columbia University, New York, 1962.

Meier, E. G. Current circumstances of former foster children. *Child Welfare,* 1965, **44,** 196–206.

Moos, R. H. (Ed.) *Human Adaptation: Coping with Life Crises.* Lexington, MA: D.C. Heath, 1976.

Murphy, D. L. and R. J. Wyatt. Reduced monoamine oxidase activity in blood platelets from schizophrenic patients. *Nature,* 1972, **238,** 225–226.

Murphy, L. *The Widening World of Childhood.* New York: Basic Books, 1962.

Murphy, L. B. and A. Moriarty. *Vulnerability, Coping, and Growth from Infancy to Adolescence.* New Haven, CT: Yale University Press, 1976.

Murray, H. A. *Explorations in Personality.* New York: Oxford University Press, 1938.

National Institute of Child Health and Human Development. *Perspectives on Human Deprivation: Biological, Psychological and Sociological.* Publication No. 0-328-458, Washington, DC: U.S. Department of Health, Education and Welfare, 1968.

Nuechterlein, K. H. Competent Disadvantaged Children: A Review of Research. Unpublished *summa cum laude* thesis, University of Minnesota, Minneapolis, 1970.

Nuechterlein, K. H. Dysfunctions of Sustained Attention and Personality Attributes of Children Vulnerable to Schizophrenia and Other Adult Psychopathology. Unpublished doctoral dissertation, University of Minnesota, Minneapolis, 1978.

Nuechterlein, K. H. Sustained Attention and Social Competence among Offspring of Schizophrenic Mothers. Presented at the 87th Annual Convention, American Psychological Association. New York, September 5, 1979.

Offer, D. and M. Sabshin. *Normality.* New York: Basic Books, 1974.

O'Malley, J. M. Research perspective on social competence. *Merrill-Palmer Quarterly,* 1977, **23,** 29–44.

OSS (Office of Strategic Services) Assessment Staff. *Assessment of Men: Selection of Personnel for the Office of Strategic Services.* New York: Holt, Rinehart and Winston, 1948.

Pellegrini, D. Social Cognition: The Social Competence of Stress-Resistant Children. Doctoral dissertation, University of Minnesota, Minneapolis, in preparation.

Phipps-Yonas, S. Visual and Auditory Reaction Time in Children Vulnerable to Psychopathology. Unpublished doctoral dissertation. University of Minnesota, Minneapolis, 1978.

Phipps-Yonas, S. Reaction Time, Peer Assessment, and Achievement in Vulnerable Children. Presented at the 87th Annual Convention, American Psychological Association. New York, September 5, 1979.

Rachman, S. J. *Fear and Courage.* San Francisco: W.H. Freeman, 1978.

Reider, R. O. Children at risk. In L. Bellak (Ed.), *Disorders of the Schizophrenic Syndrome.* New York: Basic Books, 1979, pp. 232–263.

Renaud, H. and F. Estess. Life history interviews with one hundred normal American males: Pathogenecity of childhood. *American Journal of Orthopsychiatry,* 1961, **31,** 768–802.

Roe, A. and B. Burks. Adult adjustment of foster children of alcoholic and psychotic parentage and the influence of the foster home. *Memoirs of the Section on Alcohol Studies,* No. 3. New Haven, CT: Yale University Press, 1945.

Roff, M., S. B. Sells, and M. M. Golden. *Social Adjustment and Personality Development in Children.* Minneapolis, MN: University of Minnesota Press, 1972.

Rolf, J. E. The academic and social competence of children vulnerable to schizophrenia and other behavior pathologies. *Journal of Abnormal Psychology,* 1972, **80,** 225–243.

Rosenthal, D. *Genetic Theory and Abnormal Behavior.* New York: McGraw-Hill, 1970.

Romano,. Personal communication, 1977.

Roskies, E. and R. S. Lazarus. Coping theory and the teaching of coping skills. In P. Davidson (Ed.), *Behavioral Medicine: Changing Health Life Styles.* New York: Brunner Mazel, in press.

Rutschmann, J., B. Cornblatt, and L. Erlenmeyer-Kimling. Sustained attention in children at risk for schizophrenia. *Archives of General Psychiatry,* 1977, **34,** 571–575.

Rutter, M. Early sources of security and competence. In J. S. Bruner and A. Garton (Eds.), *Human Growth and Development.* London: Oxford University Press, 1978.

Rutter, M. Protective factors in children's responses to stress and disadvantage. In M. W. Kent and J. E. Rolf (Eds.), *Primary Prevention of Psychopathology: Social Competence in Children,* Vol. III. Hanover, NH: University Press of New England, 1979, pp. 49–74.

Rutter, M., B. Maughan, P. Mortimore, J. Ouston, and A. Smith. *Fifteen Thousand Hours: Secondary Schools and their Effects on Children.* Cambridge, MA: Harvard University Press, and London: Open Books, 1979.

Schaefer, E. S. Converging conceptual models for maternal behavior and for child behavior. In J. C. Glidewell (Ed.), *Parental Attitudes and Child Behavior.* Springfield, IL: Charles C. Thomas, 1961.

Selye, H. *The Stress of Life.* New York: McGraw-Hill, 1956; revised ed. 1976.

Shakow, D. Psychological deficit in schizophrenia. *Behavioral Science,* 1963, **8,** 275–305.

Shakow, D. Some observations on the psychology (and some fewer, on the biology) of schizophrenia. *Journal of Nervous and Mental Disease,* 1971, **153,** 300–316.

Shepherd, D. M. and B. M. Barraclough. The aftermath of parental suicide for children. *British Journal of Psychiatry,* 1976, **129,** 267–276.

Shure, M. B. and G. Spivack. *Problem-Solving Techniques in Childrearing.* San Francisco: Jossey-Bass, 1978.

Silverman, I. Self-esteem and differential responsiveness to success and failure. *Journal of Abnormal and Social Psychology,* 1964, **69,** 115–119.

Slater, E. The neurotic constitution. *Journal of Neurology and Psychiatry,* 1943, **6,** 1–16.

Smith, M. B. Explorations in competence: A study of Peace Corps teachers in Ghana. *American Psychologist,* 1966, **21,** 555–566.

Smith, M. B. *Humanizing Social Psychology.* San Francisco: Jossey-Bass, 1974.

Sobel, R. "What went right?" The natural history of the early traumatized. In E. G. Witenberg (Ed.), *Interpersonal Explorations in Psychoanalysis.* New York: Basic Books, 1973, pp. 275–295.

Spivack, G. and M. B. Shure. *Social Adjustment of Young Children.* San Francisco: Jossey-Bass, 1974.

Spivack, G. and M. Swift. *The Devereux Elementary School Behavior Rating Scale Manual.* Devon, PA: The Devereux Foundation, 1967.

Spivack, G., J. J. Platt, and M. B. Shure. *The Problem-Solving Approach to Adjustment.* San Francisco: Jossey-Bass, 1976.

Stephens, J. H. Long-term prognosis and followup in schizophrenia. *Schizophrenia Bulletin,* 1978, No. 4, 25–47.

Stewart, P. R. *Children in Distress: American and English perspectives.* Beverly Hills, CA: Sage Publications, 1976.

Stone, L. J., H. T. Smith, and L. B. Murphy (Eds.), *The Competent Infant.* New York: Basic Books, 1973.

Strauss, J. S., R. F. Kokeo, R. Klorman, and J. L. Sacksteder. Premorbid adjustment in schizophrenia: Concepts, measures and implications. *Schizophrenia Bulletin,* 1977, No. 3, (Parts I–V, author order varied), 182–244.

Theis, S. V. S. *How Foster Children Turn Out.* Publication No. 165. New York: State Charities Aid Association, 1924.

Thomas, A. and S. Chess. *Temperament and Development.* New York: Brunner Mazel, 1977.

Thomas, A., H. Birch, S. Chess, M. Hertzig, and S. Korn. *Behavioral Individuality in Early Childhood.* New York: New York University Press, 1963.

Tinbergen, N. Foreword to *Ethological Studies of Behavior,* N. B. Jones (Ed.). Cambridge, England: Cambridge University Press.

Tonge, W. L., D. S. James, and S. M. Hillam. *Families without Hope.* Ashford, Kent: Headley, 1975.

Vaillant, G. E. *Adaptation to Life.* Boston: Little, Brown, 1977.

Vaillant, G. E. Prognosis and the course of schizophrenia. *Schizophrenia Bulletin,* 1978, No. 4, 20–24.

Varma, V. P. (Ed.), *Stresses in Children.* London: University of London Press, 1973.

Vaughn, C. E. and J. P. Leff. The influence of family and social factors on the course of psychiatric illness: A comparison of schizophrenic and depressed patients. *British Journal of Psychiatry,* 1976, **129,** 125–137.

Warden, S. A. *The Leftouts.* New York: Holt, Rinehart and Winston, 1968.

Wedge, P. and H. Prosser. *Born to Fail.* London: Arrow Books, 1973.

Welter, M. *Adopted Older Foreign and American Children.* New York: International Social Service, 1965.

White, B. L. and J. C. Watts. *Experience and Environment,* Vol. I. New York: Prentice-Hall, 1973.

Wolff, S. *Children under Stress.* Middlesex, England: Pelican, 1973.

Wynne, L. C., R. L. Cromwell, and S. Matthysse, (Eds.) *The Nature of Schizophrenia: New Approaches to Research and Treatment.* New York: Wiley, 1978.

Young, L. *Wednesday's Children.* New York: McGraw-Hill, 1964.

Zuckerman, M., R. N. Bone, R. Neary, D. Mangelsdorff, and B. Brustman. What is the sensation seeker? Personality trait and experience correlates of the Sensation-Seeking Scales. *Journal of Consulting Psychology,* 1972, **39,** 308–321.

Author Index

Subject Index

Psychology and Psychiatry in Courts and Corrections: Controversy and Change
by Ellsworth A. Fersch, Jr.

Restricted Environmental Stimulation: Research and Clinical Applications
by Peter Suedfeld

Personal Construct Psychology: Psychotherapy and Personality
edited by Alvin W. Landfield and Larry M. Leitner

Mothers, Grandmothers, and Daughters: Personality and Child Care in
Three-Generation Families
by Bertram J. Cohler and Henry U. Grunebaum

Further Explorations in Personality
edited by A. I. Rabin, Joel Aronoff, Andrew M. Barclay, and Robert A. Zucker

Handbook of Clinical Behavior Therapy
edited by Samuel M. Turner, Karen S. Calhoun, and Henry E. Adams

Handbook of Clinical Neuropsychology
edited by Susan B. Filskov and Thomas J. Boll

Hypnosis and Relaxation: Modern Verification of an Old Equation
by William E. Edmonston, Jr.